GOLF

PLAY THE GOLF DIGEST WAY

HONE YOUR GAME—FROM GREEN TO TEE

Early-morning practice during the 2004 Ryder Cup at Oakland Hills.

GOLF

PLAY THE GOLF DIGEST WAY

HONE YOUR GAME—FROM GREEN TO TEE

UNIVERSE

Famed golf instructor David Leadbetter keeps a sharp eye on three-time major winner Ernie Els.

Published by Universe Publishing
A Division of Rizzoli International Publications, Inc.
300 Park Avenue South
New York, NY 10010
www.rizzoliusa.com

Golf Digest is a part of Condé Nast Publications and is the largest golf publication in the world. Condé Nast, a unit of Advance Publications, includes consumer magazines and their websites, Condé Nast Digital, the Fairchild Fashion Group, the Condé Nast Media Group, and the Shared Services Centers.

Photography by Stephen Szurlej, Dom Furore, J.D. Cuban, and from the *Golf Digest* archives. All photography is the property of Golf Digest Publications.

Text: Ron Kaspriske
Book Design: Opto Design

2012 2013 2014 2015 / 10 9 8 7 6 5 4 3 2 1

Printed in China

ISBN-13: 978-0-7893-2485-6

Library of Congress Catalog Control Number:
2011935200

Butch Harmon helps fine-tune the driver swing of star pupil Nick Watney.

FOREWORD

by David Leadbetter

I have been proudly associated with *Golf Digest* for nearly 20 years, and when I think back on that time, it never ceases to amaze me the quantity of instructional material the magazine has published. One has to think that *Golf Digest*, which has been around since 1950, has to produce this incredible amount of material to satisfy the huge appetites of its golf-hungry readers. It has been my experience that *Golf Digest* subscribers certainly play the game with passion. Their emotions about the sport run the gamut from absolute elation to absolute frustration—often in only a few minutes time. I often wonder if those readers need their monthly fix of how-to stories to maintain a sense of hope that they're only one magic tip away from a career-best round. Perhaps this is the reason why the magazine enjoys the success that it does.

But then I'm reminded that it's not just the message *Golf Digest* presents. It's the people behind the message who keep readers coming back for more. The magazine's list of instructional contributors—the world's finest players and teachers—isn't just impressive, it's unrivaled. *Golf Digest* has been extremely influential in all aspects of the game over the years, but thanks to the magazine's playing editors and teaching professionals, its biggest contribution has been in presenting golf instruction in a clear, concise, and original manner. It has been the standard-bearer for printed instruction around the world, revealing new approaches to learning the game, offering in-depth articles and debates on how to swing the club, and providing thousands of tips to every level of player. For millions of people, *Golf Digest* has provided countless hours of entertaining and informative reading.

This book was produced in the same vein. It's a compilation of instruction from the best players and teachers to ever grace the pages of the magazine. It's possibly the greatest collection of tips ever put together—although the word "tip" doesn't really do this information justice as the book is loaded with in-depth instruction.

Unlike other instructional books you might have read, the tips included here have been assembled in a manner that is not only logical, but also most beneficial to the golfer from a learning standpoint. Putting instruction is offered first, followed by the short game, then iron play, fairway woods/hybrids, and finally the driver. The message here is that the

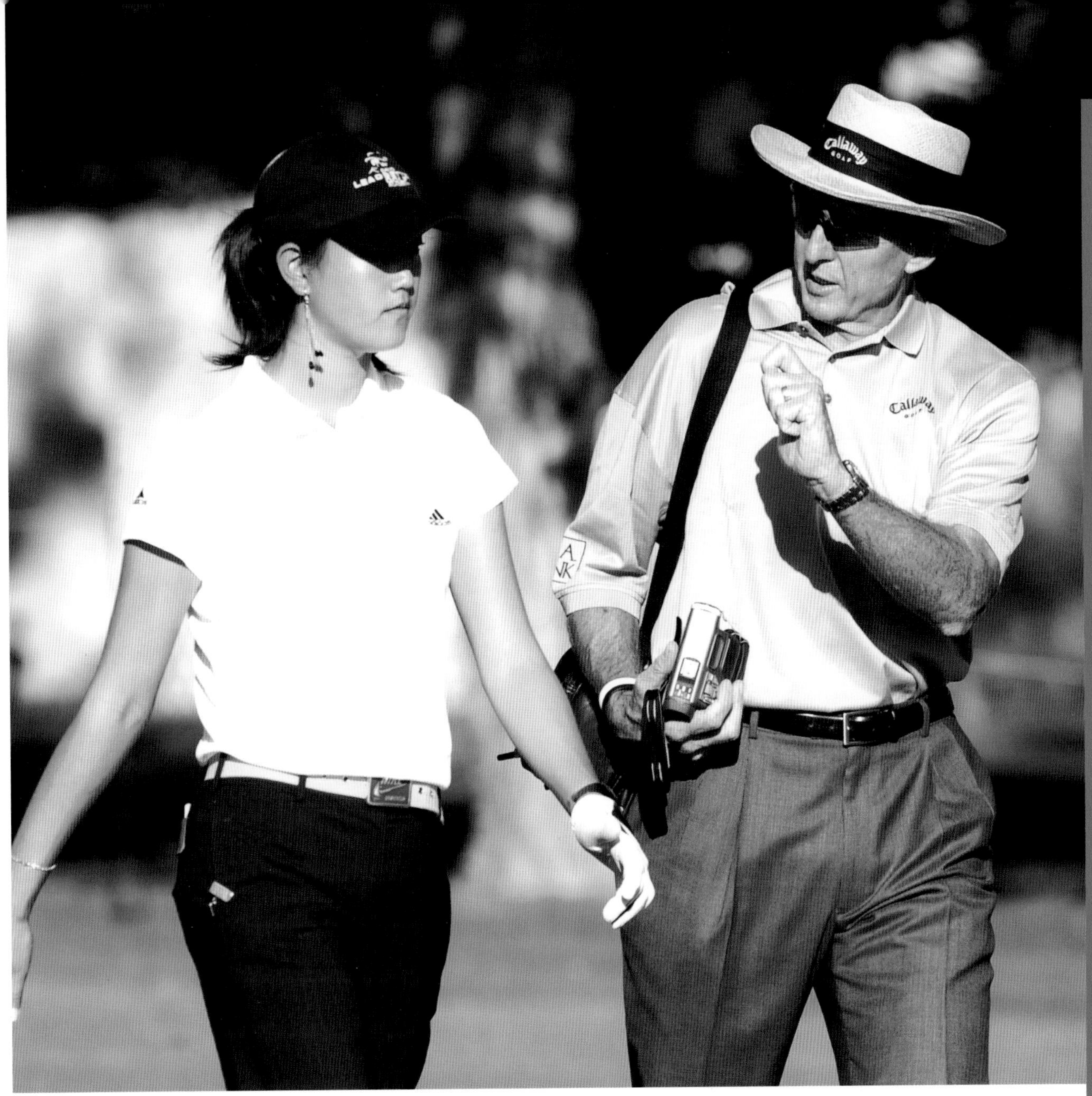

David Leadbetter consults with one of his star pupils, Michelle Wie.

game should be practiced and learned from the putting green backward to the tee—not the other way around. More strokes are taken on and around the green than anywhere else, so doesn't it make sense to learn putting and short-game skills before worrying about how far you can hit your driver? Taking the logical approach a step further, the chapters are broken down into two sections: Practice Tips and Playing Strategy. The instructors want you to crawl before you walk, and walk before you run. If you follow this format, it will give you the best opportunity to improve your game.

Part of the fascination with this great game of ours is the trial-and-error aspect of it—trying a new putter or driver; working on a new swing key; trying a different beer at the turn—whatever it takes to play our best. As one of golf's great icons, the late Ely Callaway of Callaway Golf, once said to me, "David, you and I are in the same business—we are in the business of selling hope to golfers." With this book we can all live in hope. Enjoy the read.

INTRODUCTION

by Bob Carney, GOLF DIGEST

"Learning to play golf," someone once said, "is like learning to play the violin: It's not difficult to do, but it's very painful to everyone around you."

Let the mission of this book be to make the process as painless as possible, not only for your friends and family, but especially for you.

And without further ado, here's the secret: Learn golf "backward"—that is, from green to tee. From short game to long game. From ground to air. From short club to long.

Most golfers approach the game with the opposite emphasis, whether they're just taking up golf, or they're working out the kinks of a swing that's pretty set in its ways. They start—and often end—with full shots. Ever watch beginners at a driving range? Nothing but drivers. Admirable, perhaps, but futile. Trying to learn golf this way is akin to attempting Paganini's Caprice No. 13 at your first violin lesson. If, as Bobby Jones said, the secret to golf is turning three shots into two, then making the short game your first priority is critical. You can't argue with the math: If you shoot 90, not a bad score, short-game shots account for more than half of it—46 shots—according to Peter Sanders of Shot-by-Shot, a firm that analyzed 185,000 amateur rounds.

This short-shots-first approach also eases novices into the clubs they find hardest to use. What's the thing that most amateurs struggle with? Getting the ball in the air. If you master the shots along the ground first, takeoff won't be such an obstacle. It'll come naturally.

You'll notice that this progression also takes you from the shortest club in your bag to the longest (unless you happen to use a long putter). Why? Because—no secret if you think about it—the shorter the club, the easier it is to control. So why would you start learning golf with the club that's hardest to manage? You wouldn't.

This approach is not just for beginners, either. It's the way accomplished golfers practice, and it's the process single-digit players—even tour pros—follow to get their games back on track. Former PGA Tour star and popular NBC broadcaster Roger Maltbie says that the secret to golf is, "Distance, distance, distance." Maltbie isn't talking about how far you hit it, but how close you hit it to your target. "I cannot stress it enough," he says. "Know what a 40-yard shot is. Know a 20-yard shot. A 60-yard shot. Get that down."

And just how do you get that down? By practicing the little shots that are easiest to control first, working your way up to the more challenging ones.

This past summer one of my son Matthew's friends came with us on vacation. One afternoon we visited a practice range, where the boys spent more than an hour hitting chip shots to holes on the practice green. In that time Eric, who had never played golf before, holed eight chips shots with a 6-iron. That's more than some golfers hole in a lifetime. And he did it because he was hitting a shot that was pretty easy to control and he had no goal but to get the ball in the hole. The boys' practice session reminded me of something *Golf Digest* Playing Editor Phil Mickelson said: "My dad gave me the best advice I ever received, which is to have fun. That's why, when I practice, I'm always having fun and enjoying it." Mickelson's specialty? The short game.

OK, now that I've made the case for the short game, let me assure you that this book is about much more than that. In fact, several chapters are devoted to the full swing. But getting a firm grasp on the short shots will make those long shots easier. This is how so many great teachers develop their students: Start a lesson on the putting green and work up to the range. Unfortunately, instructional books aren't usually organized that way, so that's why *Golf Digest* wrote this one.

Golf: Play the Golf Digest Way takes advantage of a "Murderers' Row" of great teachers and tour players who contribute tips to the pages of *Golf Digest* every month. Teachers like No. 1-ranked Butch Harmon, as well as David Leadbetter, Hank Haney, and Jim McLean. Sport psychologists like Dr. Bob Rotella and Gio Valiante, who have had dozens of tour winners. In fact, you'll find mental-side advice in every chapter, in addition to practice drills and playing strategies. And tour pros like Phil Mickelson, Rickie Fowler, Luke Donald, Jack Nicklaus, Tom Watson, Arnold Palmer, and David Toms, who will show you what great swings look like.

You'll love this book. We're sure of it. It's learning golf the right way. It's learning golf from easy to hard, building success upon success. It's all about never forgetting those key shots that help lower your score. (And no, we don't mind if you skip around.)

PUTTIN

G

THE FIRST, AND MOST IMPORTANT, thing you need to know about putting is that there is no ONE WAY to putt. Success has come from too many different methods to even list. Unlike some other aspects of the game, how we putt seems to stem much more from the right side of the brain rather than the left. By that we mean the artistic, creative side of the brain, rather than the logical, analytical side. Some golfers use long putters. Others grip the putter like they are holding a paintbrush. Even the late, great Sam Snead spent a portion of his putting career with his body facing his target, rather than the traditional method of standing perpendicular to it.

Still, with that said, you should know that despite all the different methods of putting, some fundamentals are virtually the same no matter who is making the stroke or how it's being made. For instance, few great putters ever move their head when making a stroke. Most of the best putters typically hold the club lightly in their hands. And it's nearly impossible to be a good putter if the putter face isn't square to its path when it impacts the ball.

What we're trying to say is when you read the following chapter and absorb the practice tips and the playing strategies, keep in mind that what's being advised is terrific general information for nearly all putters and nearly all putting styles. But there will be exceptions, so if something doesn't work for you, try another tip that does.

PREVIOUS SPREAD: **True roll:** Luke Donald sinks a long birdie putt on Augusta National's 16th hole during the final round of the 2011 Masters Tournament.

OPPOSITE: Brian Gay swing sequence

40% **No matter what your playing level, putting typically accounts for 40 percent of your total strokes per round in a given round.**

- A typical pro averages 29 putts per round, while a player with a 20 Handicap averages about 37 putts per round.
- Focus your practice on getting longer putts (outside 30 feet) within three feet of the hole.
- Tour pros make 85 percent of putts from inside of 10 feet. Amateurs make 40 percent.

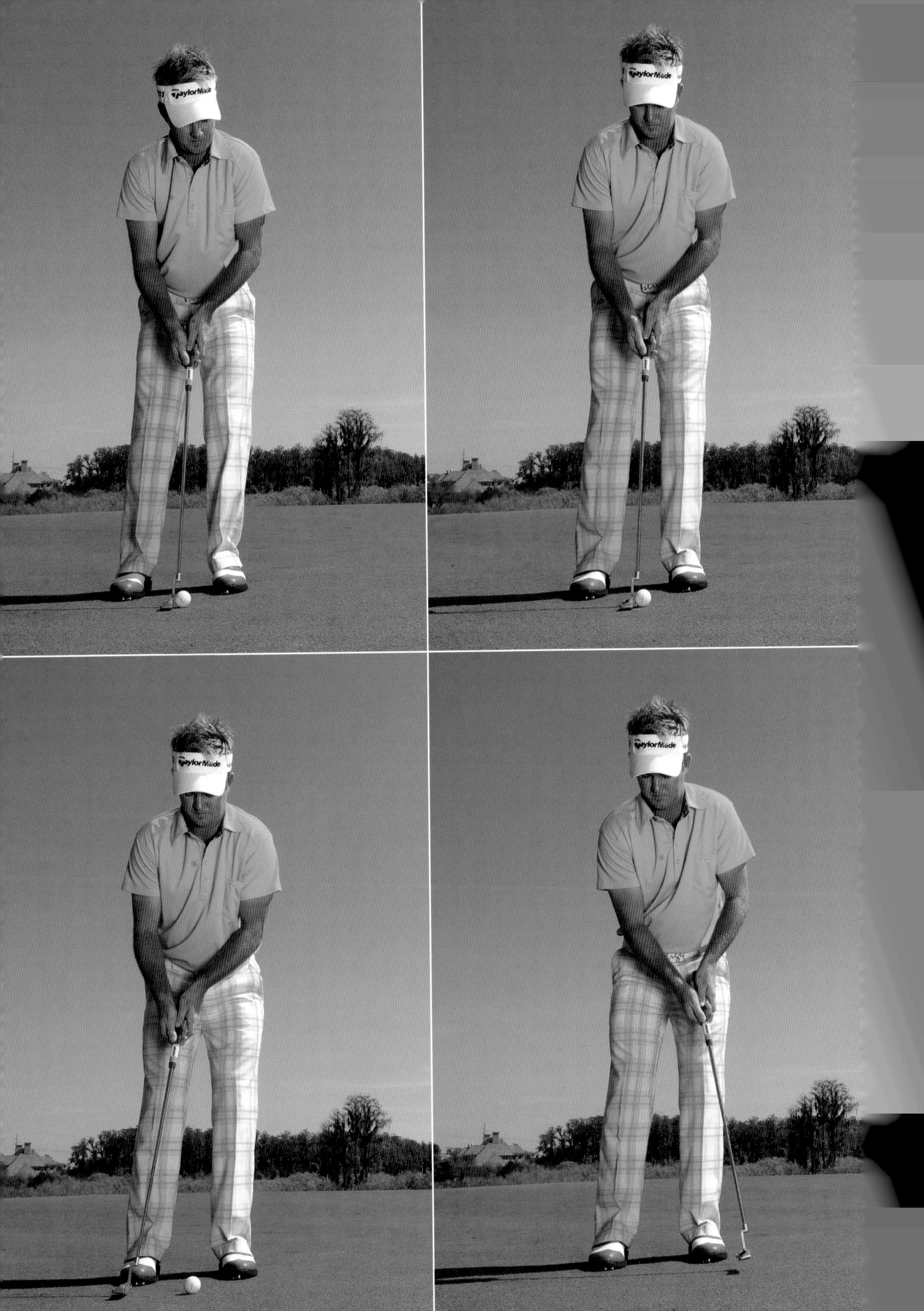
TaylorMade
TaylorMade
TaylorMade
TaylorMade

BASICS

HOW TO GRIP THE PUTTER

by Stan Utley

If you don't worry about anything else in your putting stroke, lock down these two fundamentals and you'll improve right away. First, make sure the putter grip is in line with your right forearm, not hanging below it. This helps the putter swing easily on the right swing plane. Second, set your hands so the grip runs through the lifelines of your palms and you're holding the handle mostly with your fingertips. If you were tossing a penny, you wouldn't set it in your open palm; you'd hold it in your fingertips, for feel. That's what you want when you're putting.

Practi

BASICS

LEAD WITH YOUR LEFT
by Dave Stockton

If you tried to shoot a free throw in basketball with your right hand only, you'd realize you need your left hand as a guide. The same is true on greens: The left hand is the direction hand and it's just as important as the right. Practice putting left-hand-only, or have someone hold a club in front of your hands on the target line. Bump the grip with the back of your hand, not your fingers, like David Jr. is doing in the photo below.

e Tips

BASICS

ELBOWS IN TO ROLL THE BALL BETTER
by David Leadbetter

At least 75 percent of golfers slice their full swing shots and I'd say about three out of four slice their putts as well. People who cut across the ball from outside the putting line to inside will never be able to stroke putts consistently or properly judge the roll.

To get the ball rolling on the proper line, learn to control the putter with a combination movement of the chest, shoulders, hands, and arms. Grip the putter with your palms opposing and your elbows snug against your rib cage. Make a shorter stroke going back, feeling your arms and hands staying connected and in front of your chest as your shoulders rock up and down.

PRE-SHOT ROUTINE

I've never been one to have a set routine, but I never hit a putt until I was ready. I wanted to make sure I had a good feel for the putt, that my grip pressure was light, that I controlled the putter with my right hand. And I wanted to visualize the correct line. That's why I got into my unusual crouch. I'm left-eye dominant, so bending over with an open stance was the only way I could see the line.

JACK NICKLAUS

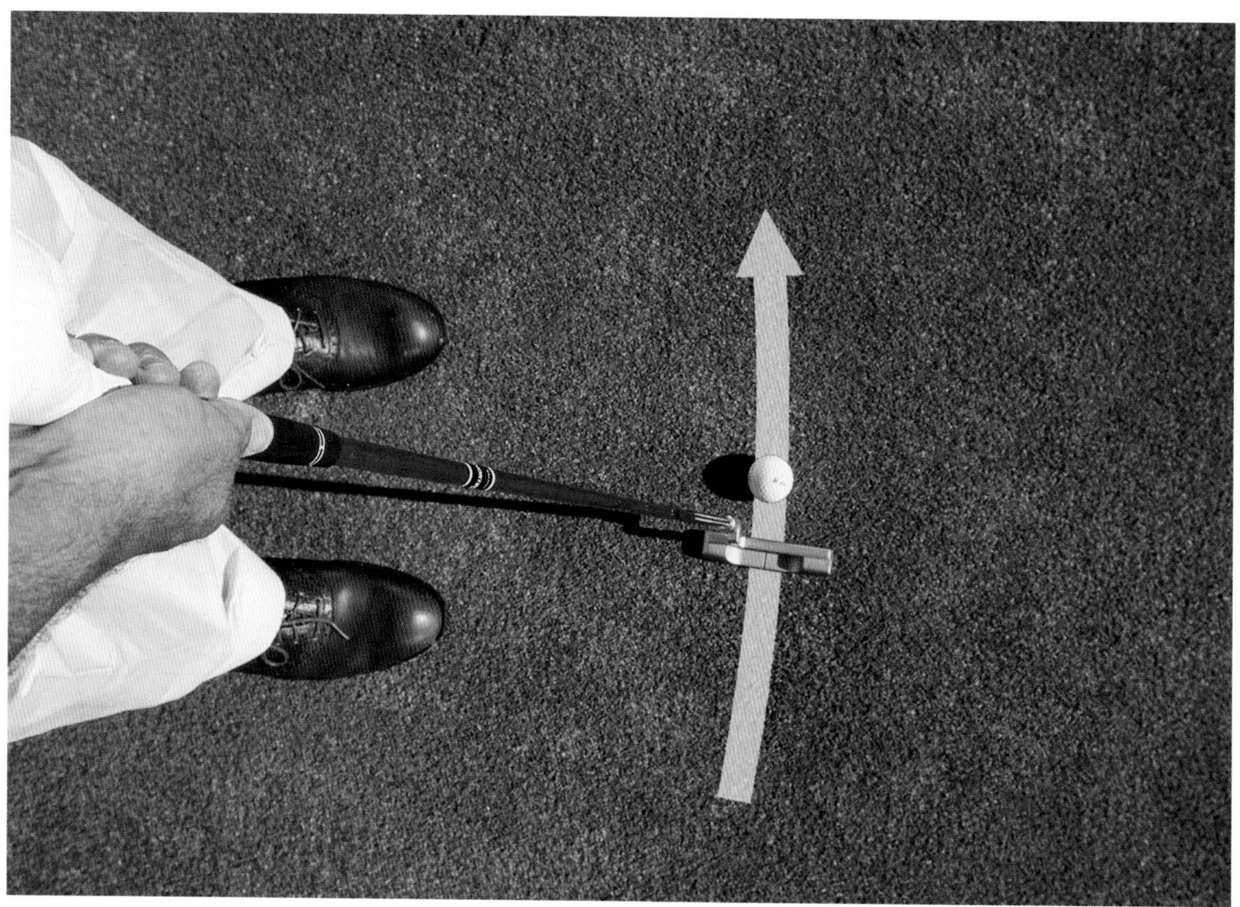

BASICS

PUTT ON AN ARC

by Rick Smith

When I'm helping people with their putting, I want their hands to be placed on the club in a natural position, relative to the way their arms hang. You get feel from the fingertips, not the palms, so in my grip, there are places where my hand isn't even on the club. The grip shown above won't allow you to swing your arms and the club naturally. Relative to the way most people's hands hang, the left hand is weak, and the right hand is strong. You'll be working against your anatomy. The hands need to be neutral and soft.

BASICS

RELEASE IT LIKE A PRO

by Hank Haney

Releasing the clubhead isn't something you hear much about on the putting green. I see it as something almost every great putter does. Certainly, two who do are Mark O'Meara and Tiger Woods. Take a look at either of them next time they're on television. Watch how there is a lack of stiffness in their left wrists as the putterhead swings through the ball. They aren't collapsing through impact, of course, but there is a definite angle at the back of their left wrists as the putter moves toward the hole.

This is what I like to see in the people I work with: the putterhead swinging past the hands as the ball is struck. There is no appearance of stiffness in the stroke. The putterhead is free to swing through and up into the finish. There have always been great putters who looked "wristy." Billy Casper was that way. And so was Bobby Locke. What they had in common wasn't wristiness, however. Both simply allowed the putter to release through impact.

MENTAL TIP

Good putters never putt out of fear. They aren't worried about how long their second putt is going to be. They're trying to make the first one. If you find yourself worrying about three-putting, your mind-set needs an adjustment. Good putters, such as the PGA Tour's Brad Faxon, stroke putts freely and don't fear a miss. They realize they can only control their own thoughts and actions.

DR. BOB ROTELLA

ADVANCED

PUTT WITH YOUR LEFT EAR

by Butch Harmon

Looking up too soon is the main reason golfers miss short putts. When you peek, your head moves, which often causes the putterface to open or close—just a touch, but that's all it takes. With short putts, there's not much room for error: If you start the ball off line, you've missed the putt. Focus on two points. First, aim the putterface precisely. After you read the break, make every putt a straight putt by looking only at the starting line. Second, keep your eyes down until you hear the ball with your left ear drop into the cup. You'll keep your head perfectly still.

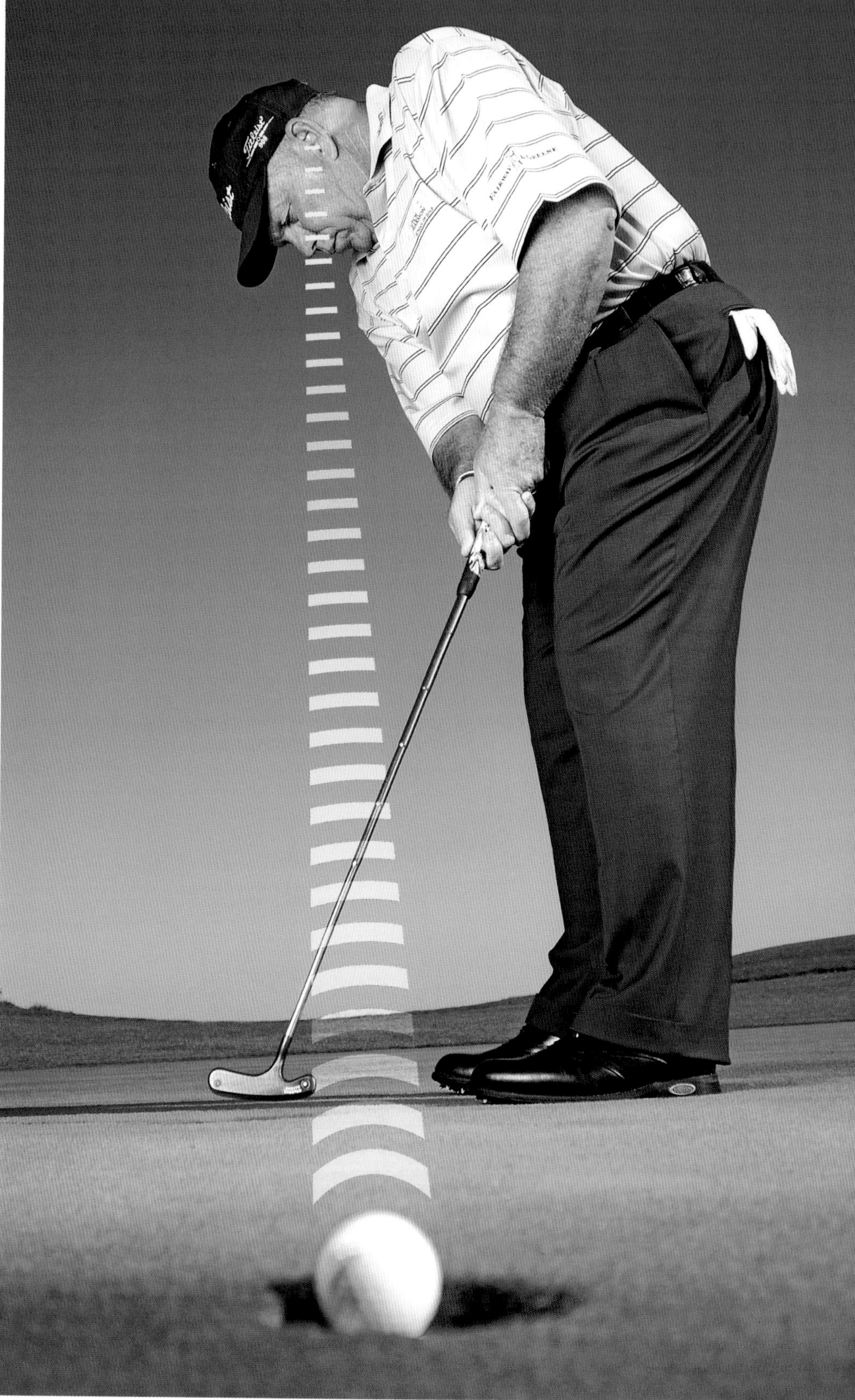

THE SETUP

When you step up to the ball, imagine a box on the ground. Your toes should be touching the corners of one side of the box. The ball should be on the opposite side, near the left corner. This image will help get your stance square to your target line and also set the ball in its proper position under your left eye (right eye for left-handed players). PAUL RUNYAN

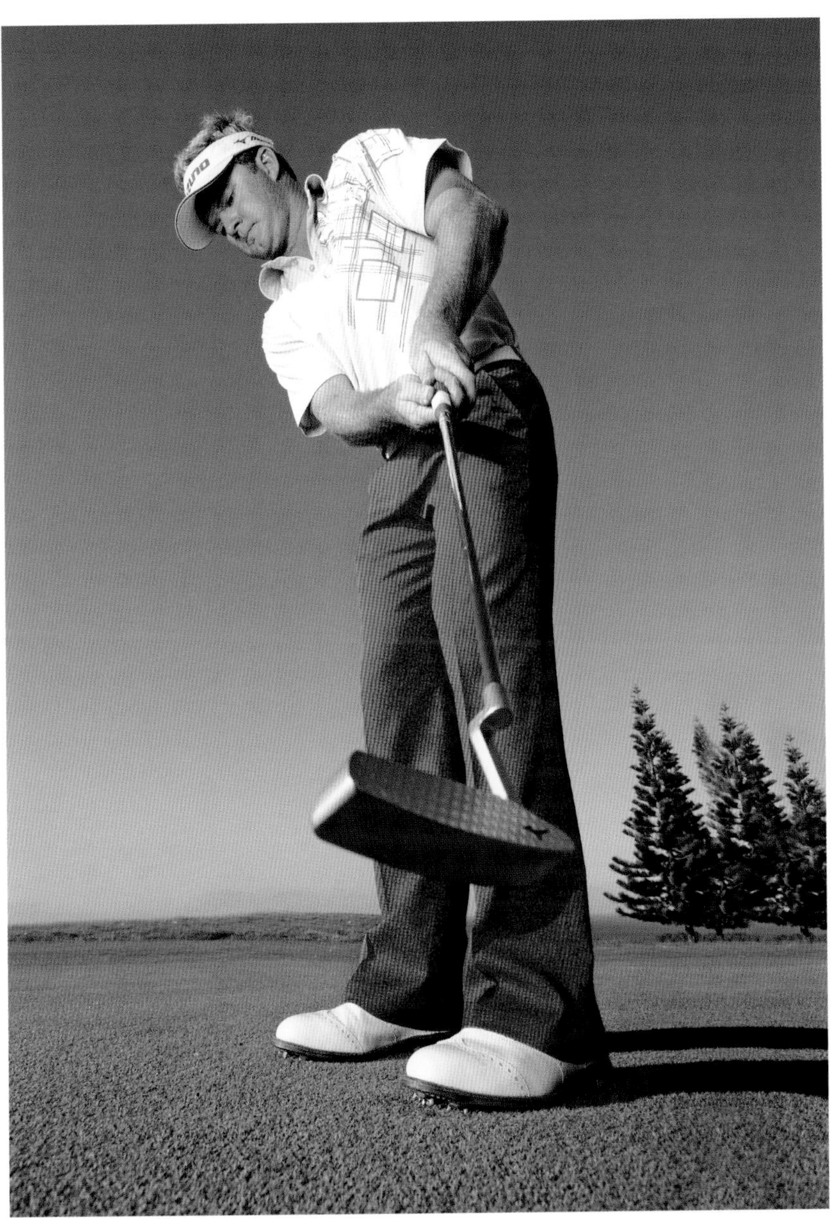

ADVANCED

KEEP YOUR HEAD STILL
by Brian Gay

I tend not to jam my putts in the hole. I like to die them in, especially from longer distances. I usually have a lot of tap-ins because of this distance control.

A great way to improve control is to hit practice putts and see if you can tell how far they've traveled in relation to the target before you look up. By the way, you should remove your glove when putting to improve feel.

FAST FACTS

Your putting vs. Phil Mickelson's

by Peter Sanders

WHAT'S YOUR 50-50 NUMBER?
Find the handicap closest to yours, and see below at what distance you should make the putt 50 percent of the time.

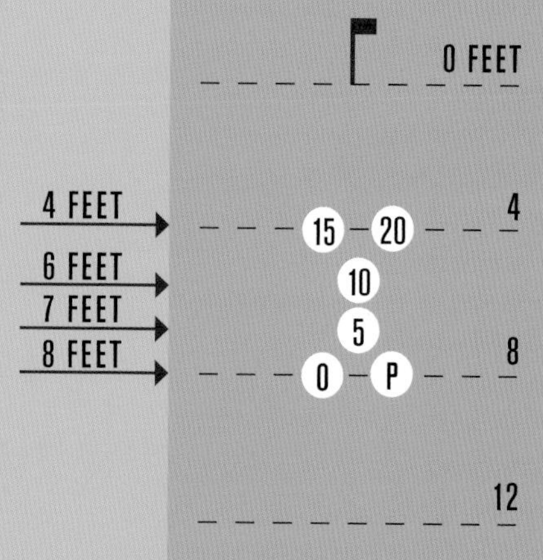

PHIL

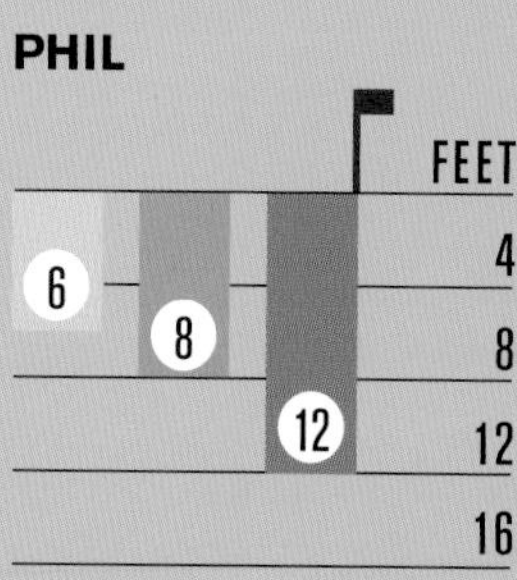

0 - HDCP

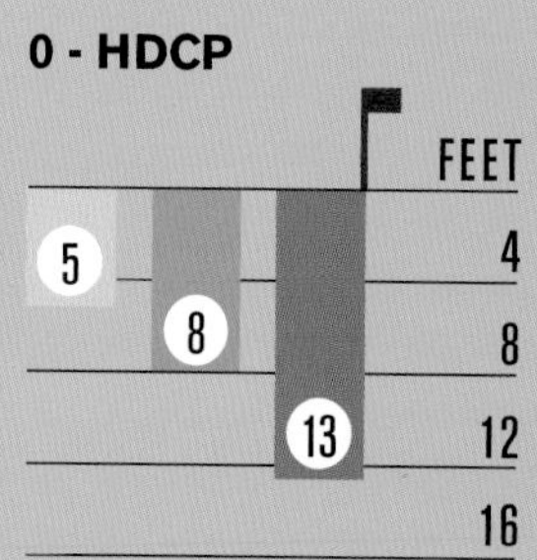

5 - HDCP

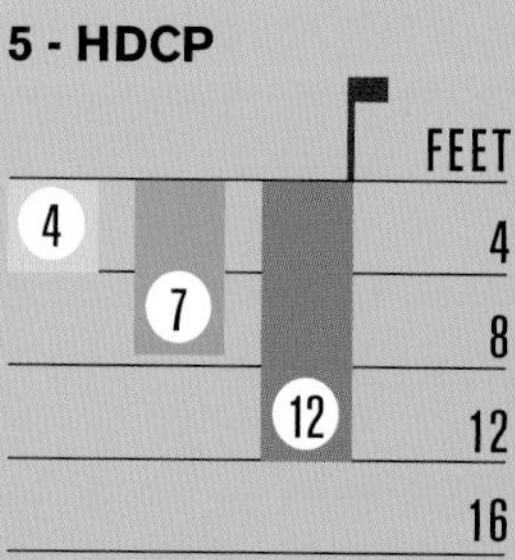

10 - HDCP

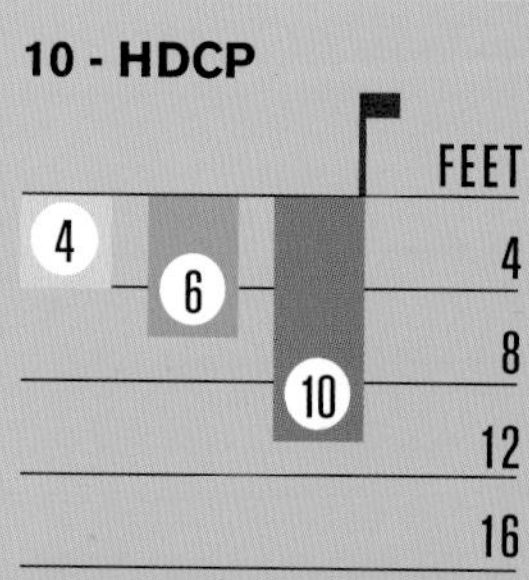

15 - HDCP

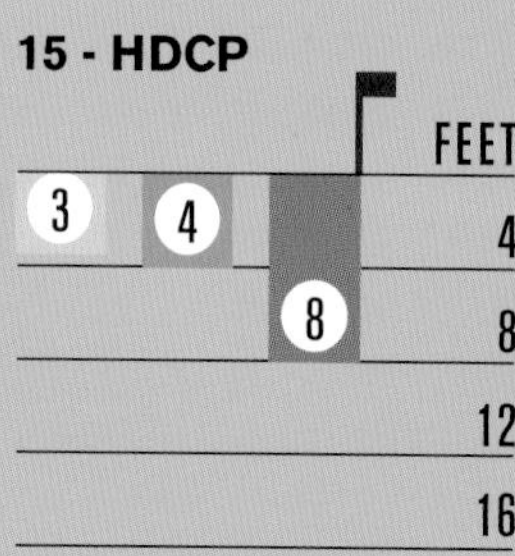

20 - HDCP

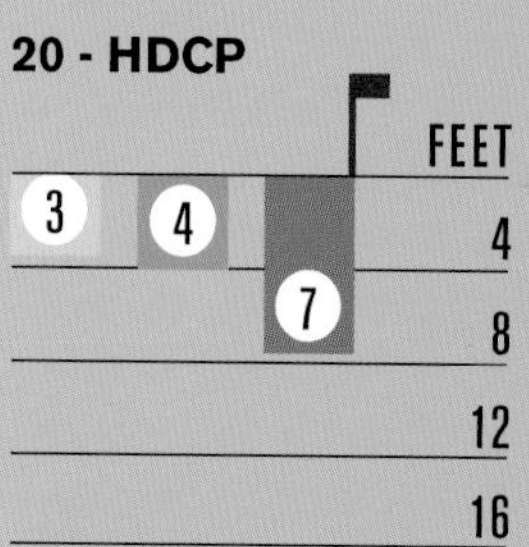

ADVANCED

THE ULTIMATE PRACTICE DRILL

by Todd Anderson

Find an area with some break on a practice tee and set up 12 tees around the hole the way I have here. The tees should be at three, four, and five feet. Now, hit one putt from each of the three-foot marker tees and repeat the loop three times (12 putts). Then, move to four feet and make two loops (eight putts). Finish with the five footers. You'll get a feel for making uphill, downhill, and sidehill putts. Keep your grip pressure constant throughout the drill and maintain a "one-two" beat for rhythm. Also keep the grip end of your putter pointing at your left side throughout. Follow these keys and you'll avoid common putting pitfalls.

ADVANCED

LEARN HOW TO PUTT IN THE CLUTCH

by Lorena Ochoa

Where I play golf, the game is about making birdies, and that means making putts. I've worked hard on my putting this year, practicing at home with my teacher, Rafael Alarcon. If you want to make clutch putts, start with these drills:

1. To keep the putter on path throughout the stroke, you should hold your head still. Rafael braces my head while I swing my arms and the putter back and through freely. Once I've made contact, I look at the spot where the ball was for a count of two.

2. After I line up, Rafael blocks my view of the ball with his hand. This encourages me to really feel the movement of my arms: The slower they move, the more consistent I putt. Plus, it's a good exercise for learning distance control. You can do it yourself by closing your eyes just before you start the stroke.

3. This drill helps keep my lower body in place during the stroke. I take my normal stance, then wedge a rubber ball between my knees. I squeeze the ball a little to keep it tight and to create a solid foundation. Hitting putts this way helps me develop the feeling of stability that is essential for a consistent stroke.

MENTAL TIP

"Bold putting isn't risky. The most important thing in putting is getting the ball to the hole. Or should I say, past the hole. In my prime, if I didn't make a putt, you could bet it was going by the hole. When you continually come up short, you open yourself up to risk because you've stopped moving the putter with authority. Before you know it, this will eat away at your confidence on the greens. You have to give the ball a chance to drop, every time.

ARNOLD PALMER

ADVANCED

SHORT PUTTS: THINK 25-75
by Phil Mickelson

On shorter putts, you must accelerate through the ball and impart a smooth, true roll. Try to make your backstroke shorter than your follow-through. The stroke should break down as 25 percent back and 75 percent through, though it varies slightly depending on the length of the putt.

As for obtaining a true roll, avoid hitting down on the ball or catching it on the upswing. You keep the putterhead moving level, with the shaft angle at impact the same as it was at address.

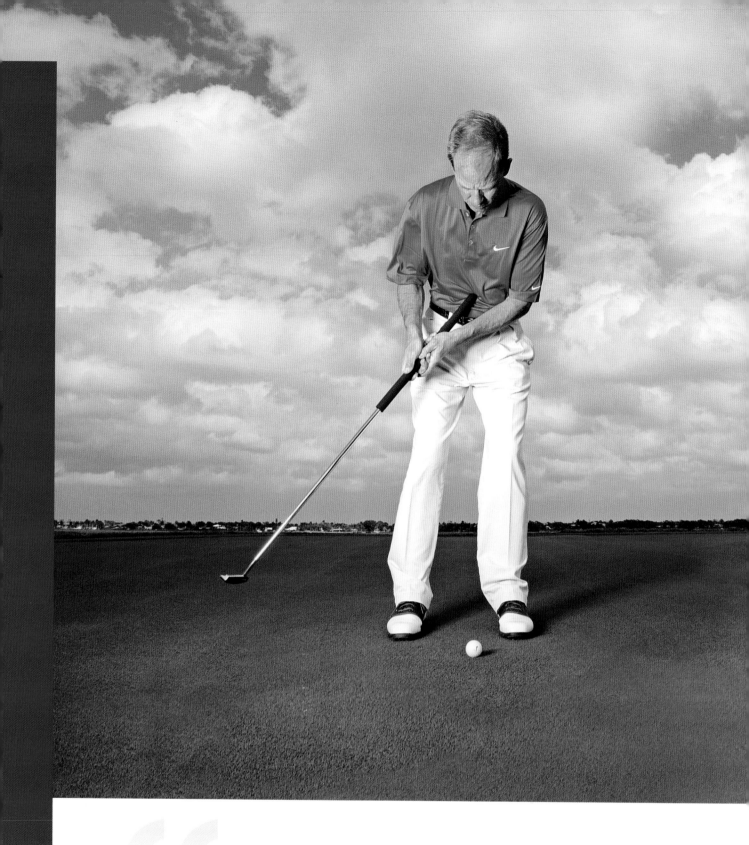

SWING THOUGHT

My conception of the soundest way to putt is that the arms and club swing exactly like a pendulum, at a very smooth, very even tempo, with the clubface square to the path of the stroke at every stage. I often visualize a pendulum action when I am putting, which helps me to make the stroke entirely with my arms, employing no wrist break or give in the hands whatsoever. My arms actually pivot from my shoulders.

BOB CHARLES

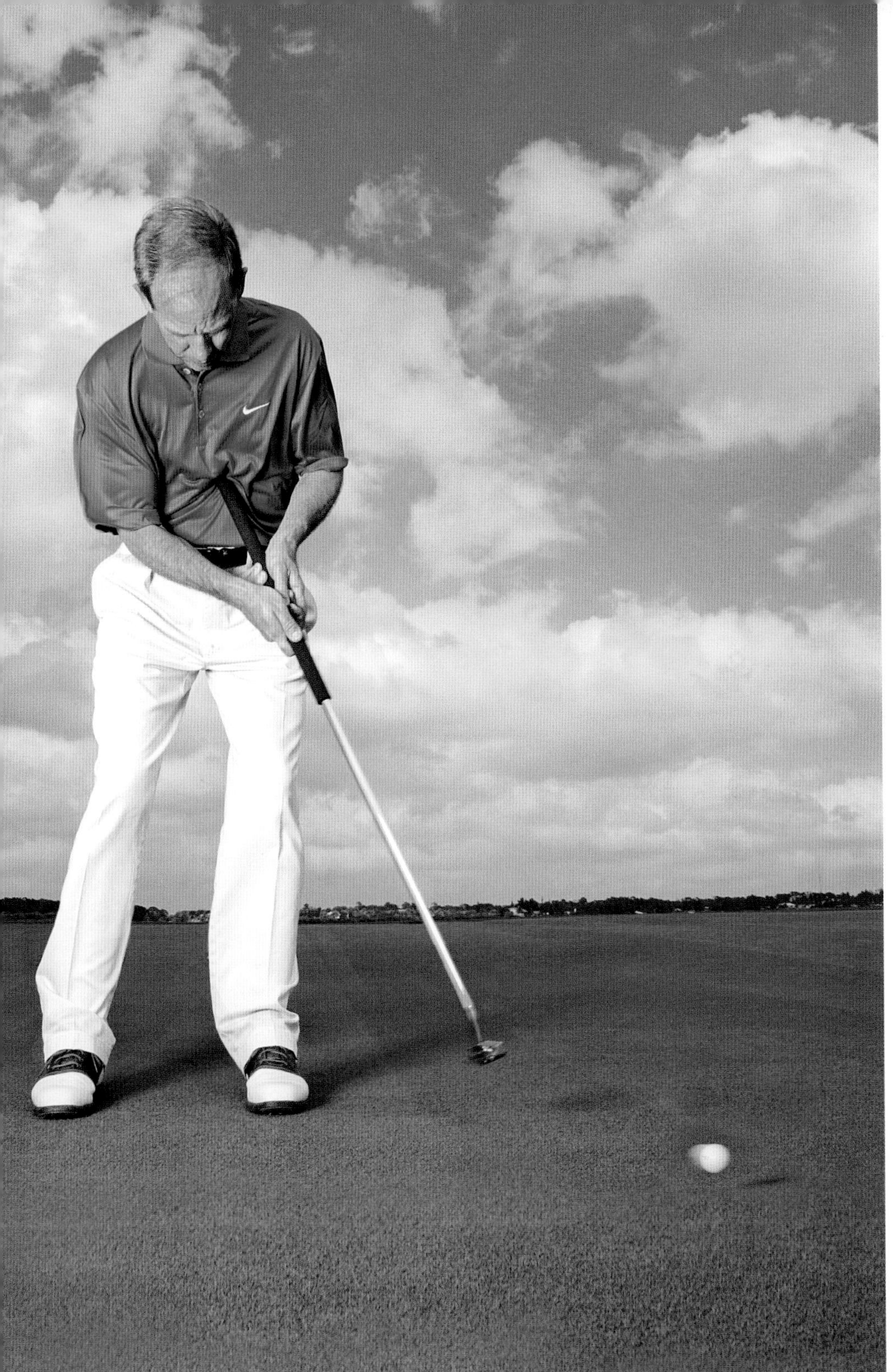

ADVANCED

HOW TO USE A BELLY PUTTER

by Mark Wood

The shaft should be secured about an inch or two above your belly button, not on it. Get custom-fit to ensure that the shaft is the correct length for you. The wrong size can alter your stroke. With the club anchored properly, the bottom of the stroke will be in the middle of your stance, so play the ball there. If you get it too far forward or too far back, you'll tend to mis-hit putts.

When you make a stroke, focus on keeping the butt end of the club pointing at your spine at all times. For longer putts, make a longer, not harder, stroke. The arc should be the same length back and through.

SWING THOUGHT

I've always been a good lag putter. I hardly ever three-putt. The reason? Even on short putts I try to drop the ball in the hole instead of banging it in. The percentages are with you because you catch more of the hole with a putt that's traveling at a slower pace. And if it doesn't go in, it's going to be in tap-in range versus a scary putt coming back. I feel like my right hand is rolling the ball up to the hole and the ball just falls into the cup.

BEN CRENSHAW

MENTAL TIP

A different thought on putting

by Ron Kaspriske

If you're struggling with distance control, or have a little "hitch" in your putting stroke that you think might develop into full-blown yips, you might want to try something radical, yet effective. Instead of looking at the ball when you putt, look at your target. Obviously, this will take some getting used to, so start by trying it on the practice putting green. If you can trust that you'll hit the ball solidly without having to look down at the ball, this method of putting can be extremely effective because it makes you forget about mechanics and instead helps you concentrate on your target. You literally stroke the putterhead toward your target. Sound strange? Look at it this way. Have you ever seen basketball players look at the ball when they shoot free throws? They look at their target—the rim. Try it and see if it brings your body's natural hand-eye coordination into play.

ADVANCED

GETTING THE RIGHT SPEED ON PUTTS

by Cristie Kerr

Putting is my favorite part of the game and you should learn to love it, too. The best way to learn to love putting is to get really good at controlling speed. If you're always around the cup, putting becomes fun. Many of the drills I do are pace-related. Here I lay a club down 1½ feet beyond the hole. My goal, if I miss, is to roll the ball up to the shaft, without touching it. That would leave an easy come-backer. I've learned a putt has the best chance of dropping when it goes a foot by the cup.

BASICS

THE BEST WAY TO READ PUTTS
by Hank Haney

Every time I play, I see amateur golfers peering at their intended line on the greens as if mysterious symbols were written on the grass. Don't get me wrong: Studying break is an important part of putting, but getting wrapped up in it at the expense of distance is a mistake.

How hard you hit a putt determines how much break you need to play. Reading break without thinking about distance leads to frustration. If you read the line perfectly on a 20-footer but hit the putt too hard or soft, you could be left with a four- or five-footer on your next putt. But get the speed down, and you can miss your read by a foot and still have an easy putt to finish.

The next time you play, approach your mid- and long-range putts thinking about a line behind the hole more than the break. This is the more important line in putting, and I visualize it 1 ½ feet behind the cup, like a little backboard. Try it. If you don't make it, you'll have a tap-in.

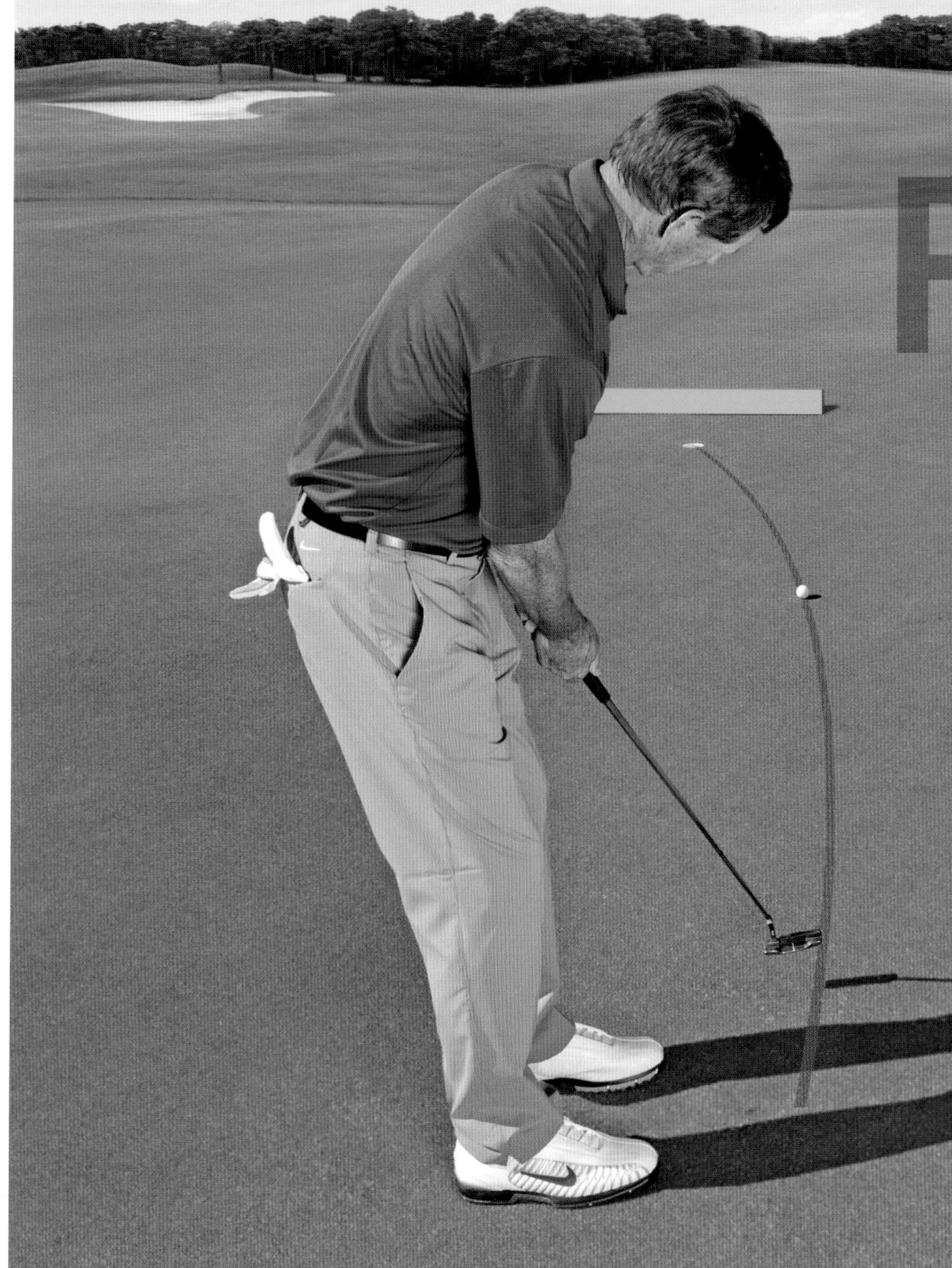

SWING THOUGHT

One way of ensuring that you don't leave a putt short is to visualize a mythical hole about a foot behind the real hole. If you don't make the putt, it's a lot better to leave it a foot long than a foot short. NANCY LOPEZ

aying Strategy

PLAYING STRATEGY

How to read a green

by Jim "Bones" Mackay

First sight is best sight. I've caddied for Phil Mickelson since 1992 and have seen some tremendous golf along the way, but the first nine holes on Sunday of the 2009 Masters was the most exciting front nine I've ever seen. Phil got it going early, birdieing the second, third, and fifth holes, and then hitting it three feet under the hole at the sixth. We grinded on that three-footer for a long time, because we had opposite reads, which is rare. Phil saw it as a left-edge putt, and I saw it as a right-edge. As I looked at it more, I began to get confused. That's the problem with studying a putt for too long; you end up seeing things that aren't there. Fortunately, I snapped out of it and stuck with my first read. Phil drilled the putt dead-center to keep his charge going. When it comes to reading greens, what the old-timers say is true: Your first instinct is best. So trust it.

Read with your feet, too. To get a perfect read on one of Phil's putts, I stand over the ball as though I'm going to hit it. I get a great sense of the break not only with my eyes, but also with my feet. When I look down at the ball, I can tell immediately whether it's a fraction of an inch higher or lower than my feet. Then I factor that in along with what I see from the other perspectives. Don't sell your sensory awareness short: Amazing as it may seem, almost everyone will get information from the stand-at-address perspective that you can't gather from reading the green with your eyes.

BASICS

TIPS FOR A 50-FOOTER

by Butch Harmon

When most golfers face a really long putt, they get so focused on hitting the ball hard that they rush the backstroke and make a short, stabby motion. The result is poor contact and a putt left short.

On those 40- and 50-foot lags, you should do just the opposite: Make a longer, slower stroke. You have to give the putterhead time to gain momentum on the downstroke, which starts with making a longer backstroke. Swing the putterhead back behind your hands, letting your wrists react to the weight of the club. Your left wrist (for righties with traditional grips) starts in a cupped position, but should flatten on the backstroke.

On the downstroke, you shouldn't have to think about adding speed. By flattening your left wrist going back, you've created a little hinge: Use that hinge by hitting with your right hand and letting your right wrist flatten through the stroke. Allow the putterface to rotate closed. Many golfers try to hold the face square, but it will close. Remember, distance control is your focus on lag putts. To get the right pace, make a long, slow stroke—and don't be afraid to allow a little wrist action.

SWING THOUGHT

I putt my best when I have a sense of gentleness in my hands, my stroke, and the way the ball comes off the putterface. I visualize the putterface as being extremely limber, almost as flexible as a length of rope, which means the only way I can get the clubhead to swing truly is to stroke very softly, smoothly, and slowly. If the limber shaft image doesn't seem to be working, I'll replace it in my mind's eye with a delicate glass shaft that will shatter if I'm even a tiny bit harsh at the ball.

JACK NICKLAUS

Titleist
Titleist
FOOTJOY

Ford

BASICS

HOW TO LAG IT CLOSE

by Rick Smith

One of the biggest problems amateurs have on long putts is controlling the stroke. Too often, they make a big, unwieldy motion and this can lead to a breakdown of the wrists. They will either hit the putt poorly or the putterface will close and they pull the putt. Or sometimes both occur.

Instead, keep your backstroke and through-stroke the same length, and put some power behind the hit. Keep the back of your top hand flat, and drive the stroke with your arms and shoulders. You'll be surprised how far you can roll the ball. You want controlled acceleration with the putter moving the fastest when you make contact (see photo). A compact stroke also reduces your margin of error and helps keep the putterface square to your target.

HANDICAP

How to spot a sandbagger

by Dean Knuth

The odds of shooting a score lower than your course handicap is 1-in-5. The odds of shooting a score three shots lower than your course handicap is 1-in-20. The odds of shooting a score eight strokes lower than your course handicap is 1-in-1,138.

BASICS

HOW TO PLAY A BREAKING PUTT

by Annika Sorenstam

Dave Stockton taught me to divide long putts into three parts: The first part is the starting line, and break is minimal; the second is where the ball reaches the apex of its curve; and the third is when the ball is rolling the slowest so it breaks the most. I use this image on putts of more than, say, 30 feet.

Here, I'm sizing up speed from the putt's midpoint on the low side of the line. I've already read the overall break from behind the ball. If I can get a feel for how fast the ball should be rolling at this point, I'll have a good idea of the overall pace. Making "air strokes" from this position helps me groove my feel.

Finally, I walk behind the ball and make a practice stroke standing perpendicular to my starting line. Looking down the line helps me visualize the pace. Don't make the common mistake of getting caught up in break and ignoring speed. I imagine a ball sitting at the apex, and I try to putt through that ball with good pace.

SOLID CONTACT

I feel that a firm-wristed stroke, with my arms swinging like a pendulum, is more consistent than a stroke that relies largely on wrist action. I try to swing the grip end of my putter back and forward so that my arms create the stroke. I try to accelerate my left hand and arm forward on all strokes so that my right hand doesn't take over and flip the putterhead upward or off line.

LEE TREVINO

ADVANCED

WHEN YOU HAVE TO MAKE, WATCH YOUR HANDS

by Tom Watson

When my short putting went sour a few years ago (it still bothers me at times), my caddie, Bruce Edwards, gave me a tip that's different. Try it if you're not making enough of those testy three-footers. Bruce suggested I look at my hands as I take the putter back instead of looking at the ball.

By doing that, you focus more on making a smooth stroke, and you don't get ball-bound and try to steer it into the hole. Practice this before you take it onto the course.

When I was a kid, my dad gave me another fun drill for short putting. I call it "putting around the clock." Ring a dozen balls around a hole three feet away. Make sure the area has some slope so you face every possible putt: downhill, uphill, right to left, left to right. On the course, the green should be relatively flat around the hole, but it often isn't.

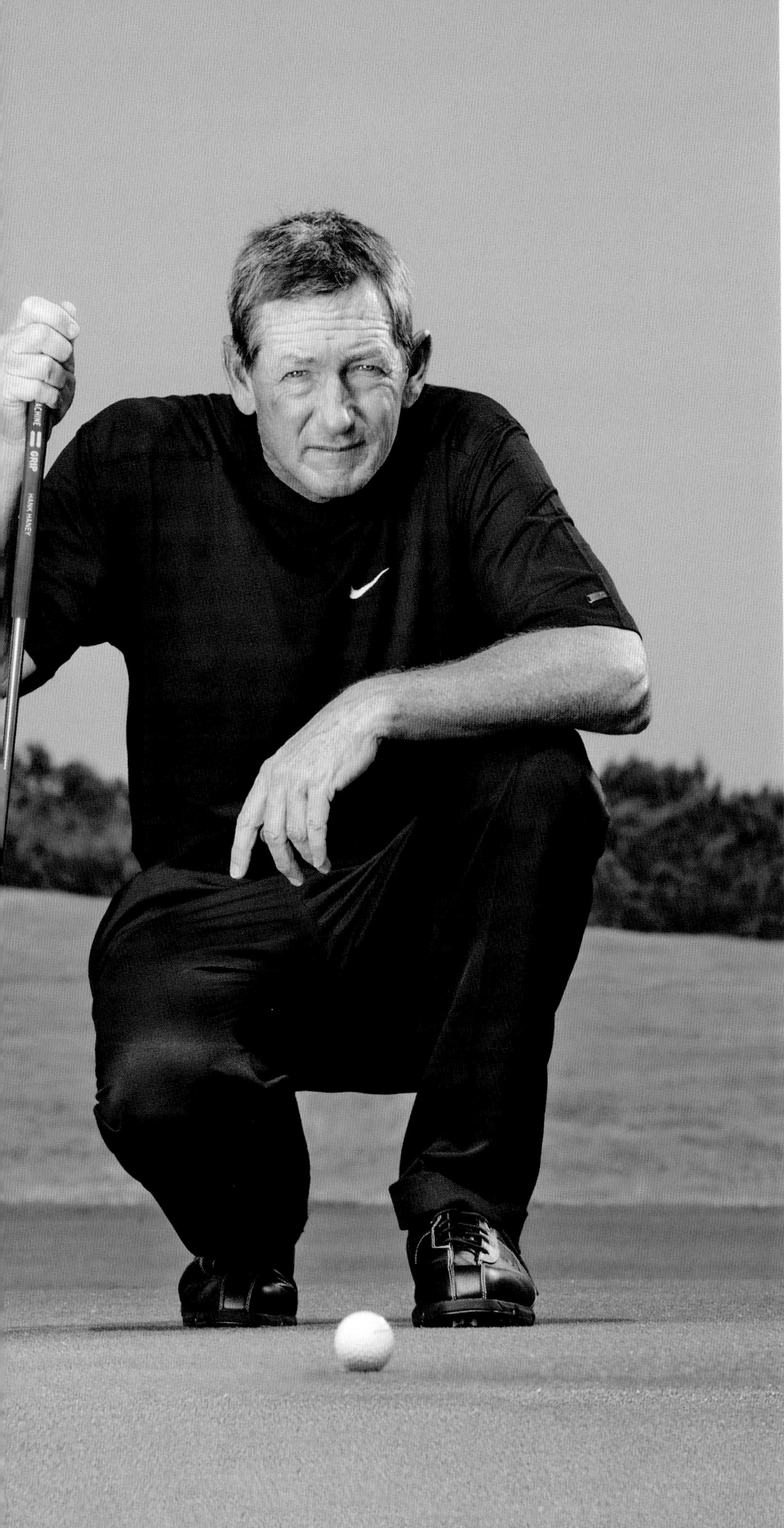

ADVANCED

HOW TO MAKE THE IMPORTANT PUTTS

by Hank Haney

The only way to take advantage of good technique is to be able to read greens accurately and aim the putter correctly. Then, you can get the ball going on the right line.

Start by looking at the entire green before channeling your attention to your putt. Imagine dumping a big bucket of water on the green. What direction would that water run off? That's going to tell you a lot about what your ball will do. Another trick is to identify the nearest straight putt to the one you have. The farther you are from the straight putt, the more your putt is going to break. As a rule, play a little more break than you think; most putts miss low. Speed is even more important than line: Try to roll the ball so it dies in the hole. The cup is more forgiving when the ball is rolling slowly.

ADVANCED

LOOK AT THE LAST FEW FEET
by Dean Reinmuth

On long lags or even putts in the 15- or 20-foot range, walk up to the hole and read the last three feet. This is where most of the break will occur, because slope and grain affect the ball most when it loses speed. Remember, the ball doesn't travel the same pace for the entire putt, so consider how it will roll when it begins to slow down. Then, allow for that extra break in your overall read.

THE STROKE

Here are some more tips for making a solid stroke.

1. Grip the putter lightly and in your fingers.
2. Keep your head still as you stroke the ball.
3. Play the ball under your left eye, near your left heel.
4. Let your arms hang naturally.
5. Keep your tempo the same throughout the stroke.
6. Make sure your putterhead is square to your target line at impact.

BILLY CASPER

ADVANCED

STAY ROOTED ON THE PUTTING GREEN

by Josh Zander

All good putters keep the lower body and the head still during the putting stroke. Although I've found it easy to keep my head still, my lower body sometimes sways a little and makes me hit putts off line. That's when I use this visualization: I pretend my legs have tree roots growing out of them. This keeps my lower body nice and still so I can take the putter back and through on the path I intended.

ADVANCED

LEAN THE HANDLE BACK ON FAST PUTTS
by Jim Flick

Former Masters champion Zach Johnson once played a practice round with my amateur pupil Philip Francis at the John Deere Classic in Silvis, Illinois. (As a freshman, Philip played on the UCLA team that won the NCAA title.) I noticed how softly the ball was coming off Zach's putter. And, of course, Zach sets up to putt with his hands behind the ball, which is quite unconventional.

Zach told me that on really slick putts, say a slippery downhiller or when the greens are extremely fast, he exaggerates this hand position. He keeps the shaft tilted back and moves the putter slowly. This adds loft to the putterface and makes the ball come off with a little more backspin. The result: a softer, more controlled roll.

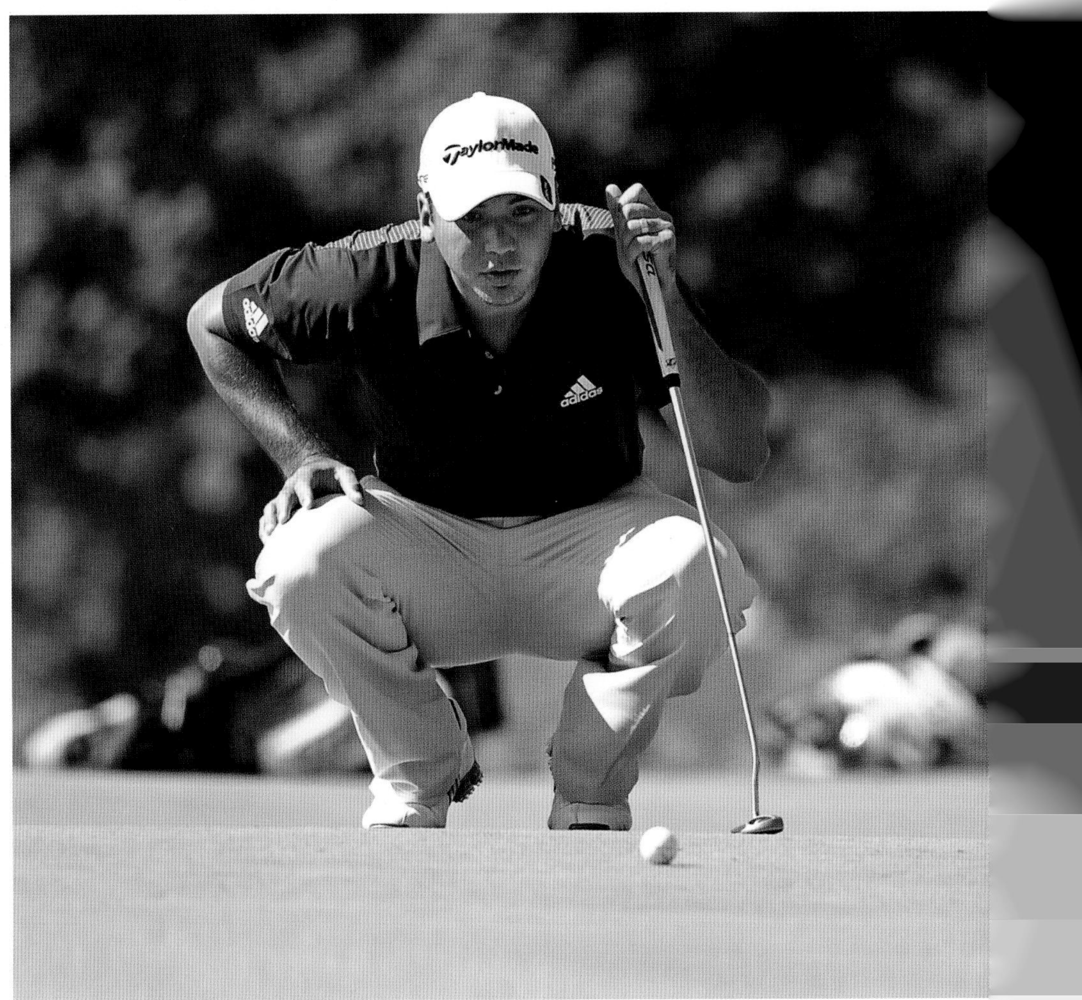

ADVANCED

TRICKLE THE BALL IN ON A DOWNHILL PUTT

by Jason Day

When you're judging speed on a downhill putt, you want the ball trickling as it gets to the hole. If you miss, you don't want it to go any farther than a foot past the cup. Missing is never good, but look on the bright side: You've got an uphill putt coming back.

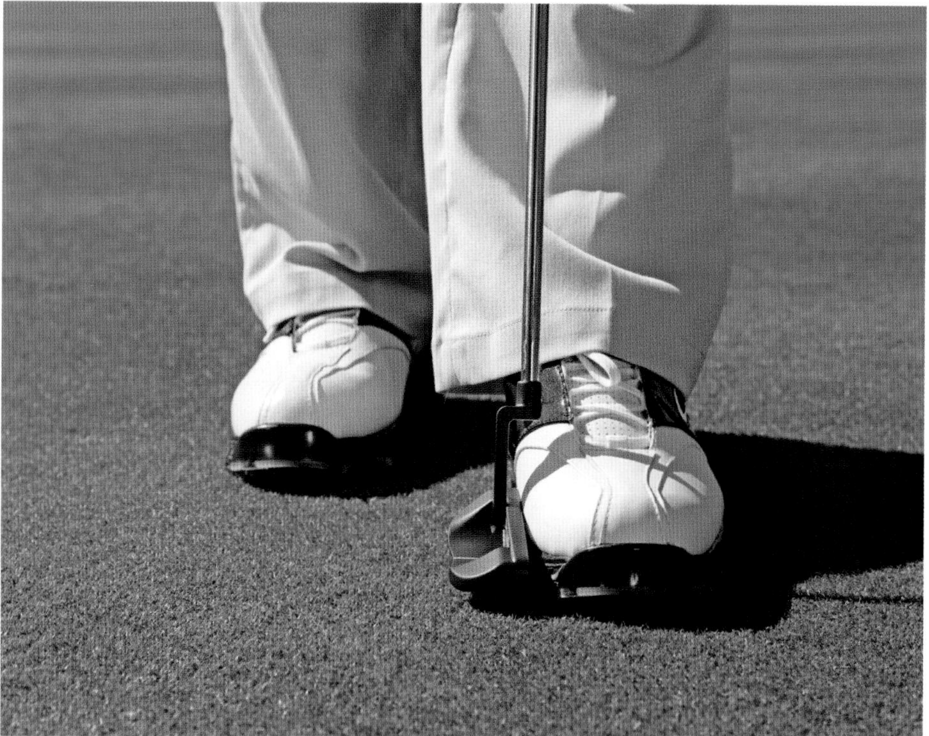

ADVANCED

POP IN THE SHORT ONES

by Jeff Ritter

To make your second putt from three or four feet, aggressive action is better than the typical soft, careful stroke. Learn to hit it like a wrecking ball with this left-foot drill.

Take your normal stance, then step forward with your left foot and set it where the ball would be. Using a short backstroke, give your foot a good pop. You'll swing the head and hit with a square face.

ADVANCED

HOW TO MASTER A TWO-TIER PUTT

by Stewart Cink

If you have a putt with a second tier, it's all about distance control. You have to mentally flatten the slope. Think of the green like a sheet that's bunched in the middle: If you pull it tight, it's a lot longer. The putt might look like 20 feet, but if you flatten the hill, it's a 22-footer. Allow for the extra length.

ADVANCED

HOW TO PUTT FROM OFF THE GREEN
by Nick Price

If there is very little grass under the ball, and there usually is when you're in a collection area or fringe just off the green, I recommend taking a 3-wood or hybrid and making a putting stroke versus chipping or pitching. The later shots are too risky for amateurs. The 3-wood will get the ball initially hopping, but then rolling like a putt. Hold the club as you would a putter, except grip down to the metal to compensate for the longer shaft.

EQUIPMENT

Let the shaft position dictate your putting path

by Jason Guss

Whether you prefer a mallet putter or a blade like the ones on this page, your putting path does not have to change. However, if you prefer a straight-back, straight-through path instead of an arcing path, a center-shafted putter could help you. Why? When the shaft is positioned in the center of the putter, instead of near the heel, the amount the putterface opens or closes during the stroke is reduced. If you putt on a straight line, you don't want the face to open or close at all.

Phil Mickelson sinks a birdie putt on the first playoff hole to defeat Ernie Els and win the 2004 Masters.

ADVANCED

UPHILL THEN DOWNHILL? SEPARATE INTO TWO PUTTS

by Tom Watson

A putt that goes up and then down is the most difficult. The key is good speed. Try separating the putt into two parts: a slow, uphill putt followed by a fast, downhill putt. Pick a point just over the top of the hill and make sure you get the ball to that spot or just past it. The hill will take care of the second part of the putt if you hit the first, part hard enough. Remember to read the downhill part first because putts will break more on the fast part of the green.

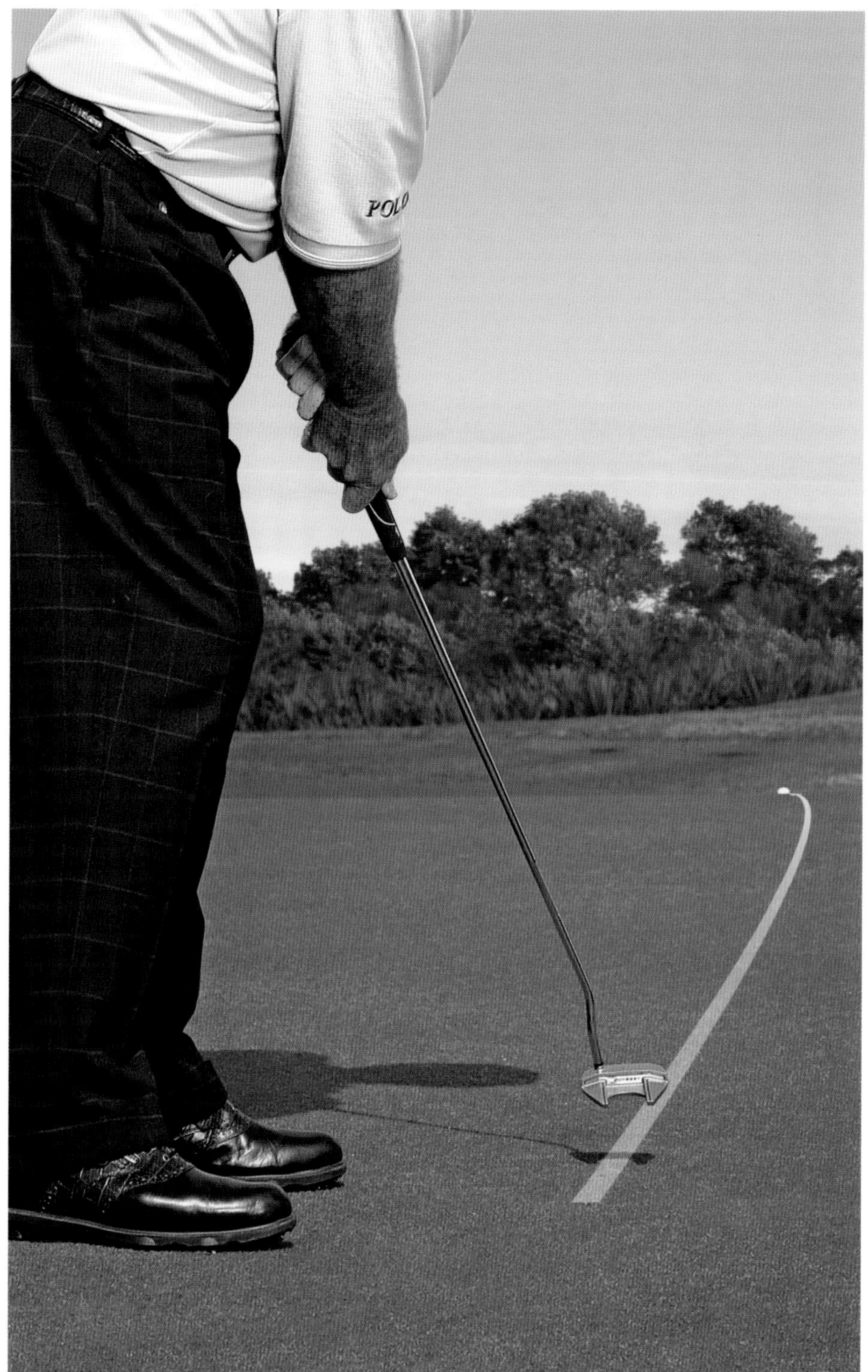

FITNESS TIP

Avoid lower back burn with glute bridges

by Mark Verstegen

Stand on the practice green long enough and you'll probably feel a burning sensation in your lower back. To avoid this type of muscle fatigue, which can also happen late in the round when you're trying to make a crucial putt, add glute bridges into your workout. It strengthens the muscles of the butt, and also the hamstrings and lower back.

Lie face up with your arms out to your sides, knees bent and your toes off the ground. Squeeze your glutes and thrust your hips upward until your body is in a straight line from your shoulders to your knees.

CHIPPI

SK telecom
N G

CHIPS ARE ANY SHORT SHOTS from just off the green where a lofted club is used to pop the ball in the air briefly, but relatively low to the ground, and then roll it to a stop as close to the hole as possible. If you want to know how important good chipping is to scoring, the very best players on the PGA Tour hit, on average, 12 or 13 greens in regulation each round. That means, when they don't, they are likely chipping close enough to the hole to make the ensuing putt (known as "getting up and down") at least five or six times a round. So you can imagine how important chipping can be to the average amateur, who only hits five or six greens a round in regulation.

Good chipping can be a real equalizer, especially to a golfer who doesn't have the swing speed to compete with bigger hitters. As the old golf cliché goes, "It's not how, it's how many." In other words, does it really matter if you made a par by hitting a green in regulation and two-putting or if you made a par by getting up and down with a great chip and a short putt?

While there is some variation to the chipping technique and club selection, most agree that an effective chip comes from maintaining your weight on your front leg and hitting the ball with a descending blow. Read on to hear what the experts have to say.

PREVIOUS SPREAD: **Deft touch:** K.J. Choi pulls off a tough uphill chip en route to winning the 2011 Players Championship.

OPPOSITE: Phil Mickelson swing sequence

90% **Tour pros save par from within 10 feet of the green more than 90 percent of the time.**

- For amateurs, lower, running chips are 58 percent more likely to stop within five feet of the hole than higher-lofted "checking" chips.
- A 20-handicap amateur gets up and down two out of 10 times from chipping distance. A scratch player does it five out of 10.
- From inside 10 feet off the green, the average tour pro chips to about three feet from the hole.

BASICS

HOW TO HIT A CHIP SHOT
by Todd Anderson

Because the chipping swing is so short, set up with your hands and club where you want them to be at impact.

1. Using a short iron or wedge, play the ball behind center and open your stance so your lower body is pre-rotated toward the target. Set more weight on your front foot, and lean the shaft forward so your left wrist is flat.

2. Swing the club back with your arms and shoulders, feeling the upper part of your arms riding on your chest as you make a little turn back. Remember, the clubhead stays below your hands.

3. Don't let your right elbow go just behind you; that would mean you're moving the club with your arms only. Start the downswing with your lower body, your right knee pushing toward the target. At impact, you want to return the club to that forward-leaning position, with the shaft in line with your left arm. Keep turning your body through and check that your left wrist is still flat at the finish.

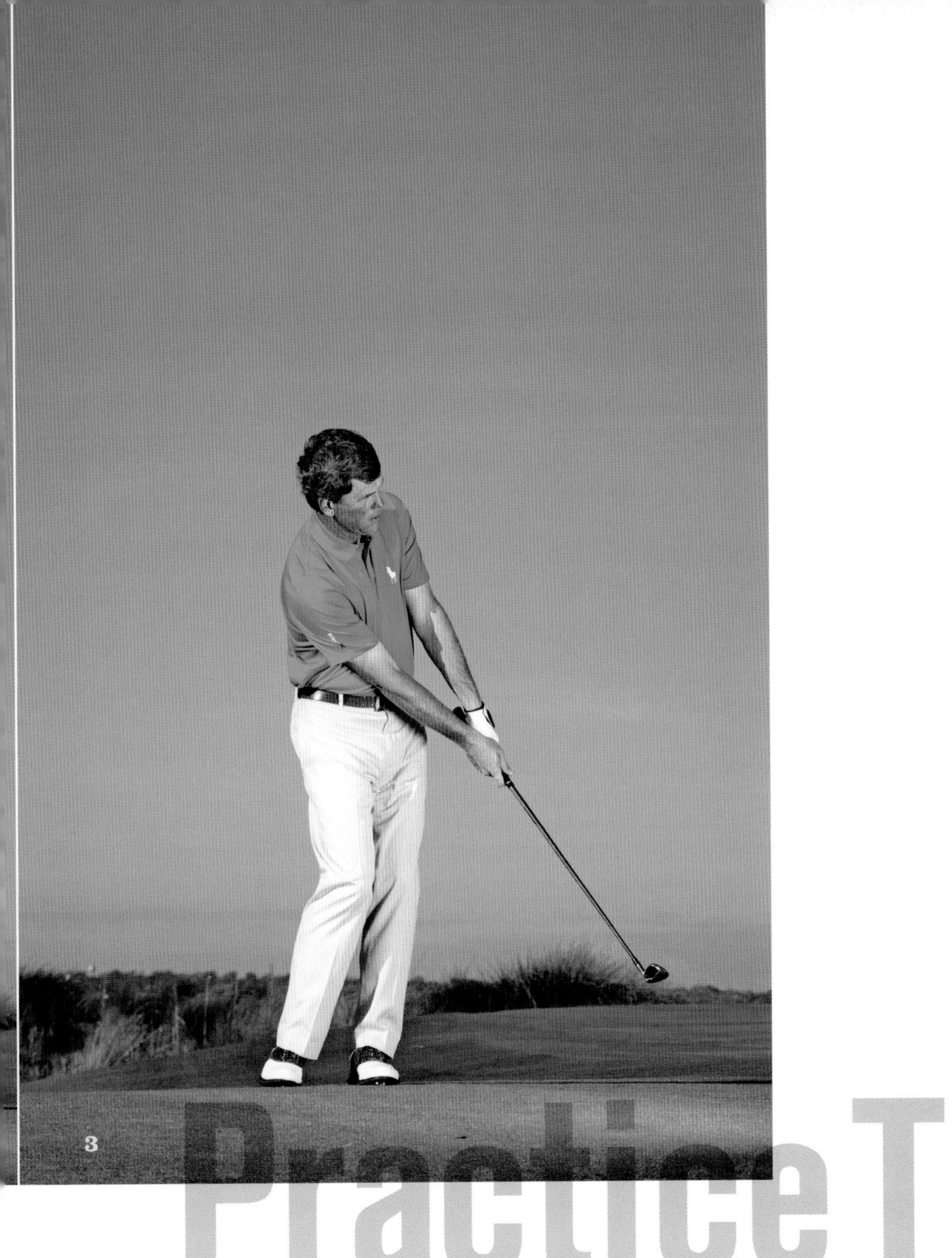

Practice Tips

SWING THOUGHT

Sometimes words sound like what they describe. A good example is the broom. Anyone who has used one knows it goes "whisk" when you sweep. I think whisk is a good sound to think about when you hit a chip shot. The clubhead should brush the grass and whisk the shot on its way. There is nothing lazy or sloppy about the chip. It's quick and firm. It whisks. So make your chips whisk. You might even imagine you're swinging a broom. ARNOLD PALMER

BASICS

SETUP: CREATE A SOLID LEFT SIDE

by Paula Creamer

When I chip, I place my left hand on my left thigh before taking my grip. This tells me that my weight is on my left side and that my center of gravity is slightly in front of the ball, two keys to making crisp contact. You can't hit the ball solidly if your weight is behind it at impact; the club will swing up into the ball instead of descending into it on the downswing. If I set up with a strong left side, my contact is much better.

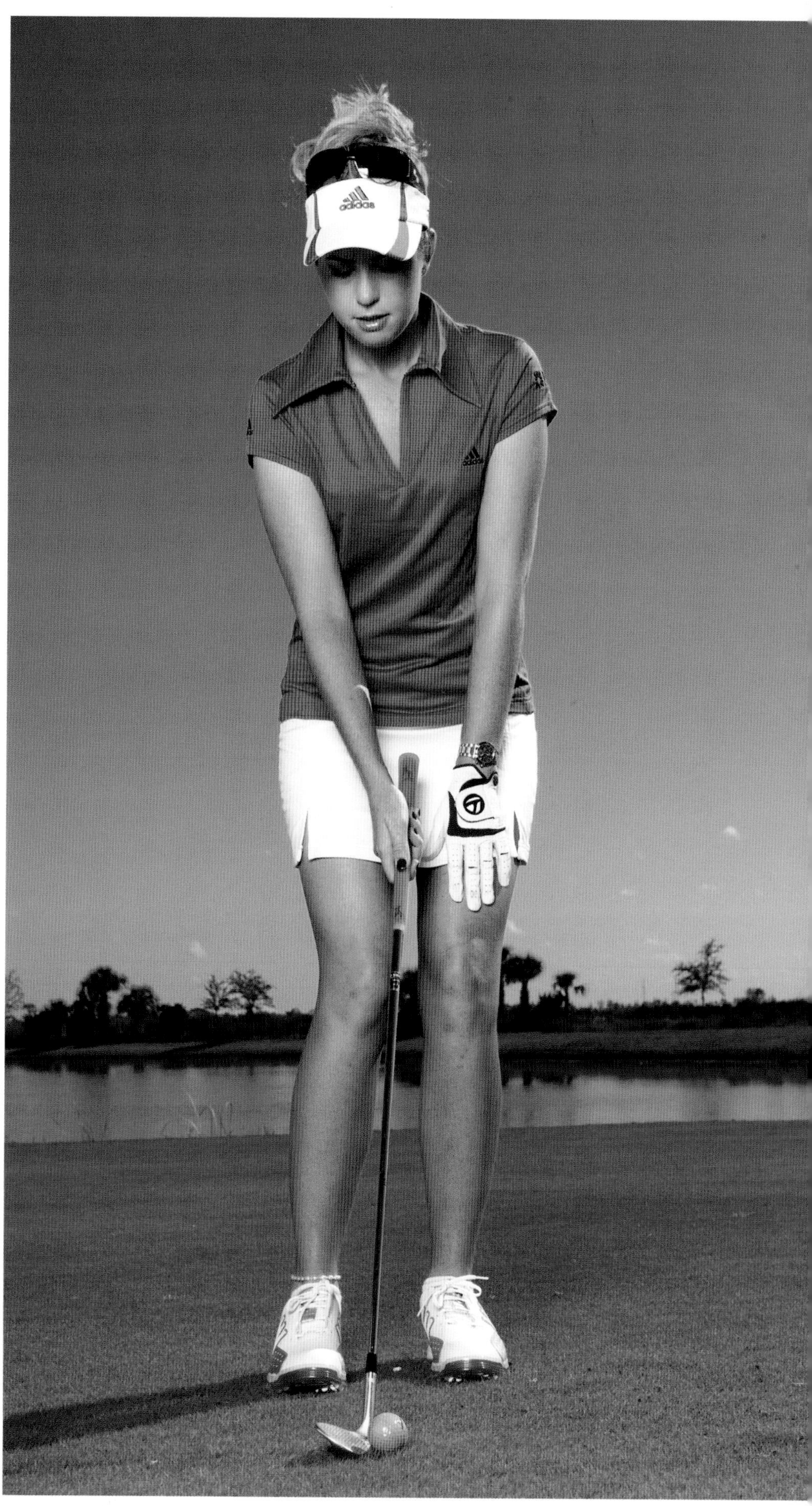

BASICS

KEEP YOUR LEFT WRIST FIRM FOR SOLID CONTACT

by David Leadbetter

Chipping, especially from longer distances, requires a lot of feel. You need some wrist action to control the distance, spin, and trajectory of the shot. Unfortunately, many golfers overuse their wrists. The left wrist breaks down at impact, causing them to blade or chunk the shot.

Your goal should be to keep your left wrist relatively firm through the swing, which helps you hit down crisply on the ball and keep the clubface square to the target. It's much easier to keep the left wrist solid by chipping with a putting-style grip, which is a variation of the common Vardon (or overlapping) grip. Simply invert the pinky and index fingers that connect your hands so your left index finger rests outside your right-hand fingers (called the reverse-overlap grip). You'll keep your left wrist firm.

Everything else is standard for chipping—slightly open stance, ball position well back of center, a little hinging of the wrists in the backswing, etc. But the grip change will stabilize that left wrist for more predictable contact.

BASICS

FEEL A CHIP IN YOUR HANDS
by Dean Reinmuth

Chipping effectively, especially off of tight lies, is a skill you can master if you focus on the grip end of the club–instead of the clubhead. Feel what your hands are doing when you chip the ball solidly. For example, your right wrist should stay cupped, or bent back, with the handle leading the clubhead throughout the stroke. To help groove this critical position, practice making right-hand-only swings with a ball wedged between your wrist and the grip.

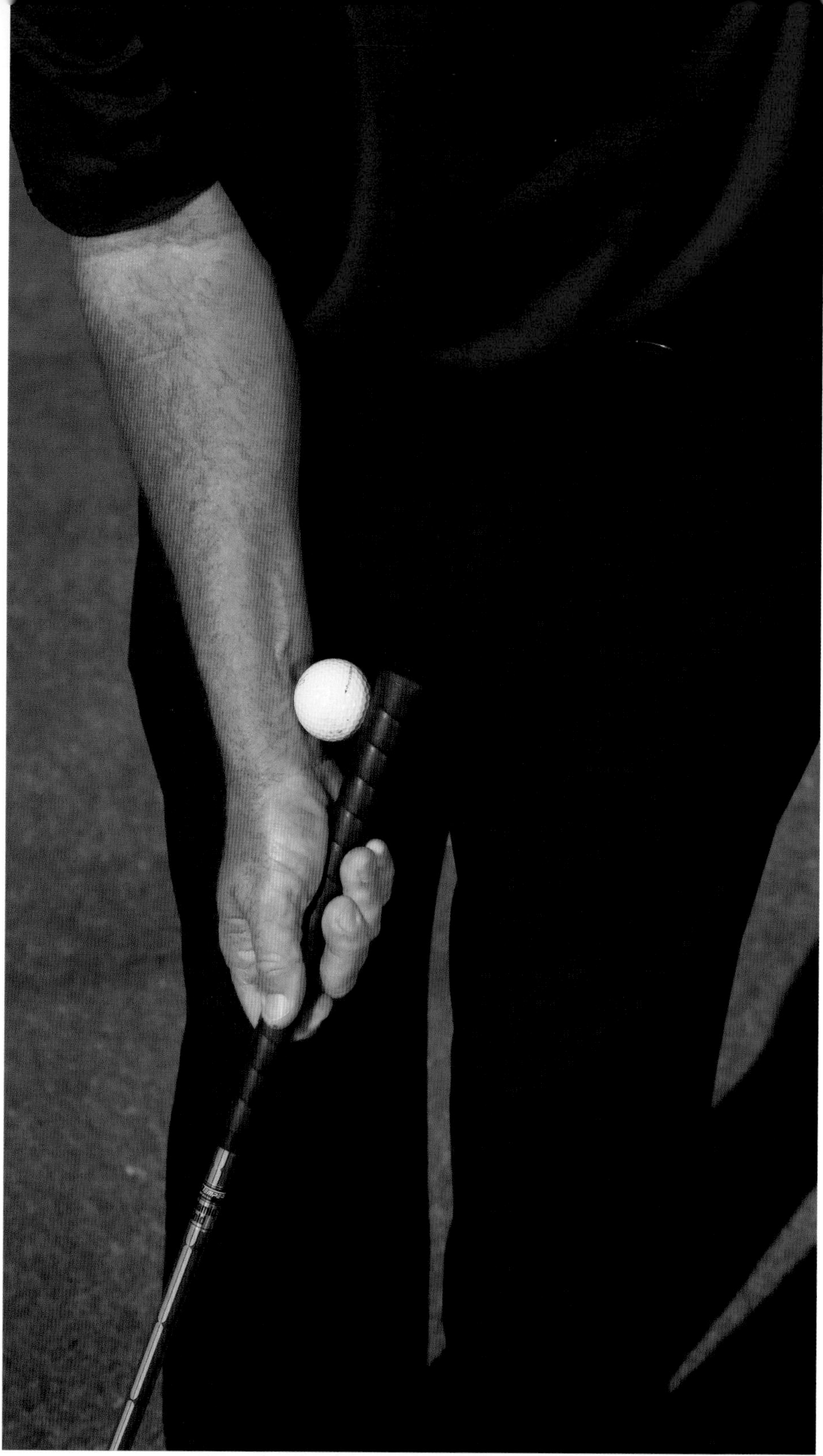

BACKSPIN

The closer you are to the green, the less chance you have for getting a lot of backspin on the ball. However, to get all the spin you can, you must swing down on a steeper angle than normal and make ball-first contact before the wedge hits the ground. But the real key is to keep swinging through the ball. Clubhead acceleration is vital to getting good backspin. Practice swinging through the ball to a full finish to improve your acceleration.

BILLY CASPER

BASICS

HIT A BACKHAND TO IMPROVE CHIPPING FEEL
by Stan Utley

It's hard for the average player to resist the urge to try to lift the ball on a chip, or to hold the face open to create loft. Imagine a ping-pong paddle in your left hand. The face of the paddle represents the face of the club. Instead of scooping or holding the face open, picture the face of the paddle turning to the ball, like a topspin backhand–the secret to crisp contact on chip shots.

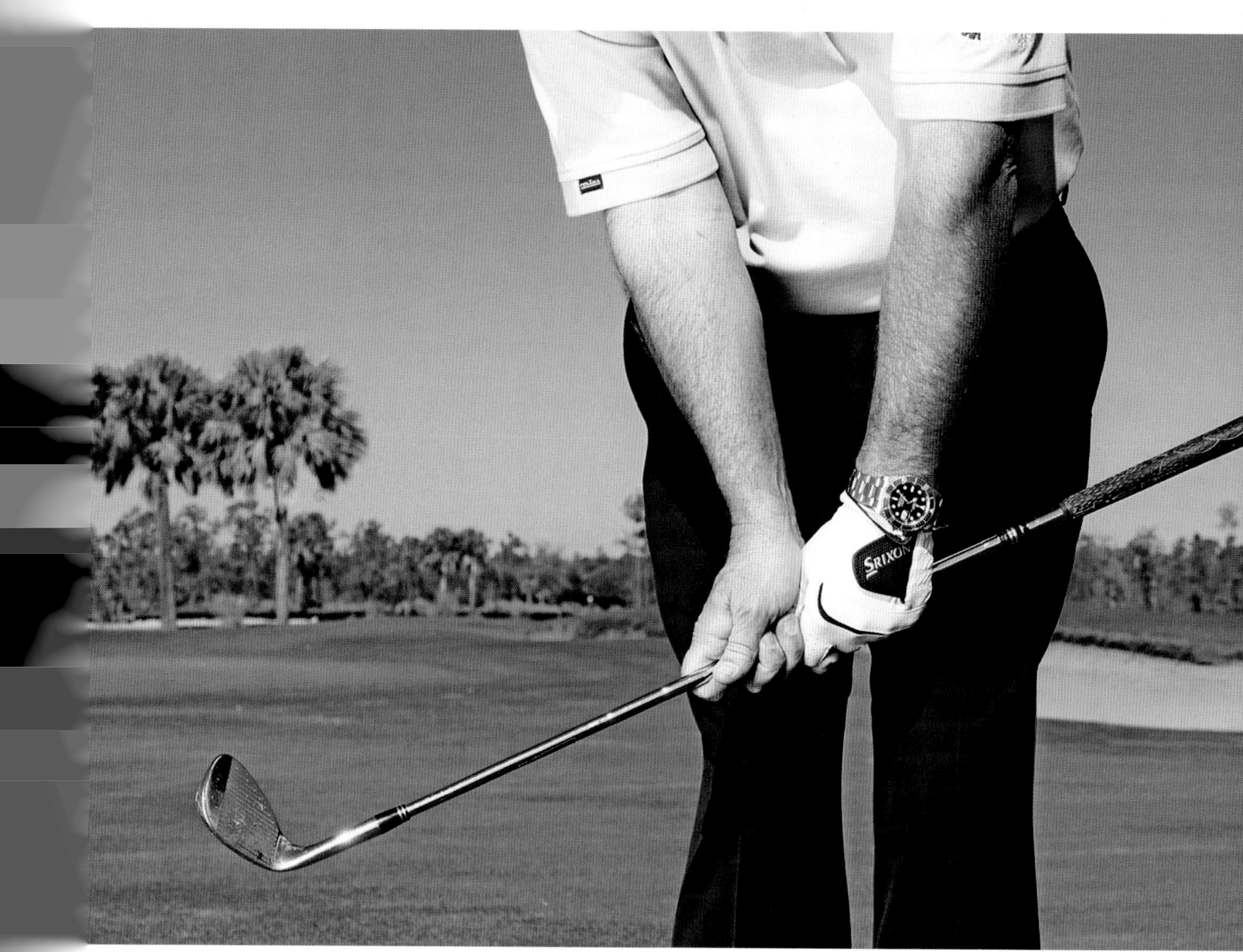

EQUIPMENT

Pick the right wedge for the right chipping situation

by Mike Stachura

When your ball is sitting in deep rough, you'll want to chip with a wedge that has considerable bounce (the bulge on the back edge of a sand wedge) so you can slide your club through the rough without it getting tangled in the grass. When your ball is sitting on a tight lie, you'll want to chip with a wedge or short iron with minimal bounce so you improve your chance of solid contact.

BASICS

A DRILL TO STOP THE CHIP FLIP

by Rick Smith

To hit this shot properly, the swing needs to be fairly long, and the wrists quiet, then the arms swing down as the body rotates toward the target. Honing this technique can take some time, especially when fighting the instinct to help the ball up with a wristy swing, but this drill will help speed up the learning process.

Grip an iron about midshaft so the butt end is pointing up and just outside your lead hip. As you take the club back, hinge your wrists slightly so the butt end of the shaft doesn't hit your side. Now start your downswing by rotating your body toward the target, maintaining the wrist hinge. The goal is to avoid having the butt end of the club touch your body during the swing. If the club hits your side, you either let your wrists break down or you failed to make a body turn.

You can try this drill with all sorts of things, including a pool cue or a broom handle. It's the fastest way I know to learn how to hit good short shots.

SWING THOUGHT

The basic fundamental in chipping to fast greens is to strike the ball with downward clubhead movement. It gives you maximum control of the shot and creates backspin, which minimizes the chance that the ball will roll too far. To achieve this downward movement, play the ball back in your stance, keep your hands ahead of the clubhead until you're well into the follow-through, and accelerate the club into the ball just as you would with a putt.

A great visual aid is to imagine how the ball would roll if you tossed it underhand onto the green. Once you have visualized that underhand toss, transfer that movement into how you hit the chip. Judging a chip will soon become easy.

JACKIE BURKE

ADVANCED

MAKE AN X TO HIT CRISP CHIPS

by Rob Akins

On chip shots, most amateurs have been told to lean toward the target at address and maintain that position through impact. The goal is ball-first contact, but the move delofts the club too much. Plus, the club's leading edge can easily get stuck in the turf. Instead, think about your spine leaning away from the target as you swing through.

Here, I'm posing at impact. The yellow stick highlights the clubshaft (leaning toward the target) and the orange one indicates the position of my spine (leaning away from the target). Notice how the two sticks converge and create an X? Next time you chip, make your own X. This allows the back edge of the clubhead—the bounce feature—to ride along the turf for crisp contact without getting stuck. Bounce equals forgiveness.

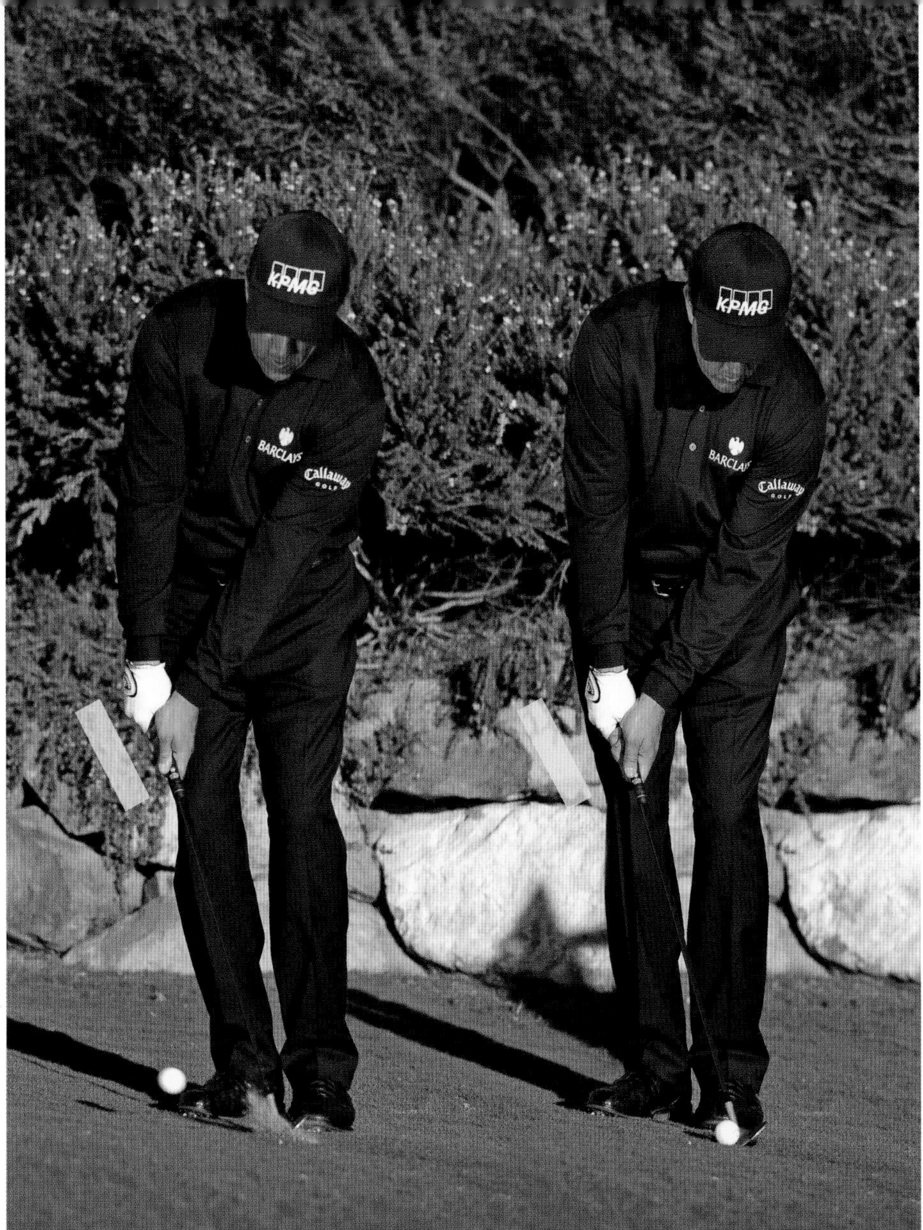

ADVANCED

MAINTAIN YOUR HINGE

by Phil Mickelson

I learned to chip as a kid by practicing endlessly in my backyard. I chipped with one club—a sand wedge—and when it came time to chip the ball low, I seldom bothered going to the garage to get my 8- or 9-iron. I simply learned to hit it low with my sand wedge, and the technique I discovered helps me to this day.

Start by playing the ball back in your stance, off the toe of your rear foot. At address, aim the clubface at the target, and position your hands well forward, in line with your front leg. That will effectively decrease the loft on your sand wedge. The backswing consists of a simple breaking of the wrists, with very little movement in your arms. On the downswing, accelerate your hands through to the finish, making sure you don't uncock your wrists. The ball will come out low, check a bit when it hits the green, and then run toward the hole.

MENTAL GAME

Good chippers have an attitude that the ball will wind up close enough to the hole that they can sink the putt. Bad chippers have the attitude that they "hope" the ball ends up close enough to the hole that they can sink the putt. Understand the difference? SAM SNEAD

ADVANCED

CHIP WITH DIFFERENT CLUBS FOR BETTER CONTROL

by Lorena Ochoa

Most amateurs I play with in pro-ams have a favorite club they use for all their shots around the green, and it's typically one with a lot of loft, like a pitching or sand wedge. This works well when the lie is a little fluffy and the design of the green calls for a high, fast-stopping shot, but it's far from ideal for all greenside chips and pitches. The key to a good short game is to chip with different clubs and pick the shot option that best suits each situation.

When I was growing up, my coach, Rafael Alarcon, had me practice chipping with every iron in my bag. From the same spot, I might have played three shots with my sand wedge, then three each with my 9-iron, 7-iron, and 5-iron. This taught me great creativity and gave me the confidence to vary my shots depending on what I need to do. I now have a variety of trustworthy options for every chip or pitch I face.

EQUIPMENT

Mind the gap

by Ron Kaspriske

When buying wedges, take into consideration their performance around the greens. Are they easy to chip with? Do they generate enough backspin on the ball to stop a short shot? Once you find a wedge you like, build the rest of your set of short irons around it. Most important is considering the difference in lofts between your pitching, gap, and lob wedges. Experts recommend a four-degree difference between these clubs. For instance, if your pitching wedge has 45 or 46 degrees of loft, your next wedge should be around 50 or 51 degrees. This is important because standard sets typically go from a 45-degree pitching wedge to a 56-degree sand wedge. That means there could be a 30-yard gap between two full-swing clubs you use often for approach shots.

Here's a sample of lofts for your wedge set:

PITCHING WEDGE	46 DEGREES
GAP WEDGE	50 DEGREES
SAND WEDGE	54 DEGREES
LOB WEDGE	58 DEGREES

ADVANCED

LEARN TO DIAL IN YOUR WEDGES

by Sergio Garcia

I've found that on chips and pitches, I can increase my feel by progressively gripping down the closer I get to the hole. It's something I picked up watching Seve Ballesteros. But remember, the more you grip down, the closer you should stand to the ball. From 30 yards, I grip down a few inches on a wedge and let my hands hang naturally from my shoulders. From 20 yards, I grip down a little farther and stand slightly closer. From 10 yards, my setup is very compact, gripping down even farther (almost to the metal) and very close to the ball.

THE SETUP

On all chip shots, keep your hands in front of the clubhead so that it will come through low to the ground and strike the ball before contacting the turf. Never try to pick the ball off cleanly. Hit down and through. In fact, many good chippers hood the clubface a little at address to ensure the club hits the ball before the ground.

GARY PLAYER

ADVANCED

TURN YOUR BODY FOR BETTER CHIPS

by Hank Haney

Believe it or not, it's actually possible to be a little too focused when you hit a chip. A lot of players get so fixated on the ball and on making clean contact that they don't let the arms extend and the body rotate through impact.

If your arms collapse and your body stops turning, the bottom of your swing is going to be behind the ball. That's how fat and bladed chip shots happen. Feel that extension and body rotation through the shot, and turn your head and eyes to where you want the ball to land. That will help move the bottom of your swing forward, where it needs to be.

The club you choose for a chip depends on what kind of shot you have to hit. I like the idea of maximum ground time and minimum air time. For a close shot from just off the putting surface, use a pitching wedge. For a 30-yard shot with lots of green to work with, try a 7- or 8-iron.

BASICS

PICKING THE RIGHT CLUB AROUND THE GREEN
by Butch Harmon

How's your lie? From deep grass, sometimes all you can do is try to wedge the ball anywhere on the green. If you're in the fairway, you have options. A wedge might still be best, but often you don't need all that loft. Whenever you can, play a running shot, down to a fairway-metal chip. And if the ground is dry and smooth, putt it.

How much green do you have? Always try to land the ball on the green, because the bounce will be more predictable. If you have a lot of green to work with, take a less-lofted club and run it. The low shot is safer because you use a shorter swing, but make sure you don't inadvertently bring trouble into play—like deep rough or water over the green.

How will the ball bounce? Look at two factors: the firmness of the green and any slopes. If the green is hard, a big bounce might make a wedge play like an 8-iron. The opposite might be true on a spongy green. The same thinking applies to landing the ball on an upslope or a downslope, where it can either die or take off. Try to picture that first bounce, and figure it into your club selection.

Playing Strategy

PLAYING STRATEGY

Some quick remedies to chipping woes

by Ron Kaspriske

The correct chipping motion seems counterintuitive to many amateurs, especially trying to grasp that such a short shot requires such a long, accelerating swing. If you are struggling to hit good chips, here are some things to try.

1. Look at your target instead of the ball when you swing. As long as you have confidence you'll hit the ball, this will help you accelerate the clubhead through the ball and toward the target.

2. Look at your hands instead of the ball. The correct chipping motion requires that the hands pass over the ball before the club hits it. By watching your hands, you can maintain a proper forward-leaning clubshaft past impact.

3. Take all your weight off your back foot. Lift it so you are balancing on your big toe. By keeping your weight off your back foot, you help ensure a downward angle of attack into the ball and help prevent a wristy, scooping stroke, which leads to poor contact.

4. If all else fails, try a chipper. There are many clubs designed to help improve the chipping stroke. Just make sure the one you buy is approved by the USGA.

BASICS

CHIP OR PUTT? WHAT SHOULD YOU DO FROM JUST OFF THE GREEN?

by Tom Watson

The 1977 British Open at Turnberry, where Jack Nicklaus and I went head-to-head the final two rounds, is a favorite memory. Jack led by a shot when I missed the green left on the par-3 15th the last day. My 4-iron stayed up on a little knob 12 feet off the green, 60 feet from the cup. My recovery shot was downhill, with a left-to-right break. Should I chip it or putt it?

If the grass between the ball and the green is similar to the green, it's almost always better to putt. You have more distance control. The fescue around the green was playing fast. I might have had better directional control by chipping to take some early break out of the shot, but I wanted to focus on the distance. I took the putter and made the long birdie putt to tie Jack, eventually winning by a stroke. (He finished 65–66 to my 65–65.)

BASICS

LONG CHIP? GET THE BALL ROLLING FAST

by David Toms

When I have nothing but green to work with, I don't have to fly the ball very far. The sooner I can get the ball rolling like a putt, the more accurate I can be. I'll chip with anything up to a 5-iron. Because I like the first bounce to be on the green, I pick the longest club that will carry the fringe. Here I'm using a 7-iron to run it up the slope; if this shot were downhill, I'd use a 9-iron and land it on the same spot.

The technique here is a compact, one-lever motion with minimal wrist hinge. I start from an open stance, which pre-sets my body to the target, and settle more weight on my front foot. I keep the backswing short and accelerate through the ball.

BASICS

VISUALIZE YOUR CHIPS LANDING AND ROLLING
by Jim Flick

We've all heard and read about visualization on full-swing shots, but you should also practice the technique on your short shots, even chips around the green.

First, check the lie to determine the shot you can play. Visualize the trajectory and rollout based on the lie. Then, select the club and swing you need to create that trajectory. I find it useful to determine the easiest putt I can leave myself if I don't hole the shot (say, two feet to the left of and beyond the pin in the photo here). That would give me a slight right-to-left, uphill putt. I visualize where my chip needs to land, hop, and roll out to give me that putt. Then, I make practice swings that would carry the ball to that landing spot.

Follow this procedure—check the lie, then visualize from the hole back—and you'll get those tricky chips up and down a lot more often.

BASICS

FROM THE ROUGH, PLAY IT LIKE A BUNKER SHOT TO ENSURE ACCELERATION

by Steve Stricker

Just like a pitch shot, I don't hinge my wrists very much when I chip. So to create the clubhead speed I'm losing by not hinging, I play chip shots out of the rough almost as if the ball were in a bunker (open face, swinging out to in). I think this method can help amateurs who struggle with this shot because they decelerate in fear of hitting it too far. Acceleration is the key to a successful chip. Set up with your feet aligned open to the target, and address the ball with the clubface open. Then, swing along your foot line, cutting across the ball. You can swing hard because the open face and out-to-in path creates a high shot that lands softly.

ADVANCED

HOW TO CHIP FROM A SIDEHILL LIE

by Tom Watson

Most players have trouble when the ball is above or below their feet. From a sidehill lie, the ball will follow the direction of the slope, and you have to allow for that.

When the ball is below your feet, it will bounce and run to the right, so aim left. Stand slightly closer to the ball, and set your weight left and more in your heels. Bend more at the waist, grip the club at its full length, and swing easier to adjust for the longer arc.

When the ball is above your feet, it's going to go left, so aim right. Stand slightly farther from the ball, and set your weight left but more on your toes to keep your balance. Grip down on the club, and swing a little harder to make up for the shorter swing arc.

Uphill

Downhill

ADVANCED

SWEEP UPHILL CHIPS

by David Leadbetter

When playing a course with elevated greens, you'll frequently find yourself chipping from an upslope to save par. But a normal chipping stroke, where you hinge your wrists and then make a steep, downward strike, can result in hitting a fat shot that comes up short. Simply put, the club gets stuck in the ground.

For this common short-game situation, you need to sweep the ball off the slope, not hit into it. I recommend taking a less-lofted club—the upslope will help get the ball in the air—and then making a swing that goes from low to high. In other words, the backswing should stay low to the ground, but the through-swing should move upward along the slope.

You'll make a clean hit, picking the ball off the grass. And when it lands on the green, it will usually roll, and not check up. That's because the sweeping action makes the ball come off the club with less backspin.

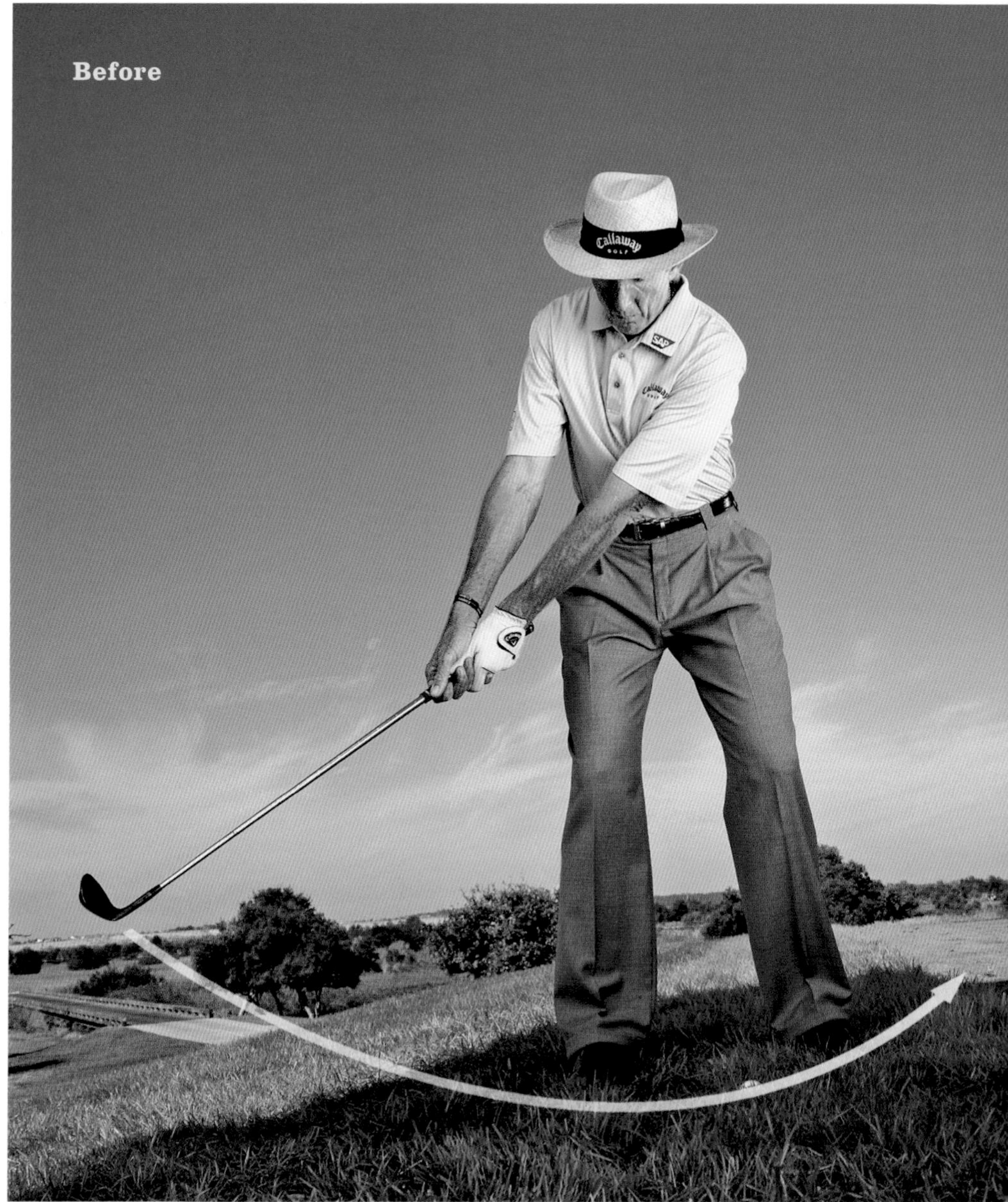

THE SETUP

Before my dad took over at Cape Fear Valley, he was the pro at Fort Bragg. The trick-shot artist Paul Hahn would come through there for exhibitions. Paul had a chest-high tee he'd stick in the ground, and he'd challenge people to try to hit a ball off the tee. It was hilarious; they'd whiff every time. I noticed that when people swung, the centrifugal force on the downswing pulled the clubhead away from them, so they'd overreach where the ball was. Then Paul would step in, fully extend his arms at address, and smoke the ball. I transferred Paul's method to chipping, keeping my arms extended at address and hovering my clubhead just off the ground. I rarely hit a chip fat after that. Making solid contact on chips can be difficult, and underreaching a bit at address will help. RAYMOND FLOYD

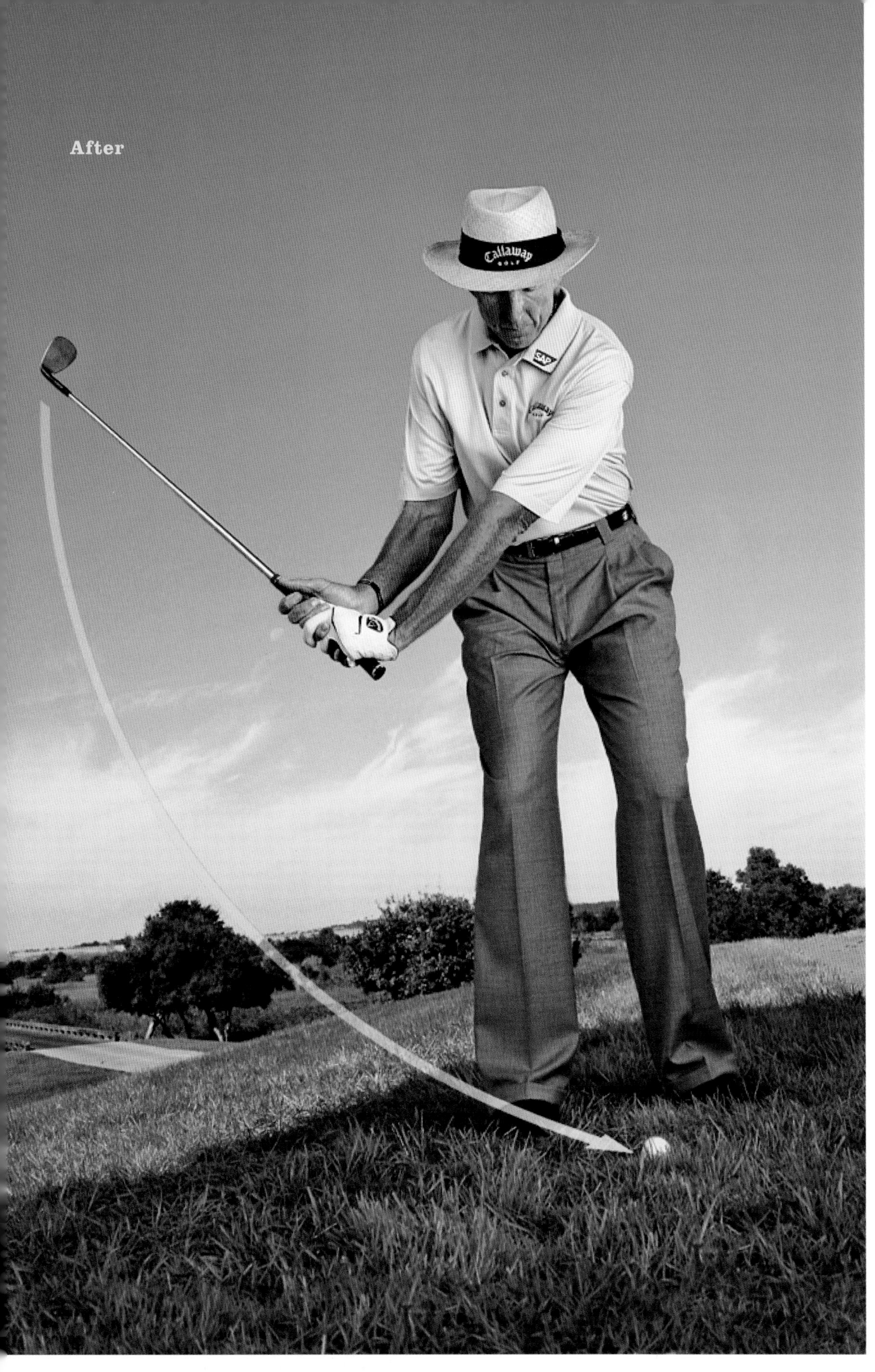

After

ADVANCED

USE YOUR PUTTER FROM A DOWNHILL LIE

by Butch Harmon

With greens rolling so fast these days, more approach shots run through the back fringe, close to the rough. You're on short grass, so you want to putt, but the rough interferes.

Use your putter, but play more of a chip shot. To play the fringe putt, take your putting setup, then let your left arm hang to your knee before taking your grip. This will lower your front shoulder, promoting a steeper backstroke that avoids the rough. (With a big-headed mallet, this shot might not work.) Lowering the shoulder is particularly important if you're going downhill, as I am here. Let your wrists hinge going back, and then stroke down and through. You'll feel more hit than you do on a putt.

STAT

How often do tour pros get up and down?

by Peter Sanders

FROM 10 YARDS OR LESS **85%**

FROM 10–20 YARDS (MEAN) **65%**

FROM 20–30 YARDS (MEAN) **51%**

FROM 30+ YARDS (MEAN) **29%**

Taken from 2010 PGA Tour scrambling stats of 192 professionals.

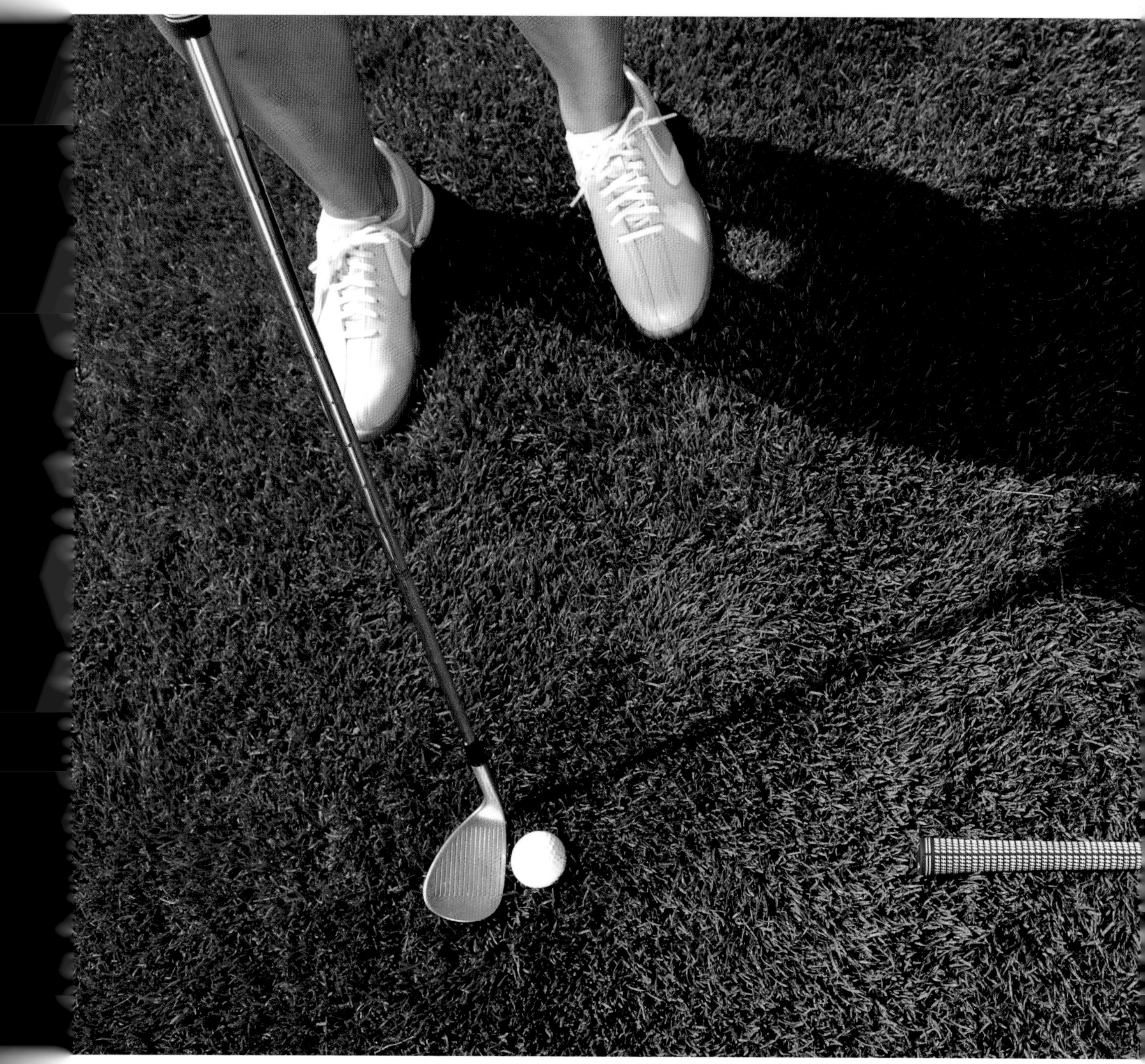

EQUIPMENT

Find a sand wedge you love. I won my three U.S. Opens, 20 tour events, and most of my 45 Champions Tour titles carrying only a 56-degree sand wedge. I'd vary the loft by opening or closing the face at address. Now I carry two sand wedges–52 and 58–but my effectiveness with the 58-degree is somewhat limited.

I think most amateurs should use only one sand wedge and get so familiar with it that they can adjust their shotmaking by choking down or adjusting their clubface position, ball position, or swing length. If you're handsy at all, lob wedges are very difficult to rely on, because you'll tend to flick at the ball with your hands and either come up short or skull it over.

HALE IRWIN

ADVANCED

WHEN YOU HAVE TO GET UP AND DOWN

by Annika Sorenstam

On short chip shots, it's important to aim the club square so you don't have to compensate during the swing. I used to have a habit of opening the clubface at address, which required me to roll the face over through impact to hit the ball on line.

Spin is another issue with chipping. Whatever amount of spin you generate—because of your club and ball choices—you want it to be predictable. That comes from consistent contact. Play the ball just behind center, put your weight on your left leg, and rock your shoulders back and through. The ball should bounce twice, check, and roll.

I also open my stance to get my left side out of the way and pre-set a little shift toward the target, but I always set the clubface square before I take my stance. If you start with a square face, the natural rotation of the club will return it to square at impact.

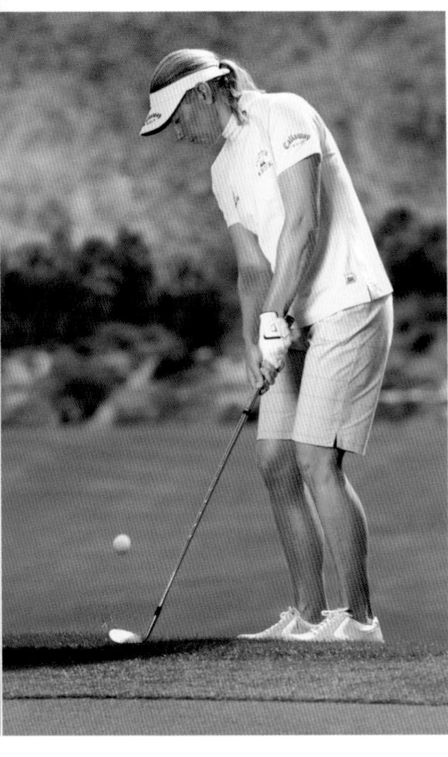

PLAYING STRATEGY

On good lies, the ball is positioned a bit farther back to the right than on putts, and there should be more weight on the left side. The worse the lie, the more weight you must set on your left foot–lean to the left–and the farther back to the right you must play the ball. The more you lean to the left and play the ball back to the right, the more lofted the club you will need to select to achieve a given height on the shot. PAUL RUNYAN

ADVANCED

HOW TO CHIP IT CLOSE WHEN YOU'RE UNDER PRESSURE

by Ernie Els

During a tournament, I'm not thinking about mechanics at all. I'm in scoring mode. But when the pressure builds on Sunday afternoon, nerves can certainly disrupt what you're trying to do, especially around the green. When you find yourself in that position late in a big match, don't get bogged down with swing thoughts.

Grip pressure–not mechanical flaws–is the biggest factor when you're nervous. You unconsciously grip the club tighter, which keeps you from making a smooth swing with a natural release. Keep your grip pressure light, and you'll be surprised how much your mechanics stabilize. I focus on light grip pressure, and then go with the shot I like to hit. For example, I've never been a good bump-and-run player, so under pressure I usually choose a lofted shot, even when I've got some green in front of me to work with.

ADVANCED

PICK A SPOT TO IMPROVE ACCURACY

by Vijay Singh

For me, chipping is completely spot-oriented. First, I decide where I want the ball to drop. Depending on if I want it to check up or release to the hole, I pick the shot I'm going to hit to that spot. I play most of my chip shots with my L-wedge. If I have to hit something longer, like a 30-yard chip, I'll use my pitching wedge. It's also a safer chipping club for most amateurs.

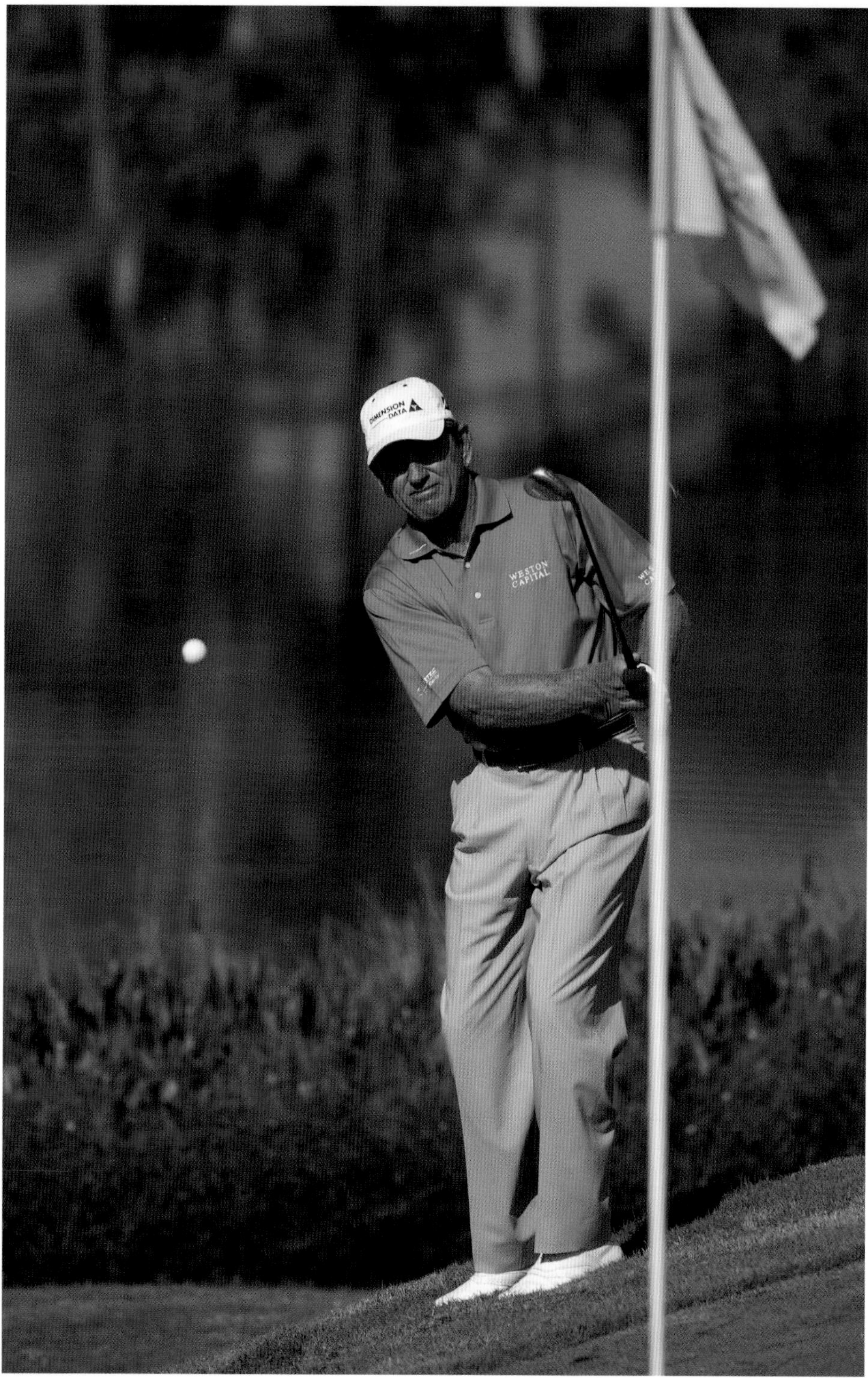

ADVANCED

HOW TO CHIP IT CLOSE FROM ROUGH JUST OFF THE GREEN

by Nick Price

When you're just off the green and the ball is sitting down, you're facing the hardest shot in golf. Commitment is everything. You have to accelerate the club underneath the ball. For this shot, I use my 56-degree wedge. The key is swinging through until your hands are about hip high. Remember, don't baby it. You want to make sure your next shot is a putt.

FITNESS TIP

Improve your posture with inverted hamstring stretch

by Mark Verstegen

The impetus to incorrectly help a chip into the air by lifting the body up and scooping the hands can often be because the golfer struggles to maintain posture. Strong, flexible hamstrings are crucial. Stand on your left leg only with your arms extended from your sides. Now bend over at the waist, and raise your right leg so it's behind you and parallel to the ground. When you feel the hamstring stretch in your left leg, return to the starting position. Switch legs and repeat.

PITCHI

N G

PREVIOUS SPREAD:
Pitcher perfect: Tiger Woods celebrates after holing out a miraculous pitch shot for birdie to help win the 2005 Masters Tournament.

OPPOSITE:
David Toms swing sequence

THINK OF THE PITCH SHOT AS THE "MIDDLE MAN." It's a longer and higher shot than a chip, but not as long or as high as a full swing. The same holds true for swing mechanics. A pitch shot is nothing more than a longer chip shot in terms of body rotation, arm swing, and club acceleration and a full swing is nothing more than a longer pitch. This concept should help you in learning how to hit quality pitch shots.

Since most pitches occur from within 50 yards of their target, you would think this is an easy shot to get close to the hole, but most amateurs struggle because they lack the confidence in the proper pitching action to execute it repeatedly. They either slow down their swing into the ball—in fear of hitting the shot too far—or they try to help the ball in the air by making a scooping motion with their wrists through impact—in fear that a normal swing and the club's designed loft won't get the ball airborne.

Remember, the pitch is a shorter full swing, but it still requires body rotation and club acceleration through the ball. If you trust this notion, and that the wedge's design will hit the ball at the right trajectory, you can learn this valuable short-game skill. Here's what the best teachers and players have to say on the subject.

8′1″ **The average proximity to the hole a tour pro hits a 30-yard pitch shot from the rough.**

- The average amount of times a 25-handicap misses the green with a pitch shot from inside 50 yards is 2.5 per round.
- The worst player on the PGA Tour saves par from off the green, known as scrambling, 49 percent of the time.
- The key to pitching is acceleration. Pros hit pitch shots with swing speeds up to 40 percent faster than amateurs.

Practice Tips

BASICS

HINGE AND REHINGE TO MASTER THE PITCH SHOT

by Luke Donald

The big thing for me on pitch shots is getting the clubhead swinging and letting that move my body, not the other way around. I start with the ball slightly forward and my hands centered in front of me. I also play the face a little open for all my pitch shots. Then, I hinge the club upward going back, not around my body, with the toe pointing to the sky. Coming down, the club should unhinge the same way it went back. I want to feel it swinging down and through. The momentum of the club pulls my body to the finish.

BALL FLIGHT

The low pitch is useful whenever you're hitting into a stiff breeze or have to keep the ball under branches, etc. First, take a narrow and slightly open stance. Move the ball back to a point about an inch inside your right foot. Now, focus on swinging the club more to the inside than before. Second, turn your shoulders more. Get your left shoulder behind the ball and under your chin. That rounded backswing will force you to rotate both your body and the clubhead more through impact. But there's no need to hit the shot hard. You only need a short follow-through.

NICK FALDO

SWING THOUGHT

Picture a sand shot to hit better pitches

by Ron Kaspriske

Most amateurs hit poor pitches because they decelerate in fear of hitting the ball too far. But if you treat a pitch like a bunker shot—open the face, hinge your wrists in the backswing, and hit behind the ball and accelerate under and through it—you'll pop the ball up on the green without letting your fear hinder the shot. Pick a spot right behind the ball, open the clubface, and then hit a bunker shot without sand.

BASICS

PIVOT AROUND YOUR LEFT LEG

by Stan Utley

The mid-length pitch is a shot average players have to hit pretty often, and they often struggle with it. You have to judge what size swing to use, and also avoid decelerating the club through impact. To get a better feel for this shot, avoid making a big, long arm swing. Keep your weight forward, let the club hinge back freely, then pivot through the shot around your left leg. Keep the arms passive. You can control distance with the speed you pivot your body.

BASICS

LEARN THE PITCH-AND-RUN FOR LONG GREENSIDE SHOTS

by Butch Harmon

With a fairway lie and plenty of green to work with, the pitch-and-run is the best shot to play. There's no reason to fly the ball all the way to the hole—even if you do see the pros doing it on TV. Using your 9-iron or wedge, play the ball middle to slightly back in your stance, and push your hands and weight forward. Get a clear focus on where you want to land the ball to run it to the hole. (It's a good idea to carry it onto the green for a predictable bounce.) Swing the club straight back about halfway, and accelerate into the back of the ball, finishing with your arms and club pointing at the hole. Think of this as an arms-and-body swing: Turn your body and swing your arms through together. Resist the urge to help the shot at impact with your hands.

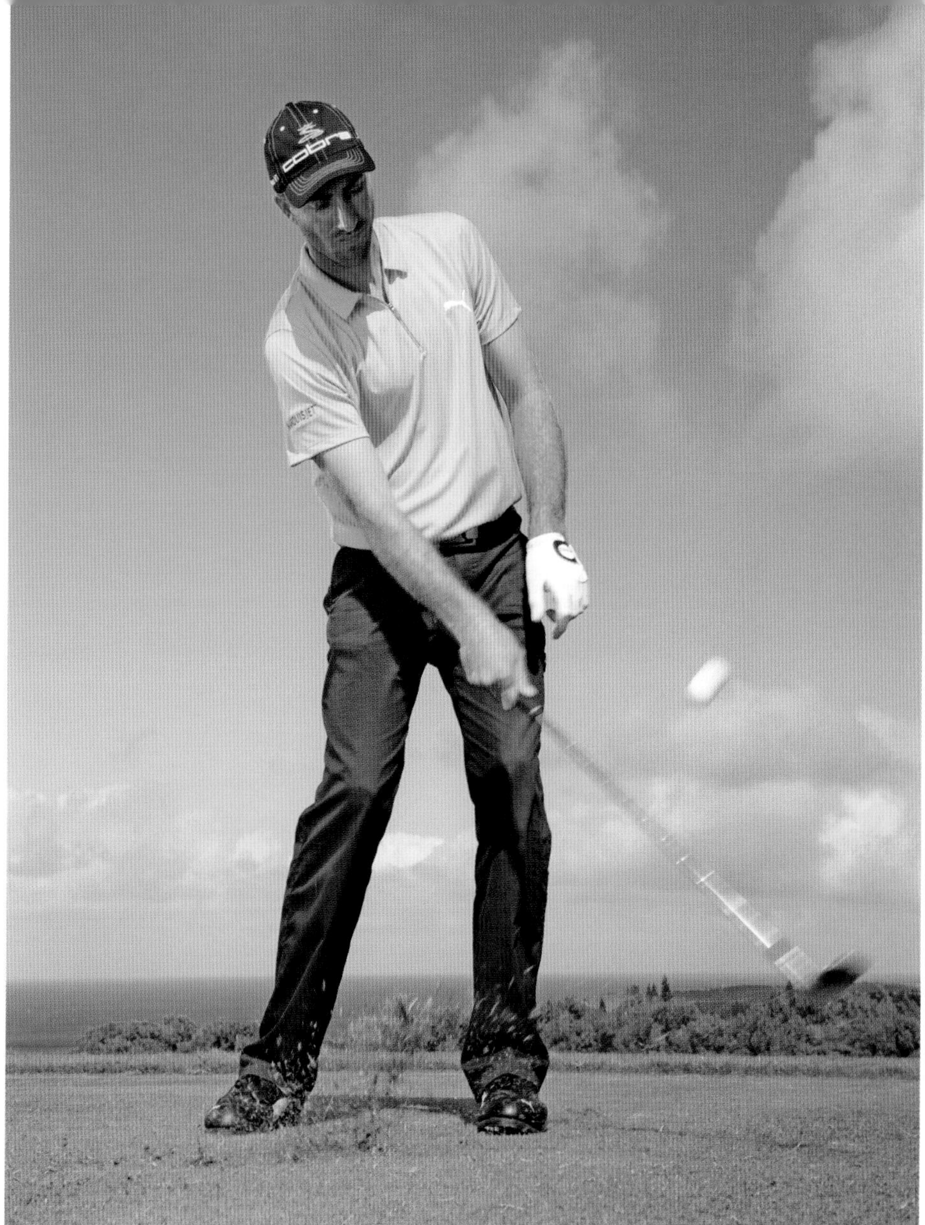

BASICS

INGRAIN THE RIGHT ACTION BY PRACTICING WITH ONE HAND

by Geoff Ogilvy

Hitting wedge shots with my right hand only really ingrains the feeling of release. Essentially, it turns my pitch shots into little full swings. I used to try to get a lot of shaft lean at impact and take the ball in low. The feeling was to hold on instead of releasing the clubhead past the hands. But it was hard to get any kind of consistency. Then, I decided to treat a pitch more like a full swing and the right-hand-only drill forces you to release the clubhead just as you would with a 7-iron out in the middle of the fairway. Now, if I want to hit a lower-trajectory pitch, I just use a pitching wedge or 9-iron.

TECHNIQUE

The short pitch shot is similar to a chip in that the stance should be narrow with the knees bent. Your weight should be toward the forward foot with the hands ahead of the clubhead at all times until after impact. There should be little body movement and the ball should be struck first, with a downward stroke. However, because I want this shot to fly high and stop quickly, I open my stance slightly so that my left foot is pulled back from the target line. This allows me to take the club back more to the outside than with a chip. It also allows me to cut across the ball and impart more spin. I also cock my wrists abruptly as I take the club back and try to maintain some wrist hinge as I swing through to add loft and spin to the shot. The wrist hinge and hold is crucial to this shot. The more forward you play the ball in your stance, the higher it will go.

GARY PLAYER

Lower

Higher

BASICS

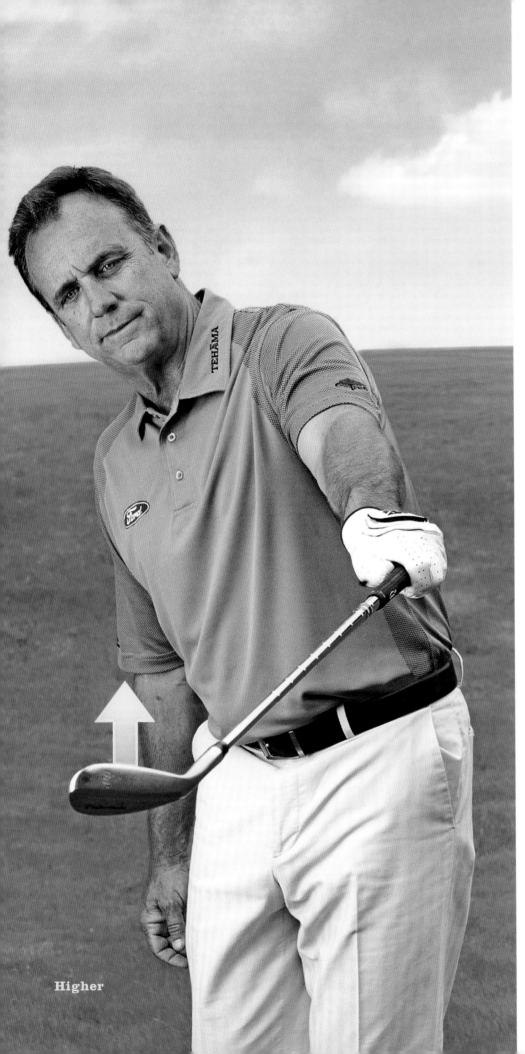

HOW TO PITCH IT LOWER
by Rick Smith

Amateur players ask me all the time how tour pros hit that 50-yard pitch shot that flies low, takes a few bounces on the green, then stops cold. Hitting down on the ball with significant clubhead speed is one key, but another important aspect is how the club moves through impact. If you want to hit a low-trajectory pitch shot that grabs on the green, make sure the toe of your wedge is pointing skyward in the follow-through.

In essence, the low pitch is like an abbreviated full shot in terms of how the club moves through the hitting area. By trying to turn the toe up through impact, you're delofting the clubface, just as you should on a normal iron shot from a good fairway lie. A side benefit of this move through the ball is that it increases clubhead speed, which produces more backspin. And that's one way to get the ball to stop quickly after it lands.

BASICS

HOW TO PITCH IT HIGHER
by Zach Johnson

First, respect the lie. The tighter the lie—hardpan, tightly mown fairways—the tougher it is to slide the clubface under the ball. If you don't have a lie where you feel reasonably confident you can do this, consider playing a different shot.

To hit it high, open your stance. Setting up with your body aimed left of the target helps get you to swing through and finish the shot. Put more weight on your left side at address for the same reason.

Set your wrists. Just like on a sand shot, you should hinge your wrists as you swing back. This will help you hit the ball higher. The higher you want it to go, the more wrist hinge you need. You don't need a lot of body rotation to hit the high pitch, so feel as if your arm swing is propelling the club. If you're shallow through the ball, the club's loft will launch it high.

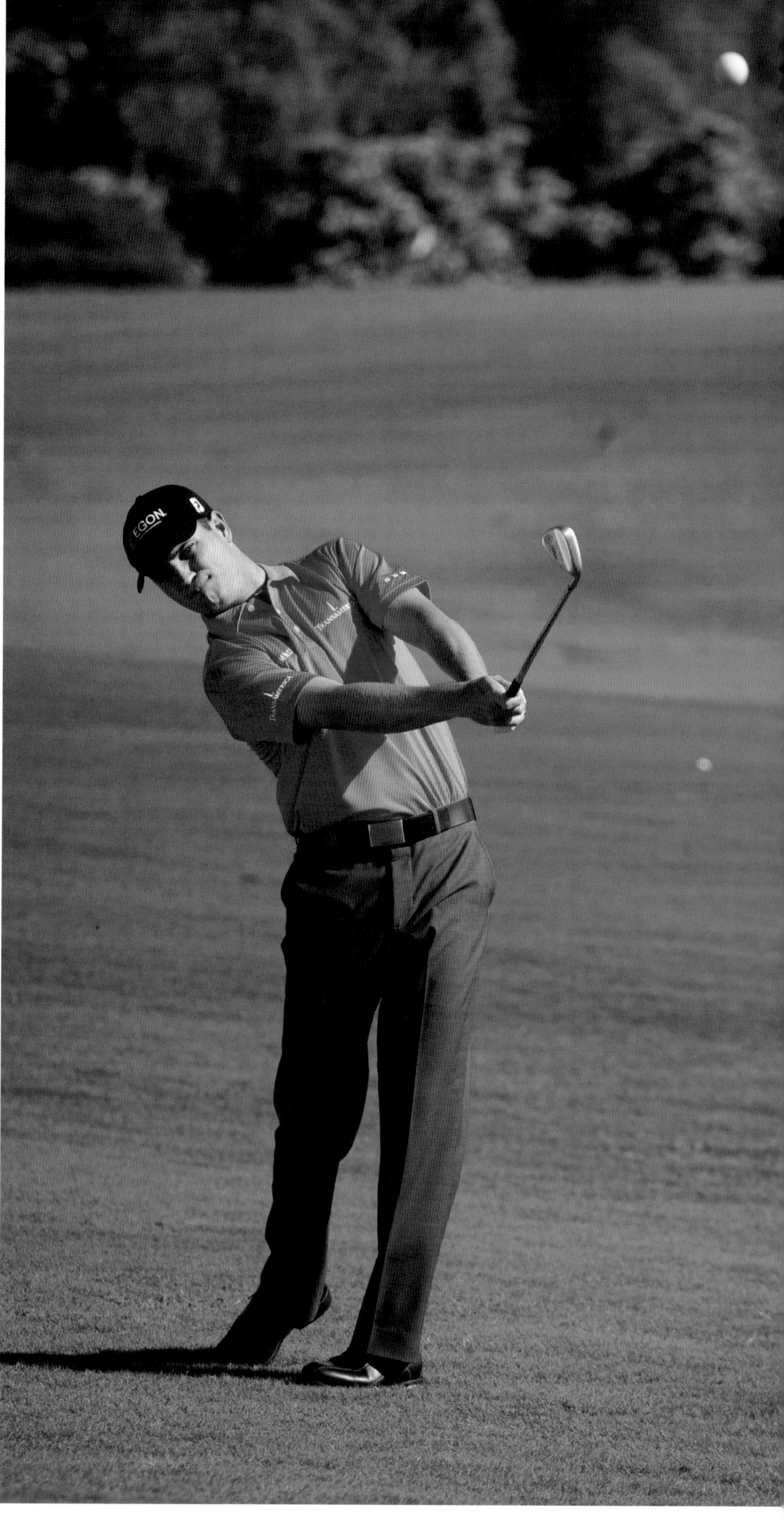

BASICS

PITCH IT LIKE THE PROS
by Butch Harmon

I see a lot of average players trying to pitch the ball way up in the air. Then I watch pros at tour events, and they keep the ball down, so they can better control how far it goes. Sure, sometimes you need a high shot, but your standard pitch should be a lower one that releases and rolls.

In these photos, you can see the differences between the low pitch and what a lot of amateurs do. The pros play the ball in the middle to slightly back in their stance and keep the shaft angled forward through impact by shifting left on the downswing. Amateurs play the ball too far forward, then hang back on their right foot and try to scoop the ball. With this much hand action, they often wind up hitting it fat or thin, which they live in fear of doing.

Think of it this way: The pros set the loft when they sole the club at address and maintain it throughout the swing. Amateurs try to add loft at impact, which isn't necessary and leads to poor contact. So play the ball back, and keep that shaft forward. Your pitching will improve, and your fear will disappear.

NO SPIN

I am very much opposed to excessive spin on the golf ball for pitch shots. For the pitch shot, it is easier to learn how to not spin it than spin it, so follow my steps. Stand tall at address with a narrow stance. Then, keep your posture constant as you swing back. You want a minimal turn of the right hip and no significant weight to the right side as you up-cock your wrists. This should create a compact backswing. Then, uncock the hands early in the downswing to promote an underhand-toss action through the ball. At impact, release the hands and wrists as the club moves under the ball. The left leg straightens and left hip turns away from the ball to promote an inside-out swing path. You want the sense the club has hit up on the ball and you should finish on your right toe.

PHIL RODGERS

BASICS

A SIMPLE WAY TO CHANGE THE HEIGHT OF YOUR PITCH SHOTS

by Jim Flick

Davis Love Jr., who died in a small plane crash in 1988, was well-known as a great teacher. But not many know that Davis Jr., father of Davis III, was also a very good player. He tied for the lead after one round in the 1964 Masters, and he tied for fifth with Jack Nicklaus in the 1969 British Open at Royal Lytham. Davis pitched the ball magically at that year's British Open, despite firm and windy conditions. He later told me one of the secrets to great pitching is controlling your trajectory. The way to do that, he said, is by adjusting your grip pressure.

Davis said that to hit high pitches, you should grip the club softly. I'd recommend a 2 or 3 on a 10-point scale, 10 being the firmest. This allows the club to release freely and adds loft as it slides under the ball through impact. For low pitches, grip the club more firmly—a 6 or 7. This allows you to keep the grip end ahead of the ball, which stabilizes the clubface through impact, keeping its loft constant. When you practice pitches, use one club and vary your grip pressure. See for yourself how it affects your trajectory.

Callaway
SAP
Jos. A. BANK
0
20
40
60
80
100
120
140
160
MPH

ADVANCED

HIT THE GAS TO IMPROVE PITCHING ACCURACY

by David Leadbetter

The most common way golfers are told to regulate distance on pitch shots is to vary the length of the backswing. But I've always found it extremely difficult to get players to know exactly how far back they should take the club. How would they know? It's not like a bell goes off when they get to the correct spot.

Instead of worrying about varying backswing lengths, focus on one length—halfway back, with the left arm parallel to the ground. From there, key on the acceleration factor through impact. For example, if you want to hit a 90-yard shot, think about making a 90-mph swing. If you want to hit it 70 yards, make it 70 mph and so on. Obviously, these speeds are not accurate, but it's a great mental concept for improving distance control on your pitch shots.

EQUIPMENT

How the new grooves affect your wedge play

by Max Adler

Our test was simple. Using identical 56-degree wedges (one with the new V-like grooves and one with the old U-like grooves), a scratch golfer hit 10 balls each from a 100-yard full-swing shot, a 40-yard pitch, a flop shot from the rough, and a greenside bunker shot. See chart below for results.

THE GAP FOR PLAYER A

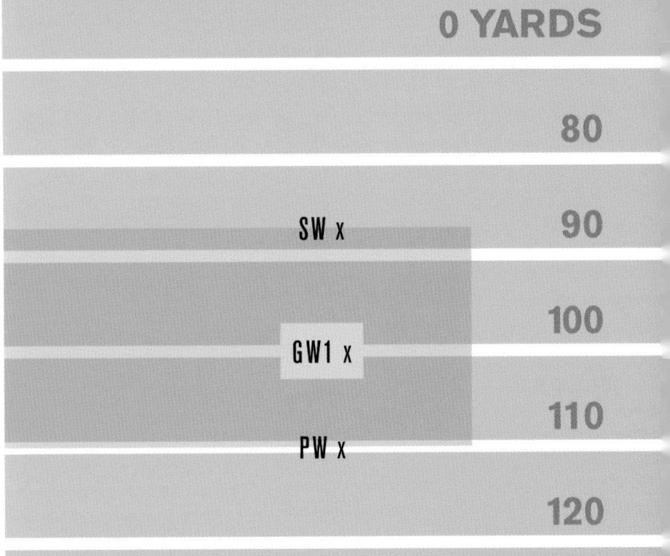

THE GAP FOR PLAYER B

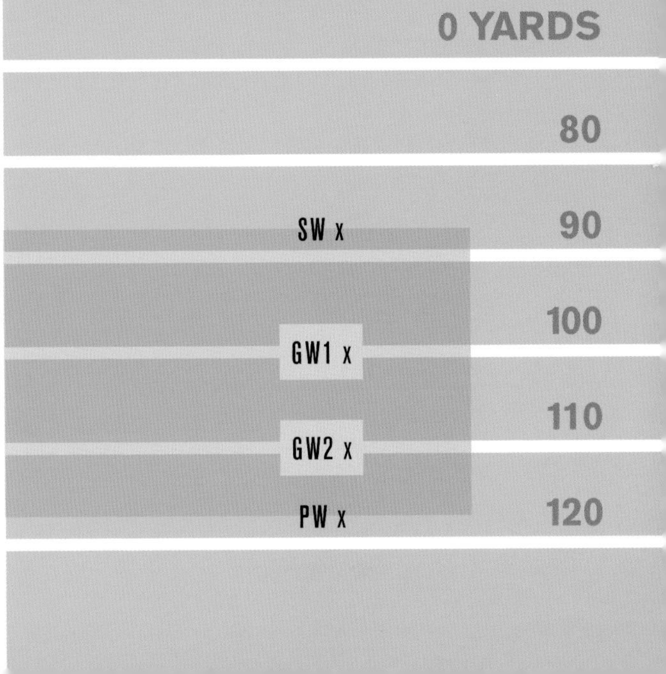

ADVANCED

HOW TO HIT THE LOB SHOT
by Sean Foley

The most common way the lob shot is taught is to open your stance and clubface at address and maintain an open face as you swing along your body line and cut across the ball. This can lead to inconsistency in distance control and direction because it's hard to judge how hard to swing and where the ball will land.

Even a great player like Stephen Ames struggled with this method. He would sometimes fall onto his back foot in an effort to help the ball in the air when his mechanics weren't quite right. That's why we changed the way he hits this shot. I had him take a lofted wedge and address the ball with his stance and clubface square to the target—not open. Then, I had him lower the shaft and lean it away from the target. This cupped his left wrist. The goal was to maintain that cupped position through impact, which exposes the bounce (the bulge on the club's sole) and increases the loft, making the ball fly higher.

With this method, it's much easier to control the direction of the shot because you set up square to your target. Exposing the bounce also gives you some margin for error because the bounce keeps the club from digging and getting stuck.

ADVANCED

HOW TO HIT THE HATED HALF-WEDGE

by Phil Mickelson

Many amateurs find the half-wedge shot to be awkward, and when sand or water are involved, downright scary. If you tend to hit the ball fat or thin, can't decide how big a swing you should make, or find yourself coming up long or short, try my system. It will erase your fear and give you the consistency and control you've been looking for. When playing this shot, open your stance, play the ball forward of center, and aim the clubface at your target. In the backswing cock your wrists fully, but limit your arm swing. Then swing down and through, but end the swing when your arms are parallel to the ground.

Playing Strate

BASICS

HOW TO ERASE TENSION ON PITCHES

by Stan Utley

If you get into a rigid, locked position, you're never going to have a good short game. To hit good pitch shots, set up so your arms hang loosely from your shoulders and your feet are close together, to make it easier to rotate. To hit the shot, pivot through instead of swinging your arms independently at the ball. The butt of the club should stay pointed at your belt buckle the whole time, which keeps the bounce on the bottom of the club exposed to the ground. If you flip your hands over, the club will dig into the turf instead of skidding the way you want.

gy

BASICS

HOW TO HIT AN UPHILL PITCH
by Jim McLean

An upslope lie has the effect of making your left side longer, which can tip you back and lead to poor contact. To compensate, drop your left foot away from the target line and bend your left knee more. Opening your stance like this pre-sets your turn through the ball. You'll need the help, because the upslope makes it tough to rotate toward the target.

Why do you want a body turn at all? Because you need power to pitch uphill. The slope adds loft, so you tend to leave the ball short. But I still like a sand wedge here, especially in heavy grass. Another benefit of setting up open is that it promotes an out-to-in swing, which is steeper and gets the clubhead through the grass and under the ball.

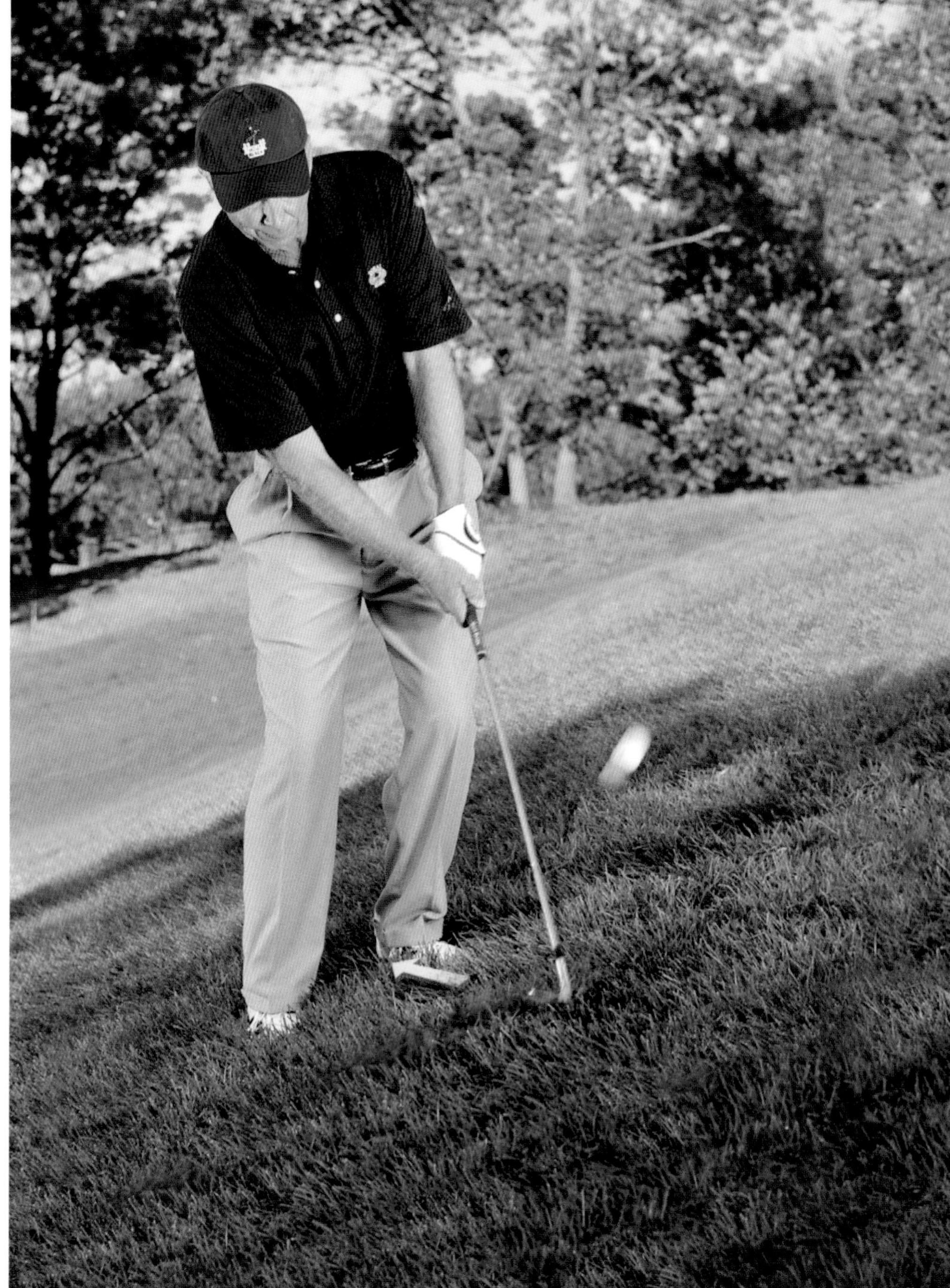

TECHNIQUE

When I'm pitching over a hazard and have little green between me and the hole, I want a shot that will fly high and slow–one that will settle in its tracks. To execute this type of shot, the first thing to do is address the ball with the clubface laid back more than normal, thus increasing loft. I take the club straight back and break my wrists early in the backswing. I strike down and through with the hands leading the clubhead, and the wrists snapping into the ball. This gives me a high lob with a lot of backspin. The entire swing should be leisurely and rhythmical.

SAM SNEAD

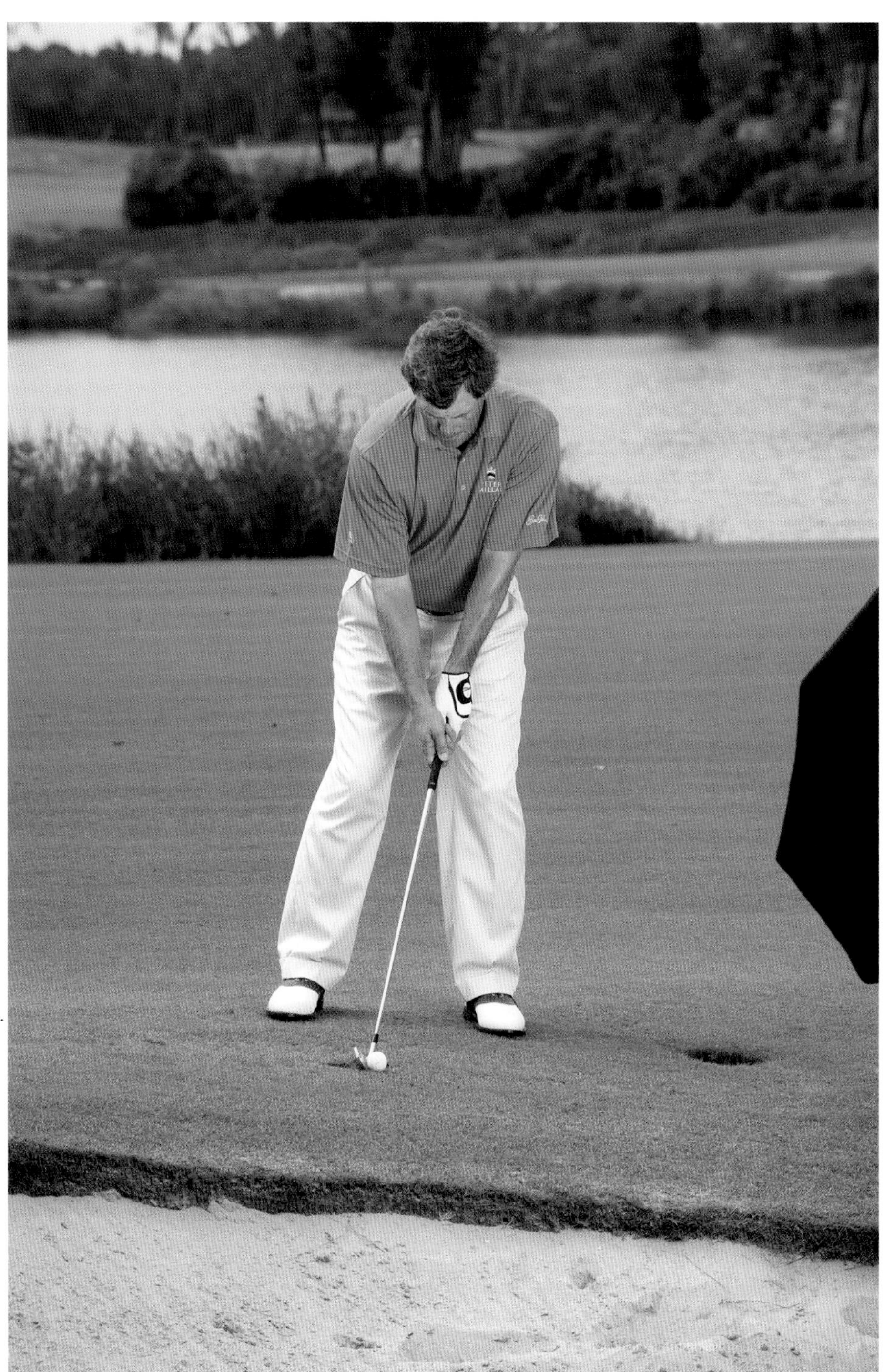

BASICS

HOW TO SURVIVE A DOWNHILL LIE

by Todd Anderson

The tendency on a downslope is to drop the handle back to try to add loft to the clubface. Make sure the club's leading edge is flush to the ground. Build your setup around the correctly soled club. Point the butt of the grip between your zipper and left hip, and play the ball farther back than normal. Shots from downhill lies tend to fly lower and go right, so take less club and aim left. Swing down the slope, and don't try to help the ball in the air.

BASICS

HOW TO PITCH IT OFF A TIGHT FAIRWAY LIE

by Annika Sorenstam

From firm ground, the tendency is to try to scoop the ball in the air, which usually leads to hitting it fat or thin. Solid contact comes from making a downward strike. For a standard pitch shot, play the ball midway between your heels and set more weight on your front foot. This promotes the steeper descent you need to hit the ball first.

The club should strike the ground immediately after the ball. Try this drill: Have a friend plant his or her heel just in front of where the ball would be. Set up to the shoe and swing, trying to wedge the clubface under the heel. If you scoop, you'll swing up into the sole. Control the pitching motion with the rotation of your upper body, not with your hands and arms. You want everything to turn back and through together, so your hips and shoulders face the target at the finish. This will help you maintain the loft on the clubface for a higher shot. Make sure the face points upward well after impact.

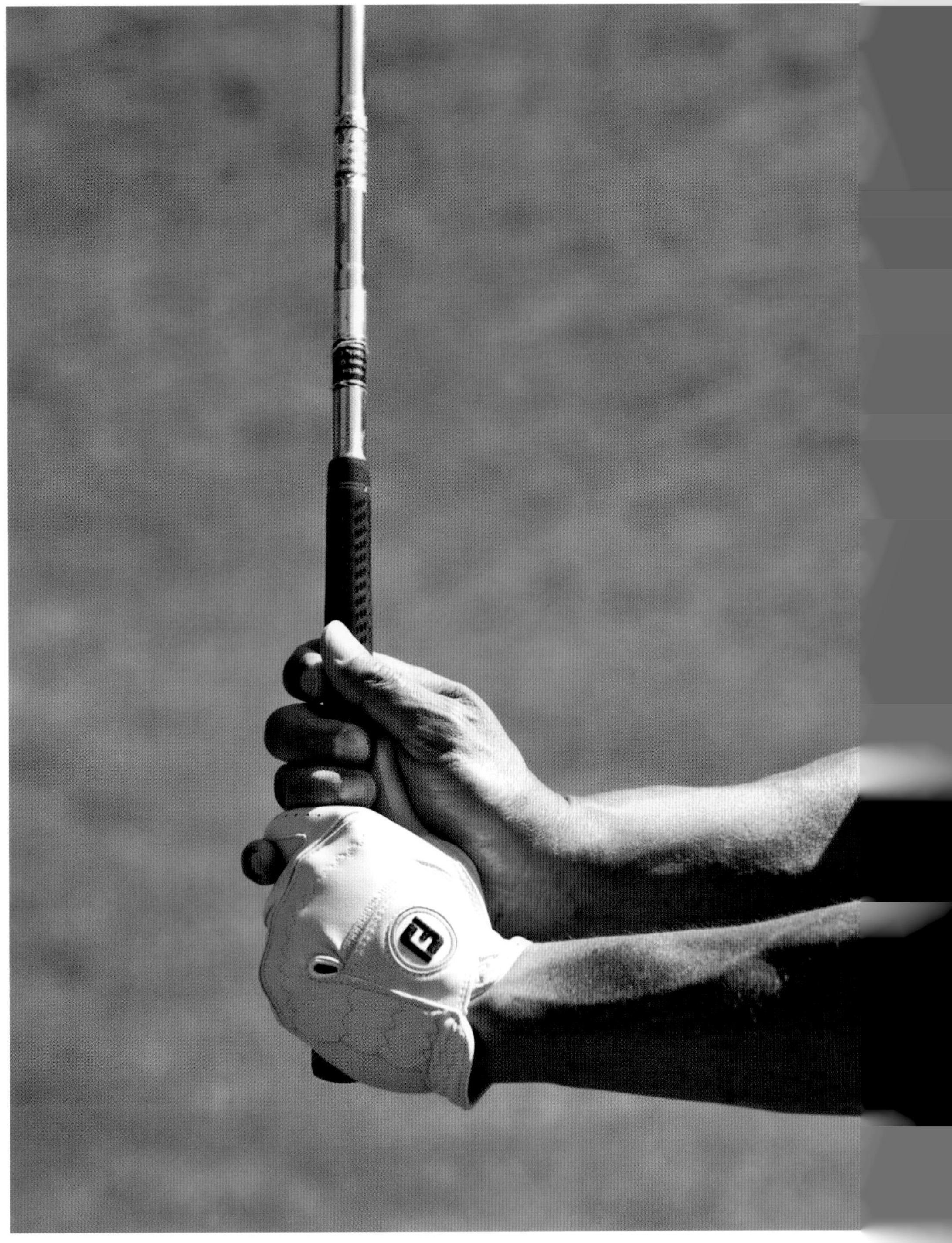

BASICS

REALLY HEAVY ROUGH? HINGE YOUR WRISTS EARLY

by Don Hurter

Thick greenside rough poses a dilemma: How do you swing hard enough to get the ball out of the heavy grass, but soft enough to land it just on the green? It's a leap of faith, but if you don't commit, you're facing the same shot all over again.

What to do: You need a fairly long swing, so hinge your wrists early going back and accelerate through the ball. What to feel: To make sure you don't quit on this shot, imagine that the clubface is looking back at you after impact.

BASICS

HOW TO HIT THE PRO WEDGE (AND MAKE IT STOP ON A DIME)

by David Toms

Want to know how I hit a low, boring pitch shot that bounces a couple of times and then stops? Gripping down an inch, I play the ball just behind center, but I set my weight left and keep it there. I also stand a little open to pre-set body rotation through impact. Before I start back, I lean the shaft a touch forward. The length of my backswing depends on the distance to the hole. This is a 60-yard shot.

My body rotation toward the target pulls the club down. My hands lead the clubhead through the ball. I release the club by turning my body and swinging my arms, not by flipping my hands. Even though I didn't hit this sand wedge full distance, I made a full body rotation.

MENTAL TIP

See where you want the ball to go before every shot. When players are properly into the target, it's as if there were a laser beam linking the mind and the spot where they want the ball to go. Nothing else exists for them. They're single-minded. Hazards such as woods and water don't distract them. Once they have picked the target, they think only of the ball going there. This is especially helpful when pitching.

DR. BOB ROTELLA

BASICS

GET WIDE TO BEAT THE ROUGH

by David Leadbetter

When your ball is sitting down in the rough, hitting a quality pitch can be difficult because it's hard to make predictable contact. Try widening your stance at address and maintaining the exaggerated knee flex throughout your swing. This lowers your center of gravity and allows you to slide the clubface under the ball. As a bonus, it keeps your body stable as the club works through the high grass. It's a lot like playing a greenside bunker shot.

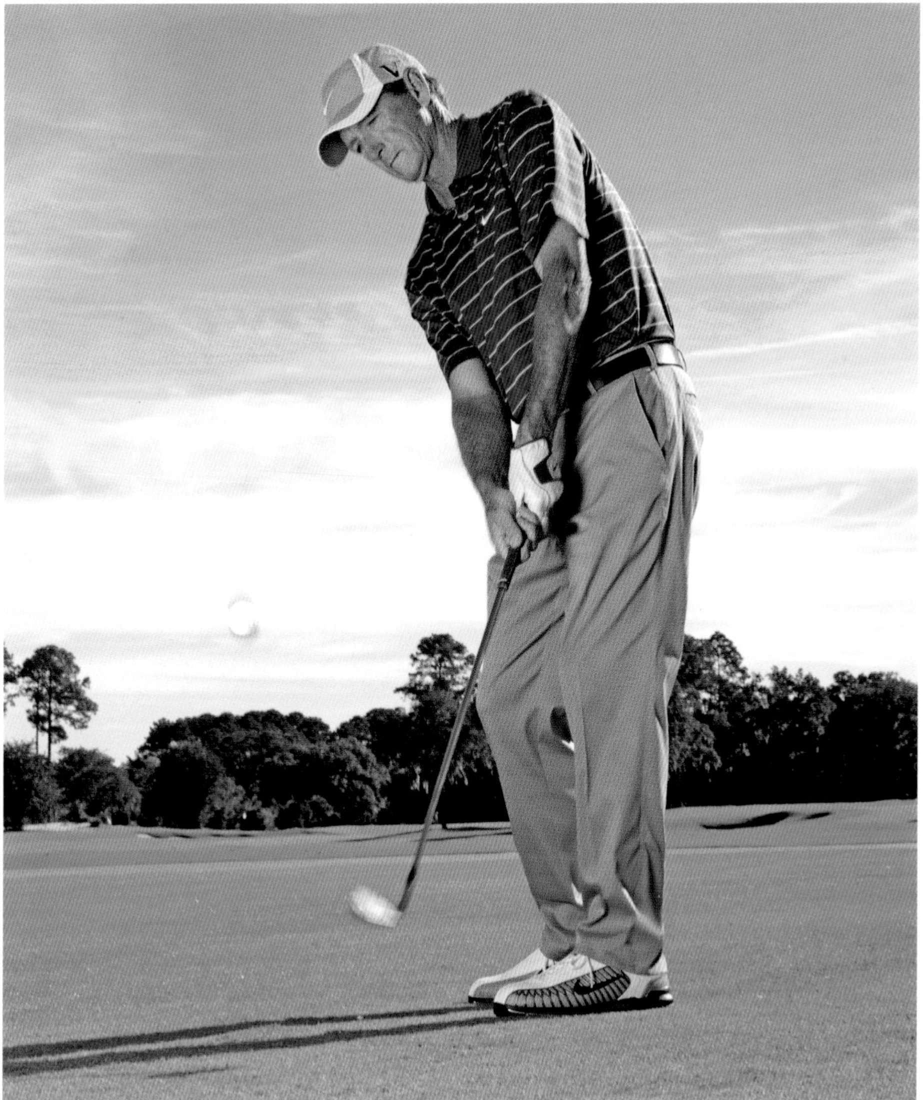

BASICS

HOW TO BEAT YOUR NERVES ON A SHORT PITCH

by Hank Haney

The most important fundamental on these little shots is moving the bottom of the swing forward so you can catch the ball slightly on the downswing. Most players have been told to keep their bodies dead still, so they lock up and try to lift the ball with their hands. This does the opposite of what they want: It moves the bottom of the swing back, leading to a fat or bladed shot.

Instead, use a firm-wristed swing, and let your body turn and move through the shot, as if you're making a smaller version of your full swing. And focus on the front side of the ball; this will also help you make ball-first contact.

BASICS

SLIDE THE CLUBFACE UNDER THE BALL TO HIT THE FLOP

by Stewart Cink

I hit the flop shot only as a last resort, and amateurs should do the same because it's hard to execute. If you don't really commit to hitting it, you'll either blade the ball across the green or chunk it. But if you absolutely have to loft the ball high and stop it quickly, then you want to feel that the clubhead is passing the shaft at impact.

This release of the club is crucial to generating enough clubhead speed and loft to get the ball up and land it softly. It's important to set the clubface open at address (pointing right of the target), which adds more loft, and then grip the club–in that order. You can even weaken your grip, your hands rotated toward the target; this will soften the shot even more. But the key is to open the clubface before you take your grip. Assuming your lie is fairly flat, you can play the ball forward an inch or two for extra height. From there, your thought should be to slide that open face under the ball as the clubhead passes the shaft.

ADVICE

Backing the ball up on the green may look impressive, but it's no way to play golf, because you can't control it. Every shot you hit should bounce forward after it lands. If the flagstick is just over a bunker, you get close by hitting the ball higher, not by backing it up. With these 60-degree wedges, hitting it high is easy.

MOE NORMAN

ADVANCED

SOLVING THE SHORT-SIDED SITUATION
by John Daly

You've short-sided yourself when you've missed the green on the side closest to the flag, with not much green between the ball and the cup. It's risky, but the only way to get the next shot close is to hit the flop shot. Like you do on a bunker shot, aim left of your target, play the ball forward in your stance, and grip the club lightly with the face open. Make a full swing, cutting across the ball like a slice. Hit the ground and ball at the same time. Don't let the clubface turn over through impact, and the ball will fly high and land with a thud.

Rory McIlroy hits a short approach in the final round of the 2011 U.S. Open at Congressional Country Club en route to his first major victory.

ADVANCED

WHEN YOU ABSOLUTELY HAVE TO STOP THE BALL

by Hank Haney

Tiger Woods will watch another player work on a skill he's really good at, and he doesn't hesitate to borrow things that will make him better. For instance, short-game masters Seve Ballesteros, Jose Maria Olazabal, and Greg Norman play pitches with a lot of clubhead speed and spin—as opposed to using a slow, lazy swing. Tiger has picked up on this. He usually wants his ball to check up, not land and roll out. By playing his pitches with speed, he can hit to a spot without worrying as much about green contours. To do this, you've got to have great technique—and great hands—or you'll risk blading it over the green.

FITNESS TIP

Train your body to rotate through on pitch shots

by Mark Verstegen

In order to hit a pitch correctly, your upper body has to rotate toward the target as you swing down and through the ball. Most amateurs try to hit this shot with their arms only, or worse, stop after impact for fear of hitting the shot too far. To train your body to rotate through, try this exercise.

The backward lunge with lateral flexion will help because it stretches the hip flexors, the glutes, the groin area, and the oblique muscles (sides of the torso). Without flexibility in these areas, you wouldn't be able to rotate your upper body very well during the backswing or through to the finish.

To do it, step back with your right foot into a lunge position, and contract your right glute. Reach your right hand over your head and laterally crunch your torso to the left. Return to the starting position. Switch legs and repeat.

BUNKE
Ford
Callaway
GOLF

R PLAY

THE GREENSIDE BUNKER SHOT is the only routine play in golf where the goal is to hit the ground behind the ball and not the ball itself. Since most golfers struggle making ball-first contact in their normal swings, you would think this purposely fat shot would be easy to master—it's not. Because it's a short shot that typically requires the ball to fly high and land soft, most amateurs either fail to complete their swing in fear of hitting it too far or they flick at the ball in hopes of using wrist-action to get the ball airborne. Neither is very effective in extracting the ball.

Fairway bunker shots also give amateurs fits because the action required to execute this shot properly—which is quite the opposite of what you'd do in a greenside bunker—is very difficult to master.

Whether your ball is in the sand near the green or near the fairway, the first thing you should know is that being a good bunker player starts as a mind-set. Players on the PGA Tour have no fear of the sand. In fact, they are so good at bunker shots, they often aim near the sand knowing it's the perfect bailout spot should their attempt to hit the target fall short. So your first piece of advice for excelling in bunkers is to embrace the challenge. Here are some tips from the masters on sand play.

PREVIOUS SPREAD: **Sand master:** Phil Mickelson escapes a greenside bunker at the 2008 Accenture World Match Play Championship.

OPPOSITE: Ian Poulter swing sequence

71.01% **Percentage Keith Fergus saved par from a greenside bunker in 1998—still the best sand-save season average since the PGA Tour began tracking that statistic in 1980.**

- A 20-handicap golfer gets up and down from a greenside bunker less than 10 percent of the time.
- The average amateur's bunker shot finishes 45 feet from the hole. The average pro's bunker shot finishes less than 10 feet from the hole.

BASICS

HOW TO HIT THE BASIC GREENSIDE BUNKER SHOT

by Hank Haney

Tour players don't fear bunker shots the way most amateurs do, but only a handful of the pros get up and down from the sand more than 60 percent of the time. What's the lesson in this? Learn the basics, so you don't fear the sand, and adjust your expectations. Make sure you get out of the bunker and give yourself a chance at a one-putt, but for the most part be satisfied with getting down in three.

To get out safely, open the clubface so the club can bounce off the sand instead of dig. You want to hit behind the ball to splash it out on a patch of sand, so play the ball forward in your stance, up by your left foot. The big key during the swing is to follow through, and turn your body to the target.

Most amateurs swing the club into the sand, and when they feel the resistance, they quit on the shot. Plus, they're fearful, so they tend to lock their bodies in place and just wave at the ball with their arms. Commit to turning to a full finish, and you'll get the ball out every time.

BASICS

GET STEEP TO AVOID SKULLING

by Jim McLean

The sand wedge is the heaviest club in most players' bags. Using that weight effectively will help you become a consistent and good bunker player. The feeling you want is the club falling from the top of the backswing. To set up that move, you must have a more vertical backswing than normal. The average player does just the opposite. He swings around his body on the way back, which sets up a too shallow entry.

Start with an open clubface and a slightly open stance and then make a steep backswing. The combination of the open face and upright swing plane will help you "spank" the sand, producing the thump you hear on a good bunker shot. Then, accelerate through impact and prove that by holding that pose for a few seconds.

SWING THOUGHT

I've always found that a good mental image makes shotmaking a lot easier. This was especially true when I was learning the game as a youngster. I was told once that the key to hitting a good sand shot was to splash the sand out of the bunker the same way you would try to splash water out of a pool. What golfers often misunderstand is that, in a sand shot, it is the sand that throws the ball out onto the green—not the clubhead. I try to make a full, slow-motion swing, hitting the sand behind the ball and splashing it out. CHI CHI RODRIGUEZ

BASICS

OPEN THE FACE TO PREVENT THE WEDGE FROM BURYING

by Jim Flick

As I've watched great bunker players over the years, namely Julius Boros and Sam Snead, I've noticed they play sand shots with a very open clubface. This exposes the club's bounce to keep it from digging.

When executing a greenside bunker shot, many golfers are afraid to open the face. They think this will cause the shot to go to the right. Not true. Remember, the ball goes the direction the sand goes, which is along your swing path, regardless of where the face is aimed.

The more you open the face, the more bounce the club has. Now you can hit down into the sand behind the ball without fear that the club will dig. You have more margin for error. The softer the sand, the more you need to open the face. In hard-packed sand, open the face only a little, but lean your weight more to the left.

BASICS

HOW TO AVOID LEAVING IT IN THE SAND
by Annika Sorenstam

1. To stop chunking your bunker shots, you must make the back edge of the clubhead enter the sand before the leading edge. Feel this with my drill. Get in a bunker and set up to a rake (right). Open the clubface, which puts the back edge lower than the leading edge, and swing, skimming the club off the rake.

2. You'll quickly sense what it feels like to hit with the back edge of the club. Now, transfer that feeling to an actual shot. First, lower your body a few inches so the clubface can slide under the ball. I do this by widening my stance (others twist their feet in). Then, play the ball off your front heel, and remember to open the face.

3. Make a three-quarter swing, accelerating the club past your hands through impact. The back edge should enter the sand two to three inches behind the ball, which will help the clubhead slide and push the ball out. To prevent the club from digging too deep, keep your body turning to a full finish.

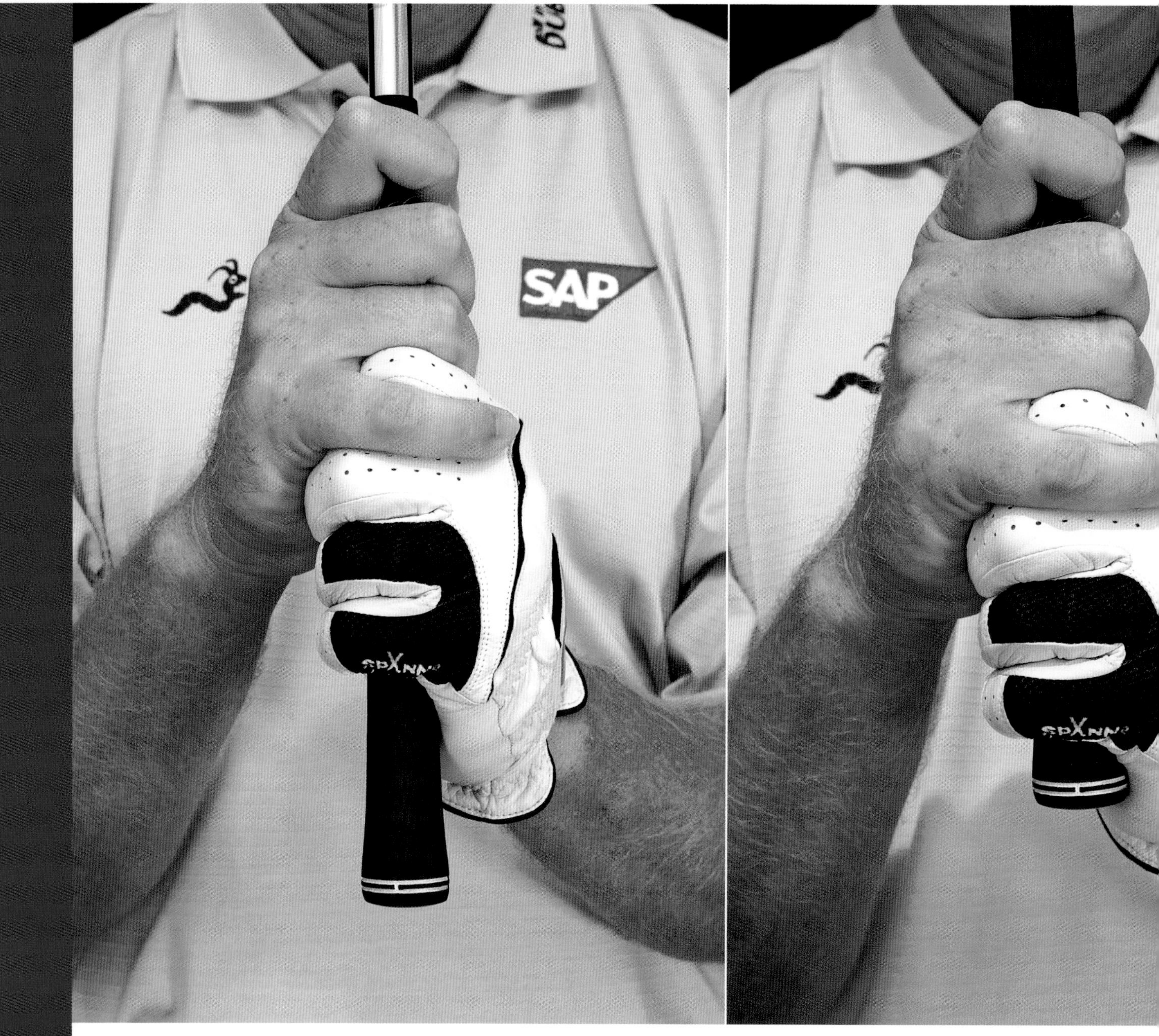

BASICS

FAIRWAY BUNKERS: CHOKE DOWN AND KEEP LOWER BODY STILL

by Ernie Els

As long as you have a decent lie, hitting from a fairway bunker isn't as difficult as you might think–you just don't have room to hit it heavy and get away with it.

I play this shot the same way I would a wind shot from the fairway. Set up with the ball in the middle of your stance, and anchor yourself in the sand by digging in your feet. Take more club, but choke down on the grip two inches, as I'm doing here. That offsets your feet being below the surface of the sand. When you hit this shot, focus on making a three-quarter backswing and keeping your lower body quiet. Hit the ball first, then the sand. The shot will come out lower than normal, because of the stronger loft on the longer club, but it'll have more backspin.

EQUIPMENT

How to choose the right wedge for a bunker

by Mike Stachura

If you rest the lowest point of the sole of your wedge on a flat surface, you're likely to see that the leading edge (the most forward part of the face) is higher than the sole. That difference is called the bounce or bounce angle of the wedge, and the greater that difference between sole and leading edge, the greater the bounce angle. A higher bounce angle helps steeper swings get through the turf. It also works well in bunkers, particularly for average golfers, because it allows the sole of the club to slide through the sand without digging. Generally, a typical sand wedge with a loft of 56 degrees should have a bounce angle of at least 10 degrees. An even higher bounce angle (12–14 degrees) is better with softer sand.

ADVANCED

PRACTICE COCKING AND RELEASING FOR BETTER SAND SHOTS

by Stan Utley

If you want to control your bunker shots, you've got to consistently hit the sand in the same spot. Keep your weight on your front foot and turn around that forward tilt; don't sway back off the ball. When you do it right, it might feel like a reverse pivot, but that's OK. The only other thing you have to think about is generating a lot of speed with the clubhead, not the grip end. Cock your wrists early, then release them aggressively through the shot. Don't move the grip end far from the center of your body on either the backswing or the follow-through.

SETUP

Tom Kite, who is as good from greenside bunkers as any player in history, has a great preshot routine for bunker play that you should follow. Open the blade of your sand wedge and place your hands high on the handle. This encourages a full finish. Point the shaft at your belt buckle with your hands slightly ahead of the ball. Take a square stance. Your open clubface will be aimed to the right. Now, move your left foot, hips, and shoulders to the left until your clubface is aiming directly at the target. Lean a little extra weight on your left foot, too. Now you're in a great position to swing along your shoulder line and hit the sand from one to four inches behind the ball.

HARVEY PENICK

ADVANCED

REGULATE YOUR FINISH TO CONTROL DISTANCE

by Rick Smith

There are many ways to regulate the distance and height of a bunker shot, but the one I find easiest for my students to execute concerns the finish position. With this method, the length of the backswing and the swing speed stay consistent, but the length of the follow-through changes depending on the distance and height you want to hit the ball.

To get the hang of it, start by hitting two shots. Take the club back to the same position and swing down at the same speed, but finish low the first time and finish high the second. You'll find the low finish is ideal for a short bunker shot that doesn't require a lot of height. The high finish, however, is better for longer shots in higher-lipped bunkers.

Whichever finish you use, remember to release the club by having the clubhead pass the hands. This ensures you won't leave the club stuck in the sand. A final thought: As you swing down, be sure to rotate your weight to the front foot. If you hang back, you'll struggle to slide the club under the ball.

ADVANCED

FOR SOLID STRIKES OUT OF A FAIRWAY BUNKER, IMAGINE GLASS

by Butch Harmon

The common miss from fairway sand is fat, and that comes from driving the legs on the downswing. The driving action lowers your center of gravity, which works great from the grass but in the softer sand often leads to hitting behind the ball. To quiet that forward leg drive, swing a little easier with a longer club. If there's a high lip, make sure you have enough loft to clear it, but if the lip is low, club up and swing easy.

Hold your chin up to set your spine angle a little more vertical. Taller posture promotes an around-the-body swing and a more level strike, so you can pick the ball without digging. Resist the urge to dive down into impact, as golfers often do to try to help the ball out of the sand.

Imagine your ball is sitting on a pane of glass: You want to clip it off without smashing the glass. Feel as if you stay tall all the way through the shot. Remember, hitting the ball thin out of a fairway bunker is a good thing, and too thin is usually better than any kind of fat.

PRACTICE TIP

"As a kid, I had nowhere to practice, so I went to the beach. It turned out to be great, because on sand you have to stay steady and hit the ball first. Try it: Get in a bunker, center the ball in your stance, with your hands ahead, and let your arms hang freely. Swing back, keeping your left arm straight, not rigid.

SEVE BALLESTEROS

ADVANCED

TURN YOUR TOES IN TO STABILIZE FAIRWAY BUNKER SHOT

by David Leadbetter

One of the biggest difficulties golfers have in a fairway bunker is keeping the lower body stable. If it's a full-swing shot, it's very easy to lose your footing, leading to mis-hit shots. Contacting the sand too far behind the ball is frequently the result. I can't stress enough that you need to be anchored in the sand.

To do this, dig your feet into the sand, then turn your toes inward as you take your stance. This secures your lower body in the bunker. Your weight should feel as if it's on the inside edges of your feet, and when you swing, keep your weight in that same position. Unlike a normal full-swing shot, there's not a lot of weight transfer. This swing is propelled more by the arms and shoulders, and the toes-in position provides the stability needed for a solid shot.

One more important thing to remember for a solid fairway-bunker shot: You should grip down on the club slightly to compensate for the amount you dig your feet into the sand. This helps you strike the ball first.

SWING MECHANICS

The sand wedge is built with a flanged sole that extends downward from the leading edge of the clubface. This flange acts as a rudder to keep the club from cutting too deeply into the sand. If, however, you allow your hands to lead the clubhead through the hitting area, you'll take loft off the club, reduce the depth of the flange, and minimize the bounce or rudder effect. My system requires that your hands be trailing the clubhead when it passes under the ball. A relatively thin cut of sand results. When you practice with just one hand, the hand has to trail the clubhead. That's the feeling you want in your real sand shots.

CLAUDE HARMON

Play

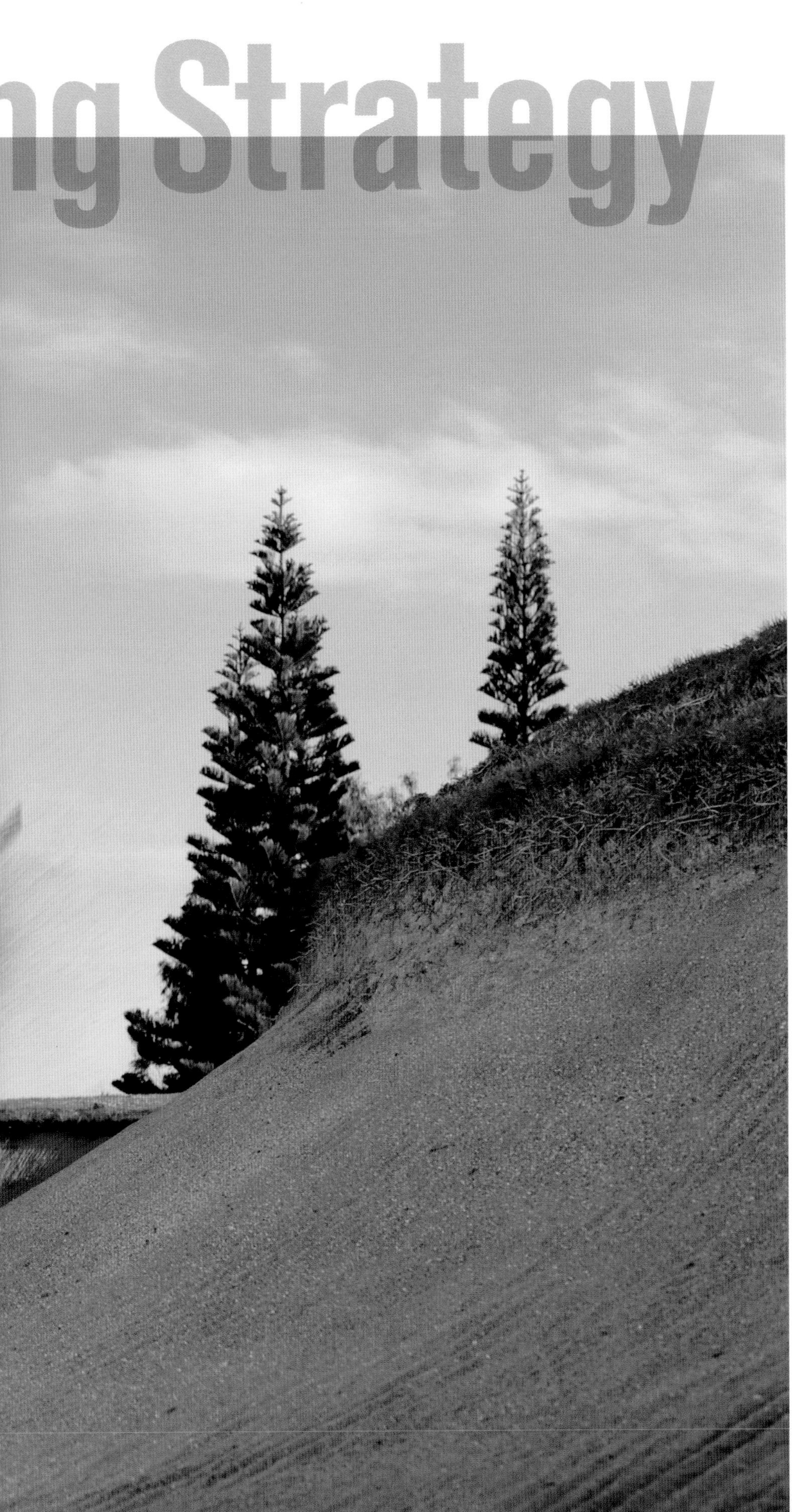

BASICS

USE YOUR WRISTS TO ESCAPE A STEEP-FACED BUNKER
by Matt Kuchar

I was always taught that the first rule of bunker play is to just get the ball out. When you have a steep face in front of you, this rule applies more than ever. Here, you have to get the ball up in the air as quickly as possible.

Start by addressing the ball with a slightly open stance. Next, open the face of your sand wedge and then take your grip, not the other way around. From there, swing the club back and rotate the face open even more.

Now comes the tricky part, where you must do the opposite of what you've been taught for other shots: You have to throw away your lag. In other words, let the clubhead pass your hands before impact and scoop under the ball. I feel as if I'm flicking my right wrist at the shot. The club should still enter the sand just behind the ball, but the full unhinging of your wrists will increase your swing speed and help pop it up. It'll land softly and stop fast.

BASICS

BURIED LIE? PICK THE RIGHT CLUB

by Tom Watson

I play a buried bunker shot one of two ways, depending on distance.

LONG SHOTS: I was playing an old Sandy Andy wedge when I first learned the standard technique from my dad: Strengthen the grip, toe in the club about 30 degrees, play the ball back of center in your stance, and make a steep downswing. Today, I might use a pitching wedge or 9-iron if I'm sure I can clear the lip. These clubs have less bounce than a sand wedge so they dig easily under the ball, rather than skim into it. The ball comes out hot and rolls.

SHORT SHOTS: Lee Trevino taught me to weaken my grip, open the face about 30 degrees, position the ball forward of center with my weight on my left foot, and swing even more steeply. I swing harder to generate enough speed to produce a softer shot that stops fast. It's even OK to leave the clubhead in the sand.

MENTAL TIP

Buried lie in a bunker? Get excited!

by Dr. Bob Rotella

Golfers who understand and love the game accept it rather than fight it. They realize the essence of golf is reacting well to inevitable mistakes and misfortunes, and a buried lie in the bunker is the perfect example. I tell players that if there's one thing they should always be proud of in their games, it's how well they react to mistakes or bad breaks. I tell them that they will never have complete control of the golf ball, but they can control their attitudes. So if the ball is buried, get excited for the challenge rather than lamenting the unlucky lie.

BASICS

GOT THE RIGHT CLUB? HERE'S HOW TO ESCAPE A PLUGGED LIE

by Ryuji Imada

When the ball is partially buried, you have to make a steeper swing to get the club under the ball. To do this, I keep most of my weight on my front foot and hinge my wrists quickly as I take the club back. With all that wrist hinge, I don't need to make as big an arm swing as I do from a standard lie, and the club still should enter the sand an inch or so behind the ball. It's not a dig, and it's not a skim. Feel the wedge exploding the sand.

SWING TIP

Here are a few tips that can help you when you face a long bunker shot. First, always take a club with enough loft to get the ball out. A long putt might not be any bargain, but it's better than playing your next shot from the face of a bunker. Next, work your feet into the sand for balance, then focus on using your legs throughout the shot. Too much of an arm swing can cause you to raise yourself up and hit the ball thin, or swing from the top and hit the shot fat. Also, don't try to help the ball into the air. Make a full, free swing, hitting down and under the ball. And don't be afraid to take a little sand. If it's really long, you can use a pitching wedge or 9-iron for this shot so long as you have enough loft to clear the lip.

BYRON NELSON

BASICS

WET SAND? FIRM SAND? HERE'S HOW TO ESCAPE
by Phil Mickelson

In packed sand, you don't want your wedge to hit the ground too early and bounce into the middle of the ball. To prevent that, set your weight forward and tilt your spine toward the target. I can't emphasize enough that your weight has to stay forward on bunker shots from firm sand. To get a feel for this, try this drill: Lift your back foot slightly off the ground and hit practice shots this way. Then, repeat this feel when you hit real firm / wet sand shots.

When you keep your weight forward, you'll automatically hit closer to the ball, which will keep you from bouncing off the sand and skulling the ball. You're playing this shot with an open clubface, so you won't have any trouble getting the ball up.

BASICS

SWEEP IT OUT ON A LONG, GREENSIDE BUNKER SHOT

by Retief Goosen

When you need more distance than your standard greenside blast shot provides, bag your sand wedge and opt for a gap or pitching wedge. The lower loft will allow you to hit the ball farther without making a bigger swing or hitting too close to the ball. With a normal lie in the sand, play the ball opposite your front foot or just inside of it. The worse the lie, the farther back you need to move the ball. But don't go too far back. Your limit should be the middle of your stance.

Try to stay as steady as possible with your legs during the swing. You need to have good footing to do this, so twist your feet into the sand a little. The long bunker swing is very much an arms-and-shoulders motion. Make a sweeping swing instead of a digging swing. You still should make an out-to-in pass through impact, but square the face a bit more and enter the sand about an inch behind the ball. Think sweep, not dig.

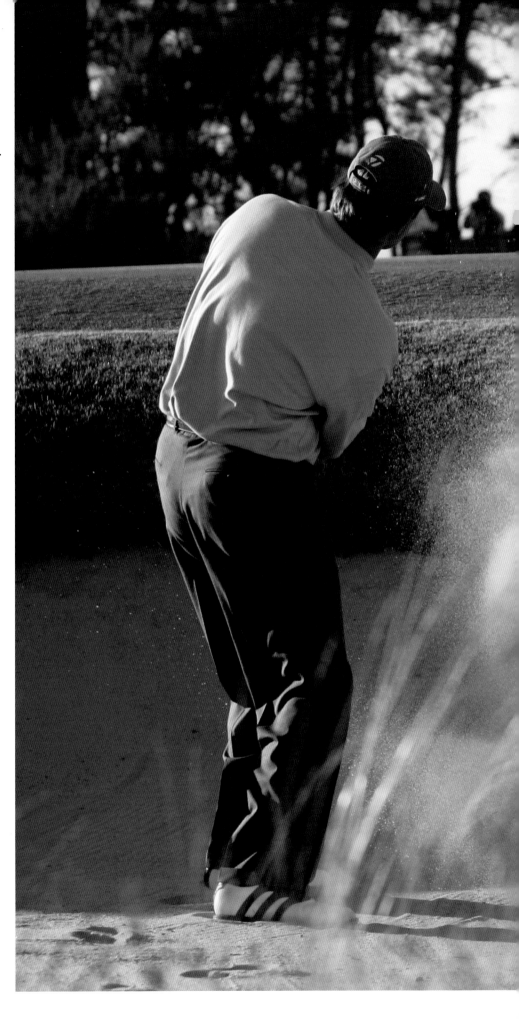

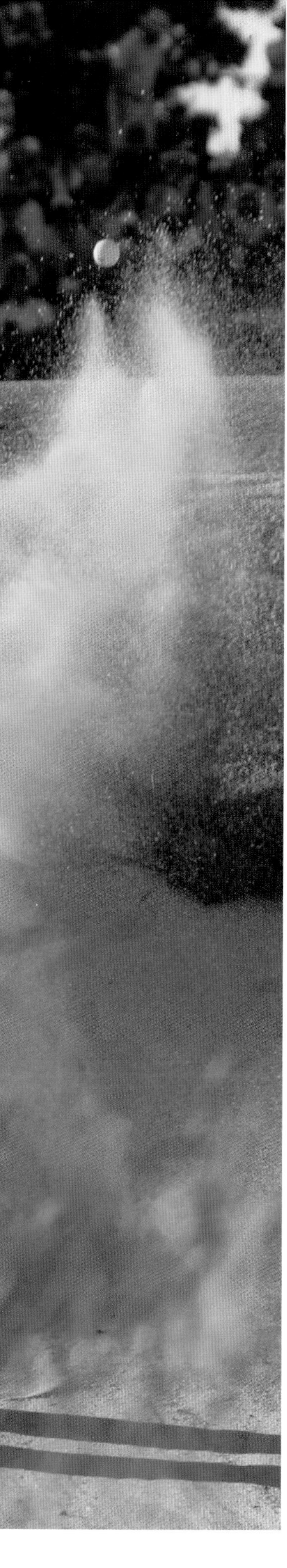

SWING TIP

Quick story: I was down in Texas and this good old boy with a big hat stopped to watch me hit bunker shots. The first shot he saw me hit went in the hole. He said, "You got 50 bucks if you knock the next one in." I holed the next one. Then he said, "You got $100 if you hole the next one." In it went for three in a row. As he peeled off the bills he said, "Boy, I've never seen anyone so lucky in my life." And I shot back, "Well, the harder I practice, the luckier I get." That's where the quote originated. You can tell a good bunker shot by the sound. From powdery sand, you want a "poof." From coarser sand, it should sound like you're tearing a linen sheet in half. Strive to make the right sound, and you'll be surprised at how fast you improve.

GARY PLAYER

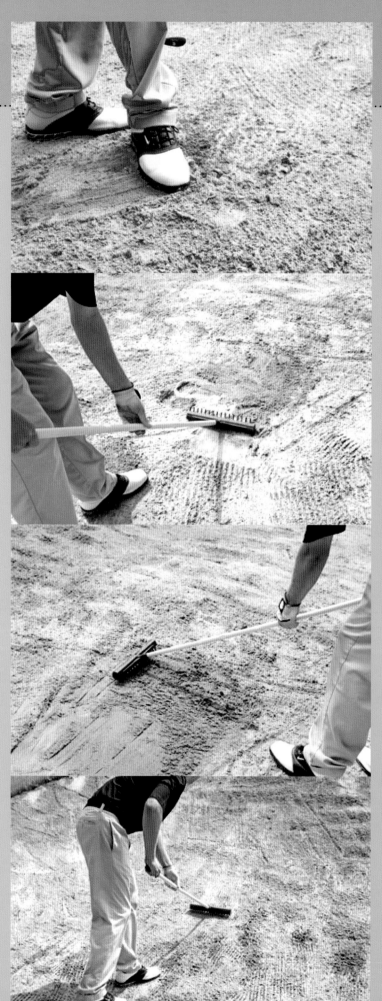

How to rake a bunker

by PGA Tour Caddies

We asked PGA Tour caddies for the correct way to rake a bunker after playing a shot. Here are their step-by-step instructions:

Use your foot to level out footprints and club marks.

Turn the rake upside down and push the sand forward.

Turn the rake over and skim the top of the sand as you pull toward you. Keep the handle down.

Push the rake toward the hole.

ADVANCED

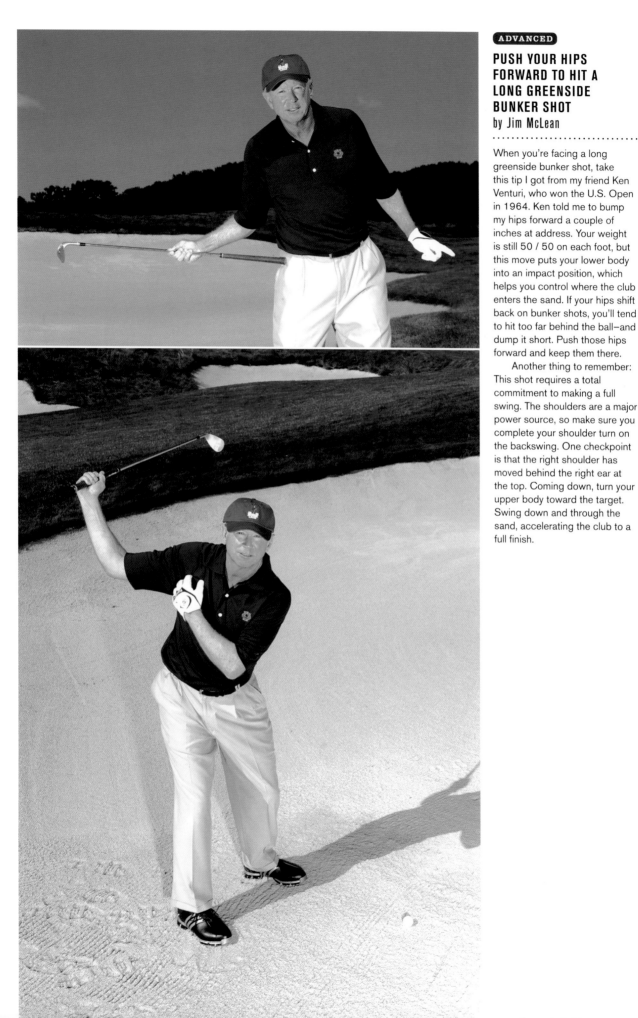

PUSH YOUR HIPS FORWARD TO HIT A LONG GREENSIDE BUNKER SHOT

by Jim McLean

When you're facing a long greenside bunker shot, take this tip I got from my friend Ken Venturi, who won the U.S. Open in 1964. Ken told me to bump my hips forward a couple of inches at address. Your weight is still 50 / 50 on each foot, but this move puts your lower body into an impact position, which helps you control where the club enters the sand. If your hips shift back on bunker shots, you'll tend to hit too far behind the ball–and dump it short. Push those hips forward and keep them there.

Another thing to remember: This shot requires a total commitment to making a full swing. The shoulders are a major power source, so make sure you complete your shoulder turn on the backswing. One checkpoint is that the right shoulder has moved behind the right ear at the top. Coming down, turn your upper body toward the target. Swing down and through the sand, accelerating the club to a full finish.

KPMG
Callaway
GOLF

ADVANCED

HOW TO GET OUT FROM AN UPHILL LIE

by Phil Mickelson

Swing the clubhead up the slope, so it passes through the sand and into the follow-through with minimal resistance. Remember to use an aggressive swing on uphill shots, because the ball will go almost straight up and land more softly.

Uphill lies in sand give amateurs trouble, because the tendency is to drive the clubhead directly into the upslope. There's no margin for error that way: If you hit behind the ball even a little too much, the clubhead will pass directly under the ball, and you'll be lucky to get it out of the sand. The key is to adjust your setup.

Rather than worry about my upper body, I focus on shifting almost all my weight to my back foot. In doing that, my upper body naturally adjusts so it's parallel to the slope. That allows me to shallow out the arc and slide the clubface under the ball.

ADVANCED

STAY LOW ON DOWNHILL BUNKER LIES
by Tom Watson

The unfortunate tendency on downhill bunker shots is to blade the ball, either by hitting it before the sand or by bouncing the club off the sand and into the ball (uphill bunker shots are easier).

When playing the downhill shot, setup is critical. I align my body with the slope of the sand. My left shoulder is lower than my right shoulder. (If you drew lines through my shoulders and feet, the lines would be parallel.) My weight is on the inside of my left foot. I play the ball in the center of my stance, opening my body and the clubface slightly. On the backswing, I set my wrists a little more quickly and take the club up abruptly with my arms. Swinging down I make sure to hit behind the ball the same as I would on a level bunker shot. I follow through down the slope, keeping the clubface open and as low as possible.

What I've done is change my address position and the arc of the clubhead to conform to the downslope. I expect the ball to come out lower than usual with more roll.

PLAYING STRATEGY

The classic blast shot will be ineffective if bunker sand is tightly packed or wet. If you open the face of a sand wedge and try to hit well behind the ball, the bounce will hit the hard sand and you will likely blade the shot. Instead, play your normal bunker shot, but use a pitching wedge (has less bounce) and hit closer to the ball. You can make a nice easy swing and the ball will pop out. The only difference is to allow for more roll since the shot will land with less backspin. BILLY CASPER

TOMMY

ADVANCED

POP IT OUT WHEN IT'S UNDER THE LIP
by David Toms

I call this my "pop shot." When I need to get the ball over a lip, I open the clubface and take a big backswing. On the downswing, I accelerate through the ball, but bring the club back before it hits the lip. It makes a pop sound, and the ball floats right out. If I have a lot of distance to carry, I'll use anything up to a 5-iron to play this shot.

ADVANCED

HOW TO HIT A SUPER-SHORT SAND SHOT
by Butch Harmon

1. Open the clubface: To do this right, turn the face open and then take your grip. Hold the club out with your right hand, rotate it open 30 or 40 degrees, take your left-hand grip, then add your right hand.

2. Lean the shaft back: Play the ball up in your stance, across from your front foot, and drop your hands well behind it. You want to hit a few inches behind this ball, so hover the clubhead over that spot, not up at the ball.

3. Accelerate, then stop: Err on the side of hitting past the hole. Swing back about halfway, then pound the sand behind the ball. Cut off your finish about waist high.

3

ADVANCED

DRAW IT IN FAIRWAY SAND
by Rick Smith

If you're in a fairway bunker at full-wedge distance from the flag, use the technique you would for hitting a draw. It's much more reliable for hitting the green—especially when your match is on the line.

First, take one more club than you normally would from that distance. This allows for some margin of error if you don't hit the ball perfectly. Next, play the ball in the middle of your stance, center your weight, and close the clubface slightly. Aim 15 yards right of your target to make room for the draw (right-to-left) ball flight. Finally, make a rounded swing back and through, allowing the clubface to turn over through impact. Allowing the clubface to turn over improves your chance of solid contact.

FITNESS TIP

Get in the gym to make more sandies

by Mark Verstegen

Getting into the correct posture, and maintaining that position through impact, is important in hitting a good bunker shot. But in many cases, holding that posture (knees significantly bent, hips and shoulders open to the target) is difficult for amateurs who have weak muscles in their thighs, hips, and butt.

Try the mini-bank sideways walk to help your sand game.

The resistance of the stretch bands against your legs activates and strengthens the hips, groin, quads, and glutes, all key to maintaining a stable base when you swing, especially at faster speeds.

Place a mini-band around your legs above the knee and another around your ankles. Walk sideways in small steps, keeping your legs fairly straight and alternating the elbows driving back with each step. Keep your back straight and your knees over your toes at all times.

IRONS

IRONS

THE SOUND A WELL-EXECUTED IRON SHOT makes is more discernible than any other shot in golf. Whether it's you or someone else, you can tell whether a ball was hit well with an iron without even watching the flight of it. We bring this up because, despite great advances in club design, full-iron shots remain the most unforgiving of all the shots you're required to learn. Granted, irons of today are far easier to use than the ones your father used—even 10 years ago. But hitting a solid iron shot requires a skill set that can't be understated.

The best golfers are often referred to as "second-shot" golfers because they are skilled enough to recover from poor drives and take advantage of good drives with the precision of their iron play. Being able to hit an iron, off the turf, that lands close to your target will dramatically reduce your scores. We're not talking about hitting straight shots with an iron, though that would help. What you should be striving for is a swing that allows you to consistently make solid contact with a predictable ball flight. To be clear, having a pretty golf swing is not a bad thing, but it's much more important to consistently hit the ball solidly. With irons, that's more difficult than other clubs, so if you can focus a good percentage of your practice on iron play, it's a good bet you will score better than ever. These practice tips and playing strategies from the best players and teachers will help you in that quest.

PREVIOUS SPREAD: **Mr. Smooth:** Fred Couples's iron swing appears effortless as he hits a shot at the 2011 Masters Tournament.

OPPOSITE: Sergio Garcia swing sequence

20% Percentage a 90-shooter hits a par-3 green in regulation. Tour pros do it 75 percent of the time.

- According to a poll of equipment manufacturers, the lowest-lofted iron they recommend for the average amateur is a 4-iron.
- A 10-handicap hits, on average, six to seven greens per round. A scratch golfer hits 11.
- In a poll of tour pros, the average effort they said they put into an iron swing was 75 percent.

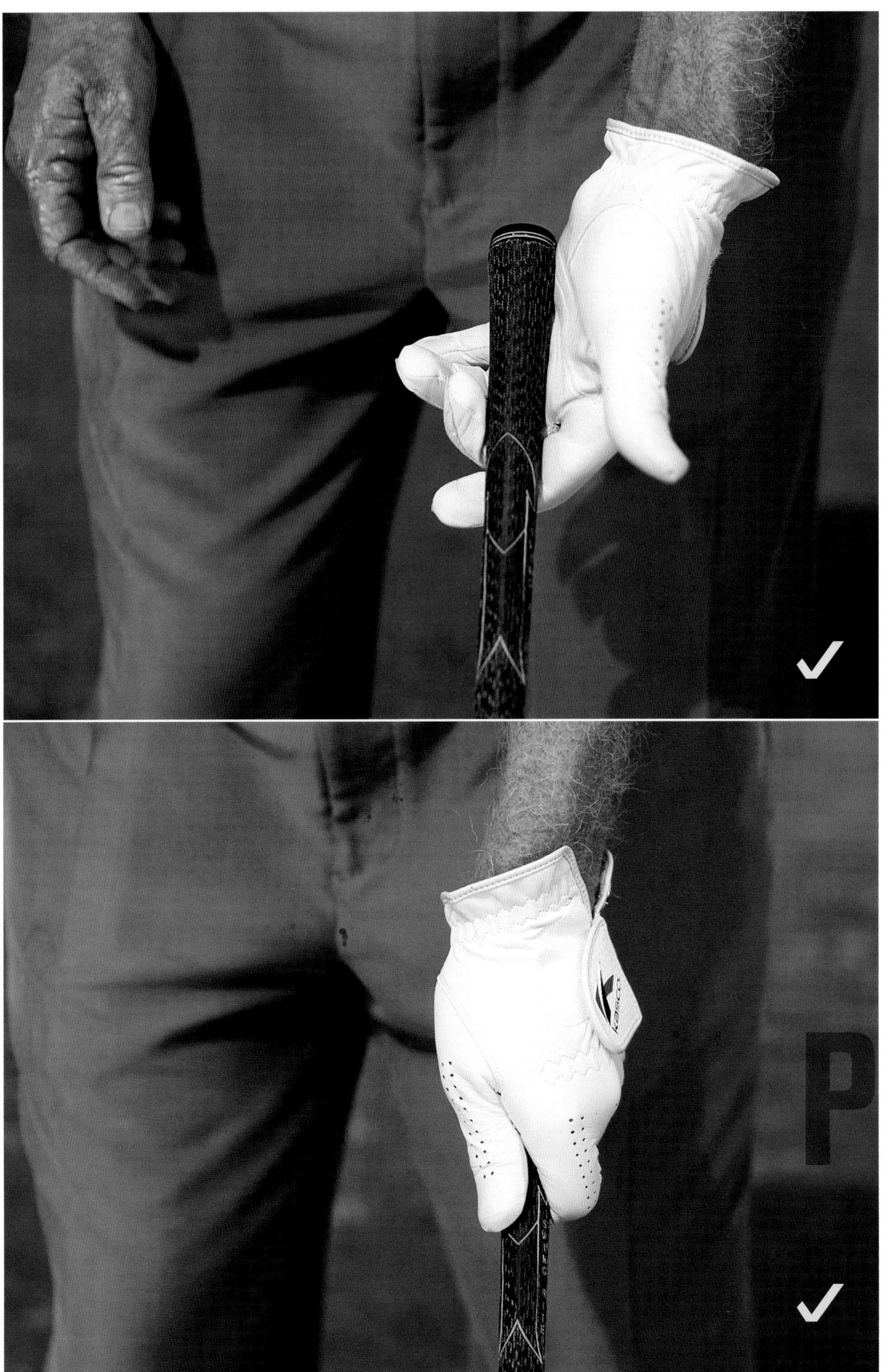
kasco

BASICS

HOW TO GRIP AN IRON: CHECK YOUR V'S

by Jim McLean

Of all the fundamentals, the grip is perhaps the most important. A good grip is essential to controlling the clubface. Show me a player with a bad grip, and I'll show you one having difficulty hitting the ball solidly and accurately. One of the most common grip errors I see with amateurs at my golf schools is resting the club too much in the palm of the left hand (for right-handed players). Gripping the club in that way makes it difficult to hinge it on the backswing and release it on the through-swing.

The handle of the club should rest diagonally across the left fingers. Be sure to grip it firmly between the heel pad and the last three fingers of the left hand to provide support throughout the swing. As the hand closes over the club, the left thumb should rest on the right side of the shaft, forming an upside-down V with the forefinger that points between the player's chin and right shoulder. This provides a wide corridor for personalizing your grip. For a draw, the V should point more toward your right shoulder.

actice Tips

BASICS

BUILD A POWERFUL PLATFORM TO SWING FROM

by Sean Foley

So many golfers would get better by simply improving their address posture. The guys I teach on tour set up in different ways, but the one common denominator is that they feel the ground under their feet. They get into a position where their legs are like shock absorbers, and they're poised to use the ground to create force. They're virtually gripping the ground with their feet. To get a feel for this, try making some swings in your bare feet. Your goal is to feel the ground under you at address, and then pay attention to your footing as you swing. Unless you're properly grounded, it's tough to control a swing with any power.

PRACTICE TIP

Pros play mind games with themselves, and I'm no exception. After I stretch and warm up my body, I start my pre-round practice with a long club rather than a wedge. The 3-iron is about the hardest club in the bag for me to hit, so I swing it first, at a moderate speed.

If I flub a shot or two, well, no big deal. It's supposed to be a more difficult club. But if I hit it dead flush right off the bat, my confidence is heightened. I think I've got it today!

There's also a physical aspect. Swinging a longer club a few times creates my rhythm for the day. My swing is stretched out. Most people take a short club first and make abbreviated swings.

TOM WATSON

BASICS

HOW TO START YOUR SWING SMOOTHLY

by Paul Casey

When I'm feeling tense, like on the Sunday of a major, I tend to snatch the club back too quickly. You can imagine what this does to my tempo during the rest of the swing. I've also seen many amateurs jerk it back way too quickly, either because they're anxious to get the swing over with or because they think a faster swing will help them hit the ball farther. Remember, a faster downswing is a good thing, but a faster backswing usually results in poor tempo.

When I feel tension creeping into my swing, I think of a drill my teacher Peter Kostis gave me for helping set my ideal tempo. On the range, he'd put a second ball right behind my club at address, and I'd make backswings where I'd roll that ball away from the target with the back of the clubhead. This helped me take the club back wider and smoother, which set up a powerful downswing. Try this drill on the range, and then mimic it on the course.

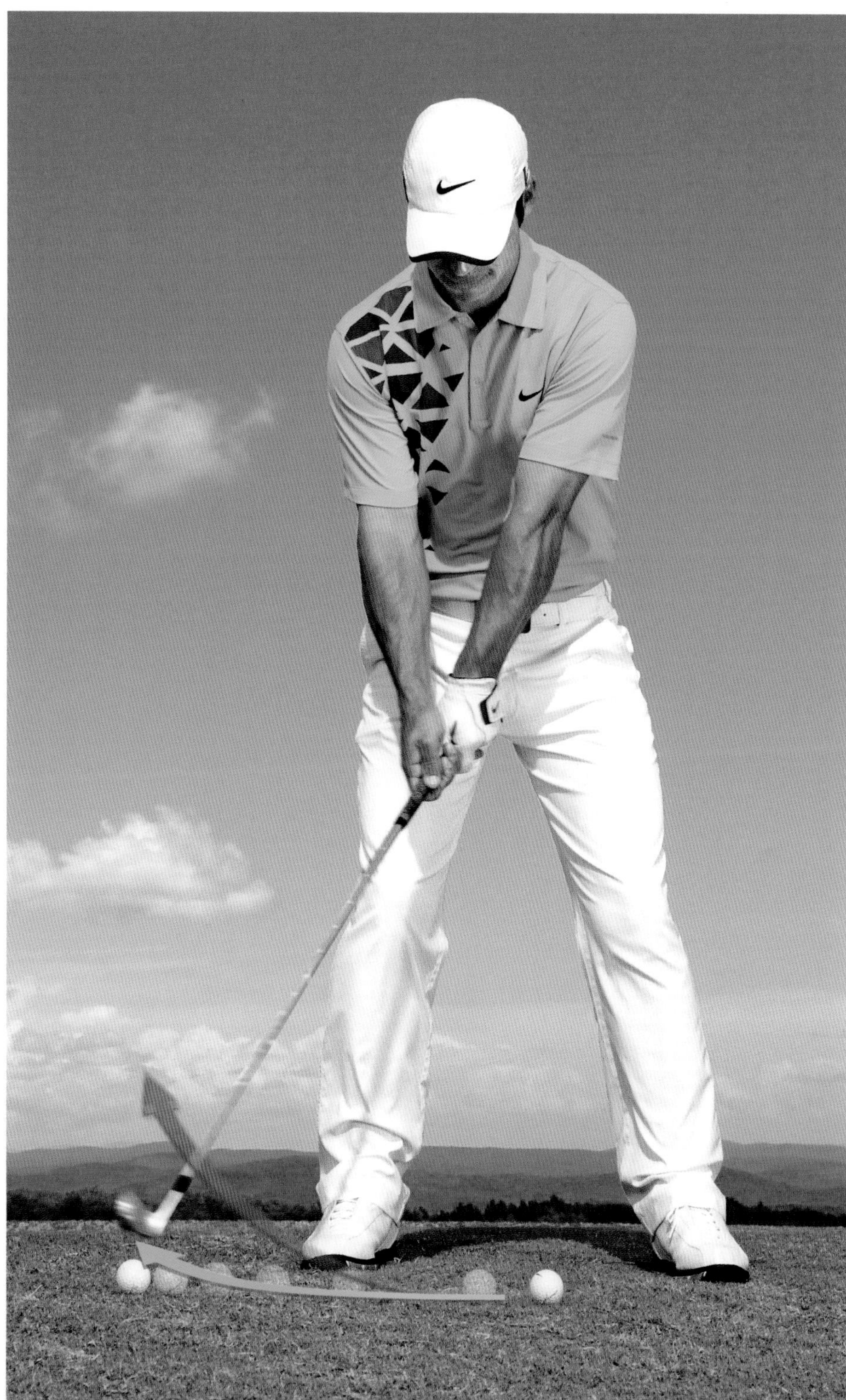

BASICS

IMPROVE YOUR BACKSWING WITH THIS DRILL

by Tom Watson

Getting into a good position at the top is important because it sets you up to make the proper downswing from inside the target line into the ball. An easy way to learn what a good position at the top feels like is to do this simple exercise: Address the ball as you normally would, bending over at the waist, with your arms and knees slightly flexed. Then, while maintaining your address posture, lift the club and lay it on your right shoulder next to your neck, with your elbows bent and close together. Now, turn your shoulders and hips away from the target exactly as you would if you were making a full backswing. When your turn is complete, simply extend your left arm out until it's nearly straight.

SWING TIP

In golf, down often means up. And that is never truer than when you are unlucky enough to finish in a divot mark. Getting a good shot out of a depression can only be achieved by hitting down on the ball. Keep the clubface square at address, hands slightly ahead, and play the ball back in your stance. Make a normal swing, but be sure to have your weight on your left side as you swing down. And never let the right hand overtake the left. The left acts as a guide and must stay firm through the shot. The ball will come out lower than normal with less spin, so allow for that.

BYRON NELSON

BASICS

DOWNSWING: LEAD WITH THE LOWER BODY

by Todd Anderson

The downswing begins with a slight lateral shift, moving the left knee and hip over the left foot. This forward movement causes the arms to drop, returning the right elbow into a position in front of the right hip. Your belt buckle should point at the ball, but your shoulders should still be closed to the target. The forward shift happens with the lower body—your head stays behind the ball. Resist the urge to throw the club from the top, maintaining your wrist hinge as you start down. Picture a karate chop, where your hand swings from the inside with your arm pulling across your chest.

Now you're in a good position at the top of your swing. Practice this whenever you can—you can even do it at home in front of a mirror—so when it comes time to play, swinging into the proper backswing position will feel like second nature.

EQUIPMENT

Are offset irons right for you?

by Mike Stachura

Offset: It's an ugly word. Yet golfers have been taught to like offset in their irons because they were told it would help them hit the ball straighter. There's a lot of misconception about what offset actually does. Most club experts say offset irons are easier for amateurs to hit solidly because the clubface is designed so it naturally lags behind the shaft—ideal for solid impact. But depending on your swing shape, the height and direction of the ball varies. If a player has a lot of clubhead lag—meaning the hands pass over the position of the ball well in advance of impact—then the ball typically will fly lower and more left with offset. Players who have scoopy swings with little lag will typically hit high-trajectory shots. This is something to consider before your purchase.

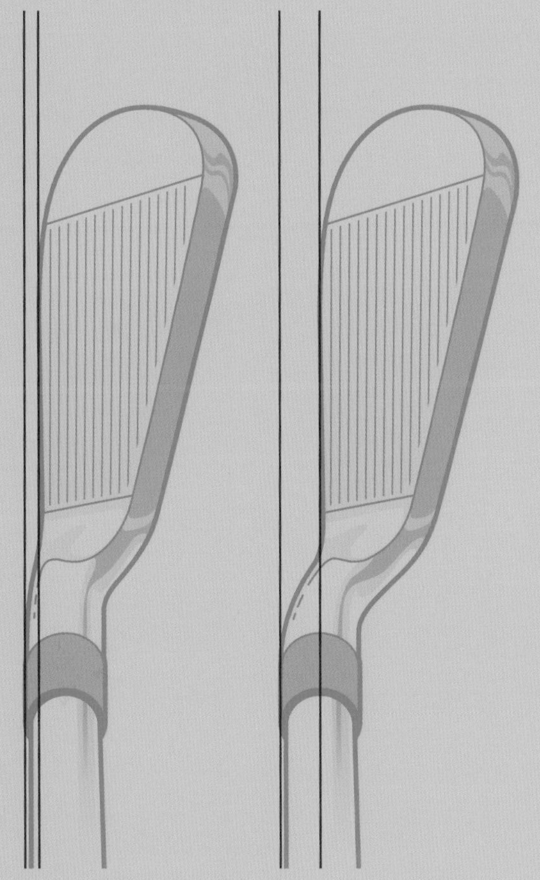

SWING TIP

Wind is such a big part of the game. When it's really howling, I widen my stance and play the ball more center. I also shorten my swing to reduce the backspin on the ball. The more it spins, the more it will upshoot and you will lose distance. Finally, remember to take more club and swing easy. **PAYNE STEWART**

EQUIPMENT

Beware of a too-light grip

by Steve Elkington

Poor grip pressure, be it too light or too firm, will channel from your hands into every part of your body and make a smooth swing impossible. Amateurs err on the side of gripping too lightly; Sam Snead's adage that you should hold the club as though it were a bird wrecked an awful lot of swings. Jackie Burke said what Snead didn't tell you was that the bird was a hawk. See, Snead had incredibly strong hands, so a grip pressure of "2" for him might be a "9" for you.

If you have average hands and hold the club too lightly, you'll instinctively tighten your grip during the swing and disrupt your rhythm. How firm should it be? You should be able to hit five practice balls in a row without having to regrip the club. Weak fingers can be strengthened. Ben Hogan squeezed tennis balls; Henry Cotton liked to hang from a metal bar for as long as he could. Remember, control of the club rests in your hands.

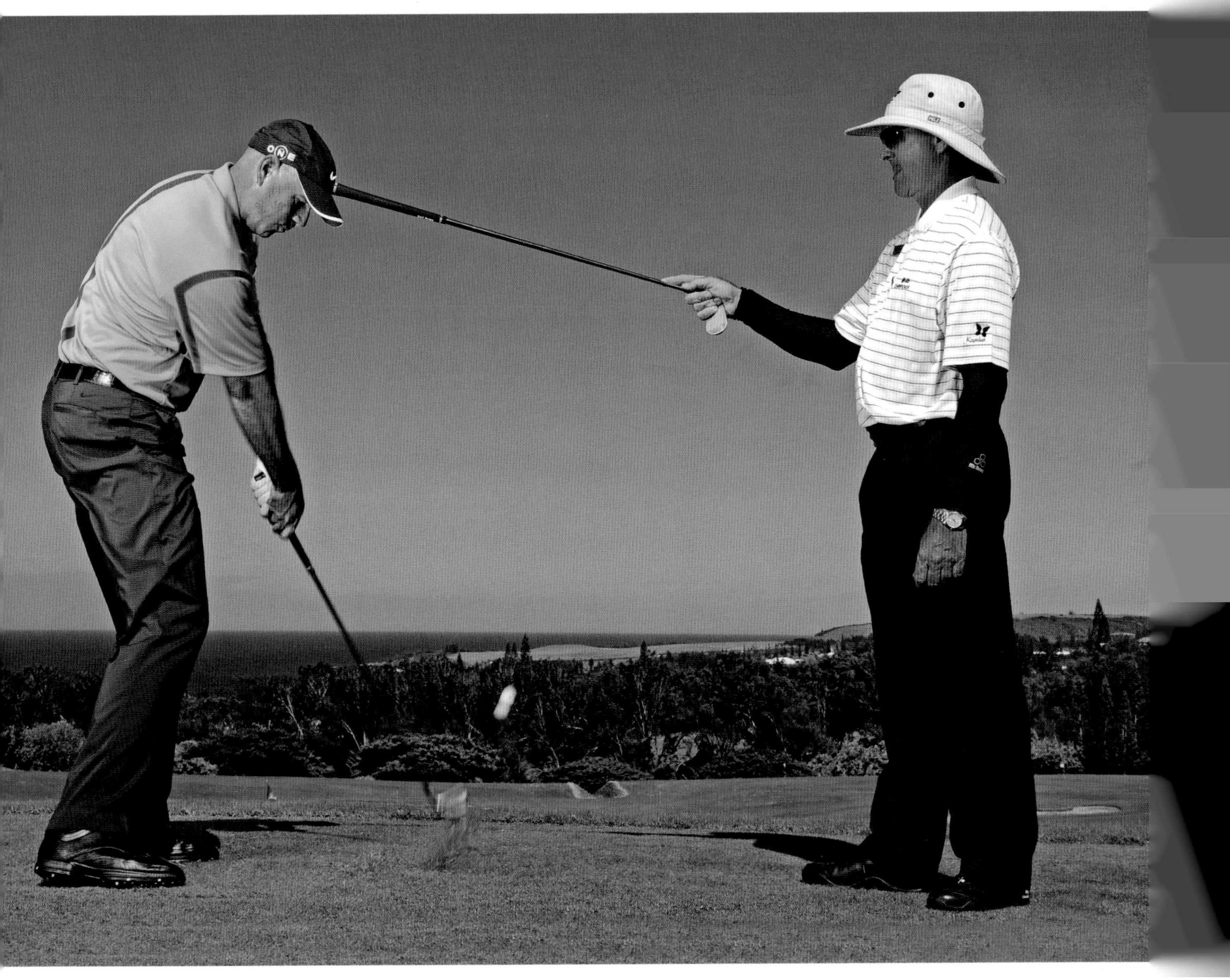

BASICS

FOCUS ON MAKING SOLID CONTACT

by Stewart Cink

The biggest problem most amateurs have on iron shots is that they swing too hard. They try to hit a 170-yard draw with a 7-iron, but an out-of-control swing produces a 130-yard slice. If you change your focus to trying to hit the ball in the center of the clubface with a little easier swing, I promise you'll hit far more quality iron shots.

Keeping your head still will help you hit the sweet spot more often. Here's a drill I've done since I was a youngster: I'd have someone hold a shaft next to my head. If my head moved during the swing, it would mess up my hair (yeah, I know, that's when I actually had hair). Try it with a friend, and remember to keep your head steady when you play.

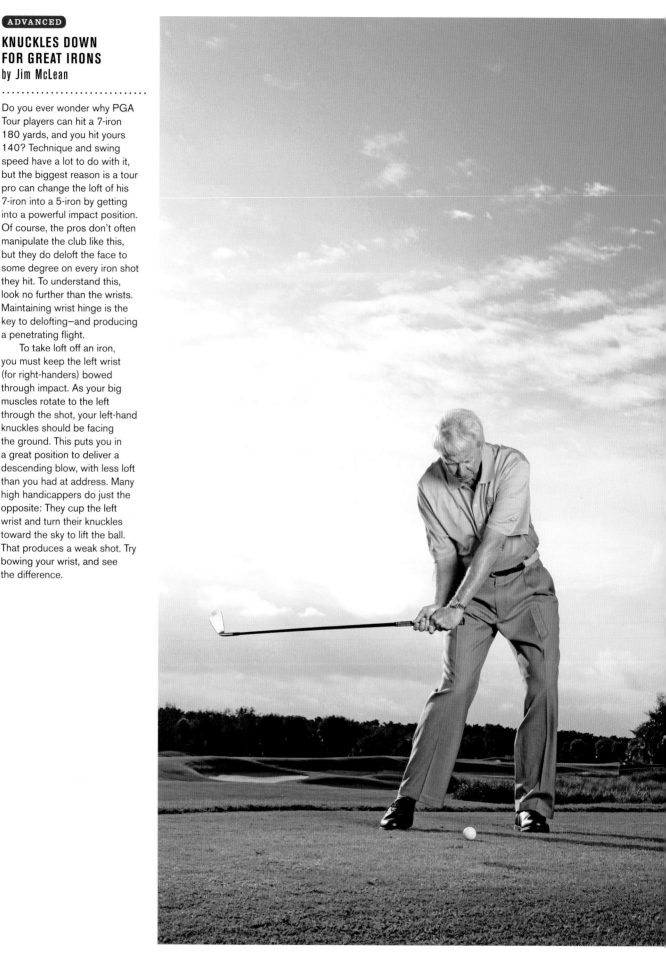

ADVANCED

KNUCKLES DOWN FOR GREAT IRONS

by Jim McLean

Do you ever wonder why PGA Tour players can hit a 7-iron 180 yards, and you hit yours 140? Technique and swing speed have a lot to do with it, but the biggest reason is a tour pro can change the loft of his 7-iron into a 5-iron by getting into a powerful impact position. Of course, the pros don't often manipulate the club like this, but they do deloft the face to some degree on every iron shot they hit. To understand this, look no further than the wrists. Maintaining wrist hinge is the key to delofting–and producing a penetrating flight.

To take loft off an iron, you must keep the left wrist (for right-handers) bowed through impact. As your big muscles rotate to the left through the shot, your left-hand knuckles should be facing the ground. This puts you in a great position to deliver a descending blow, with less loft than you had at address. Many high handicappers do just the opposite: They cup the left wrist and turn their knuckles toward the sky to lift the ball. That produces a weak shot. Try bowing your wrist, and see the difference.

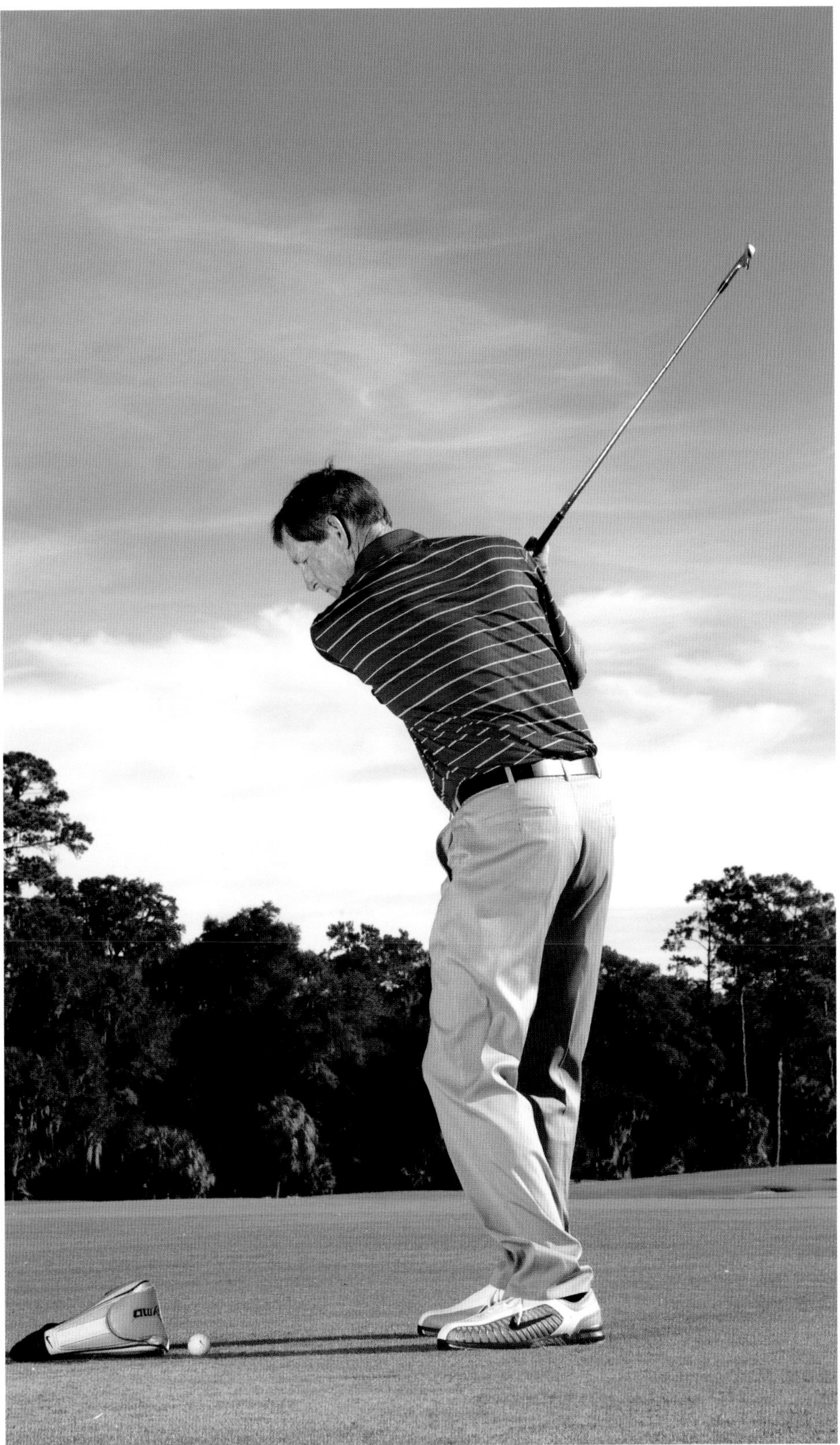

ADVANCED

USE A HEADCOVER TO IMPROVE YOUR PATH

by Hank Haney

Swing-path issues are common in the game: Many players come over the top and cut across the ball from the outside in; others come too much from the inside. The problem with path faults is that they're not always easy to see on your own. It's also hard to feel exactly what's happening when the downswing is moving at its fastest.

When you're working on improving your path, it's good to give yourself a guide. A soft driver headcover placed an inch or two outside the ball gives you a visual reference at setup, and the presence of an obstacle—even a soft one—will subconsciously push you to alter your path to avoid it. If you're trying to fix an outside-in swing, move the headcover back a little and miss it on the downswing. To fix an inside-out swing, move it forward and miss it after impact.

ADVANCED

CLEAR YOUR HIPS FOR MORE POWER

by Matt Kuchar

Hip action is extremely important in iron play. On the downswing, it's all about my left hip—actually, the left knee, thigh, and hip. I want to feel them clearing out, or turning to my left, so my right side can drive hard. From the top, my hips used to thrust toward the ball, which dropped the club too far to the inside and led to pushes and hooks. Now, I think about pushing my left hip out to left field and then turning it behind me. That keeps the club coming in steep so I can really compress the ball off the ground and hit it farther.

ADVANCED

GIVE YOUR SLICE A FACE-LIFT

by David Leadbetter

The reason you're hitting a lot of slices is because your clubface is open at impact. The problem might be in your backswing. Many slicers fan the face open during the takeaway, resulting in a weak, open position at the top. This forces them to swing down from outside the target line in an effort to square the face, but the result is a slice. Sound like you? To help square the face at impact and hit straighter shots, keep the clubface looking at the ball when you start back. Then, as you reach the top of your swing, have the face point to the sky. Getting in these two positions will greatly improve your chance of swinging down from the inside and squaring the club at impact—you might even start hitting draws.

Dustin Johnson escapes the rough during the opening round of the 2011 British Open at Royal St. George's.

UK TOUR
2011
adidas

STATS

What are your odds of making a hole-in-one?

by Dr. Frances Schneid

● ODDS	● ROUNDS NEEDED TO DO IT
TOUR PLAYER MAKING AN ACE	
3,000 TO 1	900
LOW-HANDICAP GOLFER MAKING AN ACE	
5,000 TO 1	1,250
AVERAGE GOLFER MAKING AN ACE	
12,000 TO 1	3,000
TOUR PLAYER ACING DESIGNATED HOLE	
14,000 TO 1	14,000
LOW-HANDICAP GOLFER ACING DESIGNATED HOLE	
20,000 TO 1	20,000
AVERAGE PLAYER ACING DESIGNATED HOLE	
48,000 TO 1	48,000
AVERAGE PLAYER ACING 150-YARD HOLE	
80,000 TO 1	23,000
AVERAGE PLAYER ACING 200-YARD HOLE	
150,000 TO 1	40,000
TWO AVERAGE PLAYERS, SAME FOURSOME, ACING SAME HOLE	
17 MILLION TO 1	17 MILLION

ADVANCED

THINK "LONG AND LOOSE" WITH LONGER IRONS

by Geoff Ogilvy

I've never found it hard to hit the longer irons. It mystifies me that some people can pure an 8-iron, but not a 4. I even still carry a 2-iron, but for most people, when I talk about longer irons, I mean the 4, 5, and 6. I think the problem most amateurs have is that they try to max out their distance with each club, and they have no understanding of how short they hit the ball. Say it's 160 yards to the flag. They're pulling out a 6-iron and trying to smash it when they should have a 5 or even a 4 in their hands. When I'm choosing a club, I always try to take more club than I need and swing easy. The softer you hit an iron, the better it performs. So my first piece of advice for hitting longer irons is don't try to smash it. You never look silly hitting it soft.

I try to turn my back to the target, which makes it easier to square the clubface at impact. I know some people can't turn like this, but turn as much as you can. Also, keep your grip pressure light at the top. I want some width (separation between my hands and head), but not at the expense of creating tension with a tight grip.

BASICS

PAY ATTENTION TO YOUR PRESHOT ROUTINE

by Lee Westwood

Here's my advice for building a solid preshot routine: I know this might sound odd, but if you're ready to hit and it's not your turn, that can screw up your timing. So, even when I know which club I want, I won't pull it from the bag until I can go right into my shot. Does this slow down play? Not if you move decisively from there.

From behind the ball, pick a specific target—like a tree, the edge of a bunker, even the flag. This will help you set up well and stay with the shot. If you have only a vague idea of your target, it's tough to make a committed swing. Keep your eyes on your target as you walk into the shot. If you look away, it'll be difficult to align your body correctly at address. Players who start the process standing next to the ball usually don't aim very well.

It's OK to run down a checklist as you're setting up to the ball—grip pressure, posture, aim and alignment, swing thoughts, and such. But when it's time to take the club back, forget all that and go with one thought. It could be the target you've just selected or a goal for the swing. For me, it's to take it away smoothly.

BASICS

THE EASY WAY TO SHAPE SHOTS

by David Leadbetter

There are quite a few different ideas for hitting a fade (a shot that curves left to right for right-handed players) and a draw (curves right to left). One of the simplest ways is to control the movement of your shoulders through impact.

If you want to play a fade, your right shoulder should work down and under. Think of your shoulders rotating vertically, like a Ferris wheel. That helps hold the face slightly open at impact—setting up a curve to the right.

If you want to hit a draw, your right shoulder should stay high and rotate around toward the target. Think of your shoulders rotating horizontally, like a merry-go-round. That encourages the face to close at impact—setting up a curve to the left.

BASICS

FADE IT FROM THE ROUGH
by Ernie Els

Playing from deep grass is a fact of life in professional golf. Tour courses are set up so hard now, and they're very penal for tee shots that miss the fairway. Some of the courses you play are no different. You have to know how to read your lie and take a calculated risk when you hit out of the rough.

If you aren't sure if you can get the club on the back of the ball cleanly, a cut shot is a great play. Play the ball slightly back in your stance, and account for some left-to-right curve when you pick your target. Opening the face will also give you some more loft, which helps in the tall grass.

Do not release the club early in the rough. If you don't retain your angle like I am in the pictures here, you'll make too much contact with the grass and lose clubhead speed. Resist the temptation to lift the ball out. Instead, rely on the club's loft and open clubface to do the job.

Because of the grass and open face, I take one more club for shots from the rough, unless the ball is sitting on top of dry grass. Then, I use more loft and swing softer, trying to hit it about 70 percent to avoid a flyer over the green.

BASICS

GET STEEP TO AVOID A CHUNK FROM THE ROUGH

by Butch Harmon

Hitting it fat out of the rough is a product of the backswing. If you make your normal swing, keeping the club low to the ground going back, you'll come down too shallow and catch the grass behind the ball.

To avoid this, make a steeper takeaway, hinging your wrists quicker from the start. This sets up a sharp descent back to the ball for clean contact.

It's also a good idea to play a fade from thick grass, because the normal release, with the clubface closing, might cause grass to grab the hosel and shut the face. So open the face slightly at address, aim left, and hold your wrists firm through impact. You'll catch it flush and hit a little fade.

PRACTICE TIP

To develop a feel for a proper release, assume your stance just as if you were addressing a shot. Hold the club in your left hand. With a ball in your right hand, swing your right arm back where it would be at the top of your backswing, then go ahead and throw the ball under your left arm and inside the clubshaft, which remains in address position. That feeling of turning your body and extending your right arm toward the target is one you want to duplicate when hitting the ball.

DAVIS LOVE JR.

ADVANCED

HOW TO HIT HIGHER OR LOWER IRONS

by Jonathan Byrd

There are going to be times when you need a specific ball-flight trajectory in addition to direction. To hit higher or lower shots, remember this: The farther back you address the ball in your stance, the lower it will fly. But you shouldn't move the ball too far forward or back, because that will affect the shot shape. Too far back, for instance, makes the ball go right of your target. I wouldn't let the ball position change by more than three or four ball widths.

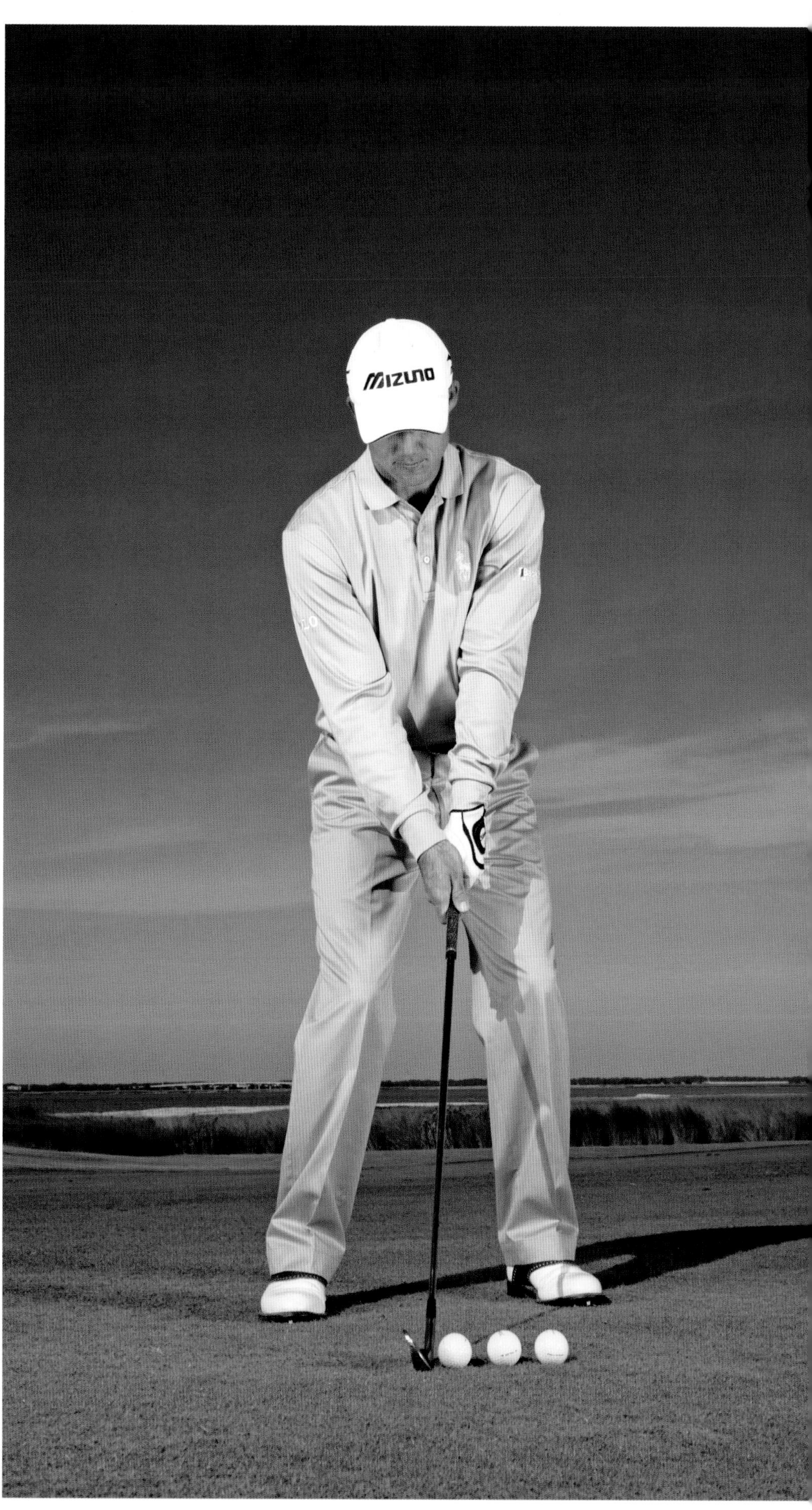

EQUIPMENT

Steel shafts aren't for everyone

by Mike Stachura

What's the difference between a steel iron shaft and a graphite iron shaft of the same flex? To study this consumer conundrum, our 5-handicapper hit two 7-irons—one with a stiff-flex shaft in steel and one in graphite. Our 14-handicapper did the same, except with a regular-flex shaft in steel and graphite.

The steel shaft worked best for the 5-handicapper. He averaged eight more yards in carry distance, and his shots had a tighter dispersion. Conversely, the 14-handicapper was more accurate with the graphite-shafted 7-iron and hit it three yards farther on average. Another bonus: His maximum trajectory was 2½ yards higher with the graphite shaft.

"Graphite shafts usually have lower bend points than steel shafts, and so they tend to kick the ball up in the air," says Mike Dickerson, president of the International Professional Association of Clubfitters. "In general, driver swings of 95 to 100 mph is the range where you can play either graphite or steel shafts. I often ask people if they're a hitter or a swinger to help them decide. A hitter is someone with tempo like Jesper Parnevik, who really goes after it. I'll steer that person toward steel. However, a swinger, or someone with tempo more like Freddie Couples, I'll steer toward graphite."

The difference between steel and graphite depends on who's swinging it.

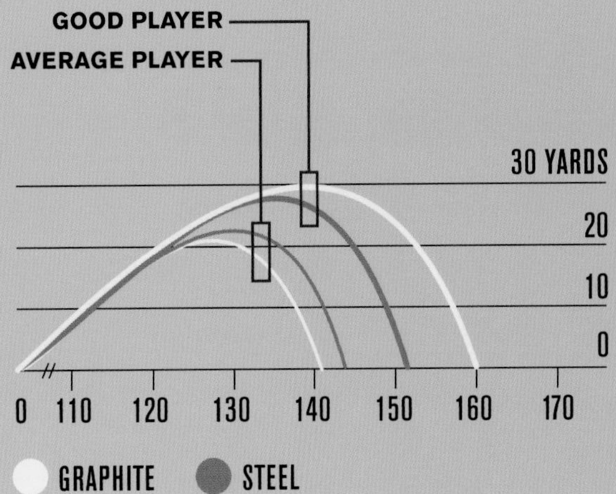

HEALTH

How to overcome golfer's elbow

by Ron Kaspriske

Tendinitis of the inner or outer tendons around the elbows, particularly the lead elbow (known as tennis elbow or golfer's elbow), is a common golf injury. It's especially prevalent in amateurs who have steeper swings since the club crashes into the ground much more violently, sending a shock wave up the arms. Here are some tips for treating tendon inflammation around the elbows:

1. Start by applying ice to the elbow (no more than 15 minutes per hour).

2. While sleeping, wear a brace on your wrist to stabilize it so the tendons that attach from the wrist to the elbow can relax.

3. Take anti-inflammatory medicine, such as ibuprofen or naproxen sodium.

4. Once the inflammation subsides, do forearm-strengthening exercises.

ADVANCED

DOWNHILL LIE? STAY ON FRONT FOOT

by Tom Watson

My experience is that you seldom see a flat lie in the Masters. The downhill lie you get if you lay up at the par-5 15th hole is a classic case. I lay up there a lot these days, especially into the wind. How do you play a shot from a downslope? Swing down the hill. To do that, widen your stance and position the ball farther back, with your shoulders parallel to the slope. If you're right-handed, your left shoulder should be lower than your right.

Now the important part: Your weight should be braced on your left foot. A slight weight shift to the right going back is fine, but your center of gravity should remain left of center throughout the backswing (on your left instep).

The tendency is to tilt back and hit behind the ball, so focus on hitting the ball first and taking a divot in front of it. Because the shot will tend to fly lower and run more, pick the club up quicker with your right hand and make a steeper swing to get more loft. On shorter shots, I'll even open the clubface.

ADVANCED

DRIVE YOUR WEIGHT FORWARD ON UPHILL SHOTS

by Jim McLean

The proper strategy on uphill approaches starts with using at least one more club—even two more for steeper hills. Play to the back-of-the-green yardage. Rarely will you knock the ball over. And be aware of optical illusions, such as large front bunkers or seeing only the top of the flagstick, because they will mess with your depth perception.

When it comes to the swing itself, the tendency is to hang back on your right side and try to help the ball up to the green. Do the opposite: Drive your weight forward and through the shot. Think of it as a level lie, and just play a longer distance.

ADVANCED

BEND MORE FROM THE HIPS WHEN BALL IS BELOW YOUR FEET

by Todd Anderson

When the ball is resting on a hill below your feet, the clubhead will tend to rest on its heel. Raise the grip so the toe is on the ground. The ground sloping away from you effectively shortens the club. Bend more from your hips and tilt your upper body forward to reach the ball. The shaft will be more vertical. When you swing, the club moves more up and down, with less face rotation, which can produce a left-to-right shot. To allow for this curve to the right, aim farther left. Expect a higher ball flight and less roll.

In a good grip, both hands act as one unit. To ensure yourself a firm two-handed grip, get your left hand on the club absolutely correctly: The club is placed in the left hand so that the shaft is pressed up under the muscular pad at the inside heel of the palm and the shaft also lies directly across the top joint of the forefinger. Now, just close the left hand–close the fingers before you close the thumb–and the club will be just where it should be. The proper positioning of the right hand is with the grip in the fingers, not in the palm. The two middle fingers apply the most pressure.

BEN HOGAN

MENTAL TIP

Greens in regulation is the stat of stats

by Johnny Miller

PGA Tour players and their fans have a dizzying number of statistics to look at these days. But one measurement of a golfer's round will always mean a little more than any other: greens in regulation.

In my heyday during the 1970s and early '80s, when players saw each other late in the day, conversations started with one question: "How many greens did you hit?" The answer didn't tell the whole story, but when you combined it with a guy's score, it told most of it. If a guy hit 15 greens in regulation but shot 74, it meant his long game was good but he putted poorly. If he hit 11 greens and shot 69, it meant the opposite—he sprayed it all over but chipped and putted like a champion. I think the GIR stat is the one pros and even amateurs should look at first. Improve by three greens a round, and your scores will improve dramatically.

ADVANCED

GRIP DOWN WHEN BALL IS ABOVE YOUR FEET

by Butch Harmon

This lie brings the ball closer to you, so you naturally stand a little taller. Grip down an inch or two to accommodate the shorter reach to the ball. Set your weight a little more in your toes; remember, gravity will pull you downhill—in this case, onto your heels.

From this upright posture, the swing will be flatter or more around the body like a baseball swing. That creates more hand and arm rotation through the shot, with the clubface closing at a faster rate on the downswing. The tendency with the ball above your feet is to hit it to the left.

FJ

ADVANCED

HIT IT HARD DOWNWIND
by Tom Watson

Downwind approach shots demand more adjustment than many players make. You almost always have to allow for more wind than you think. The ball will go farther and lower and will run more after it hits the ground. Sometimes you need to land the ball short of the green if it's open in front.

The 12th hole at Royal Aberdeen in one Senior British Open was an example of the ball running downwind. I had about 200 yards to the front edge of the green. The first day I hit a 6-iron, and the ball went about 240 yards. The next two days I hit a 7-iron down the same wind, and it was the right club. It landed 30 yards short of the green and rolled probably another 50 yards.

The key to hitting downwind is to swing full speed to spin the ball more and fly it higher. It's hard to do because the breeze flattens the trajectory, even though the ball will travel farther with the added roll. And downwind shots are even tougher today because the new balls spin less. So throttle up your swing speed–staying in control–to create more spin. Swing easier into the wind; swing harder with the wind. Game of opposites? Yes. And remember the roll. Think of carrying the ball to the front of the green or short of the green if it's open in front.

ADVANCED

PLAY A KNOCKDOWN WHEN YOU'RE INTO THE WIND

by Padraig Harrington

Coming from Ireland, I learned pretty quickly how to hit the ball low. It's the only way to control the ball in high winds.

The low ball might be my best shot, but it can be useless in this country. There's no point hitting a low shot into firm, fast greens, so consider what the ball will do when it lands before you hit it. If you don't think you'll be able to stop it on the green, go higher.

I'd recommend taking one club longer than normal and gripping down an inch or two. The ball will fly the same distance as it would with the shorter club, but the lower loft in the longer one will keep the shot down. You need to set up a little closer to the ball to stay over it when you swing—I'll explain this in my next point. For a middle iron, play the ball in the middle of your stance, or even a bit farther back, so you make contact with the clubface in a delofted position.

Make a three-quarter backswing and a three-quarter finish, focusing on staying on top of the ball. What I mean is, feel as if you're covering the ball with your chest as you swing through impact. This will help you trap the ball against the turf, lowering the flight.

Also, don't forget to practice this shot. You can't expect to play this shot well once every two weeks. On the range, remember to hit some of these low balls, too.

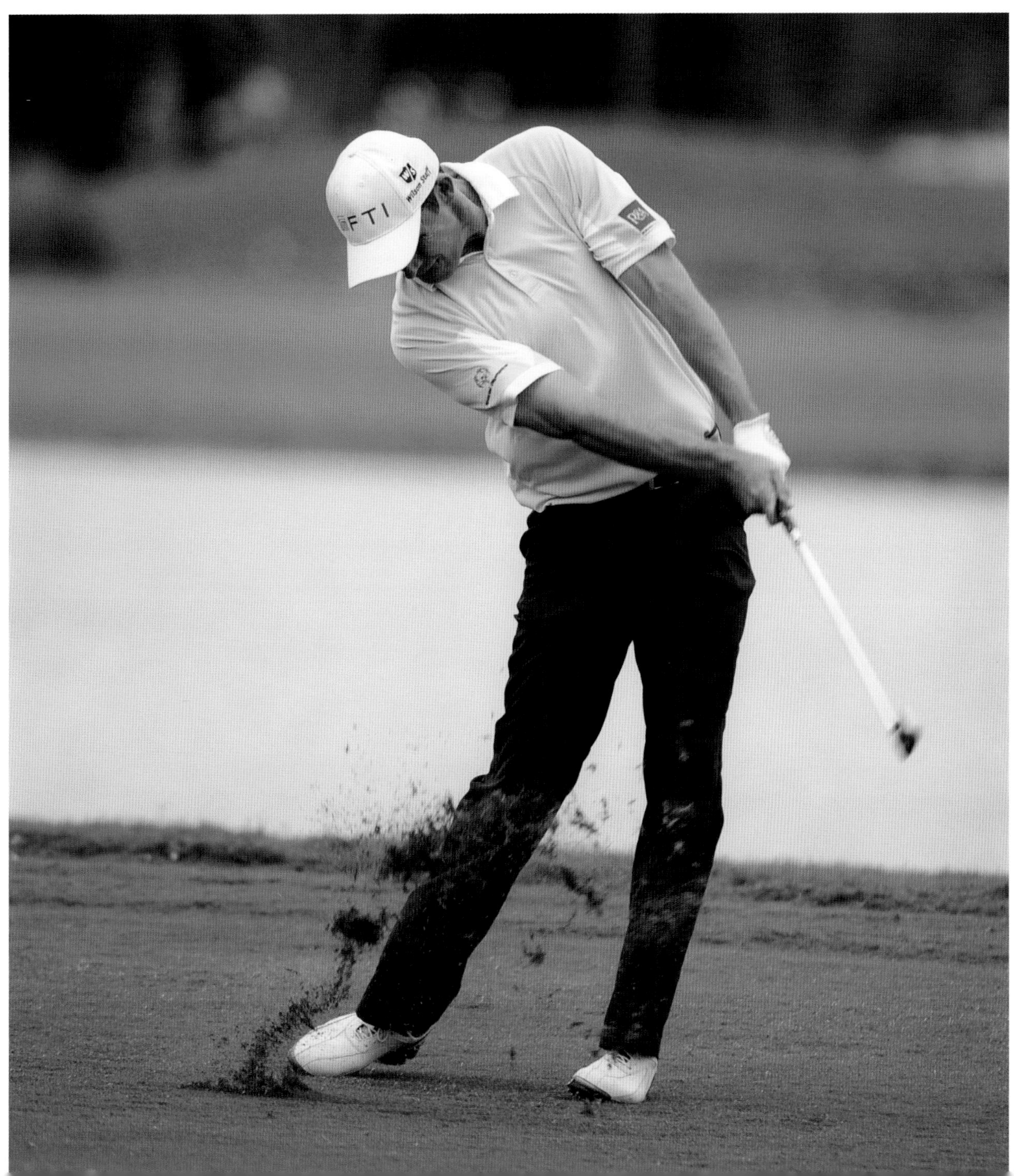

ADVANCED

HOW TO HIT IT SOLID OFF OF TIGHT LIES

by Nick Price

When you have a tight lie, it's hard to hit a medium or long iron high and get the ball to land softly without playing it way up in your stance and thereby risking a fat shot. A higher-percentage play is my knockdown draw: a lower-trajectory, right-to-left shot that lets the ball release when it lands. Aim right of your target, make a three-quarter swing, and try to trap the ball against the turf. This shot is more forgiving because to draw the ball you have to swing down from inside the target line on a shallower path than normal. If you don't quite catch the ball first, the club isn't going to ricochet off the turf the way it would with a steeper approach into hard ground. Instead, your clubhead will skim along the turf, so you might turn a mediocre swing into a good shot. The best part about playing my knockdown draw is that the shallow angle of approach gives you more room for error, especially on tight lies. You don't have to hit the ball perfectly to execute a decent shot because the club stays down longer in the impact zone.

To hit it, play the ball back in your stance, grip down an inch on the club then take the club back more inside than normal. You can even drop your trailing foot back an inch at address to help set up this inside path. By starting inside, you'll make room for the club to swing down from the inside without your body being in the way.

FITNESS TIP

Improve your iron play with hip crossovers

by Mark Verstegen

Without flexible hips, you can't fire your body through the ball or maintain your posture, two important ingredients to making solid impact with an iron. The hip crossover will help improve the range of mobility in your hips as well as help reduce the stress placed on your lower back as a result of stiff hips.

To do a hip crossover, lie face up on the ground with your arms to your sides, your knees bent, feet wider than shoulder width, heels on the ground. Now, twist your bent legs to the left until they reach the ground, then twist them to the right. Continue, alternating sides, for about 8–10 turns per side. Keep your shoulders on the ground and your stomach tight. You should feel your hips and lower back stretching.

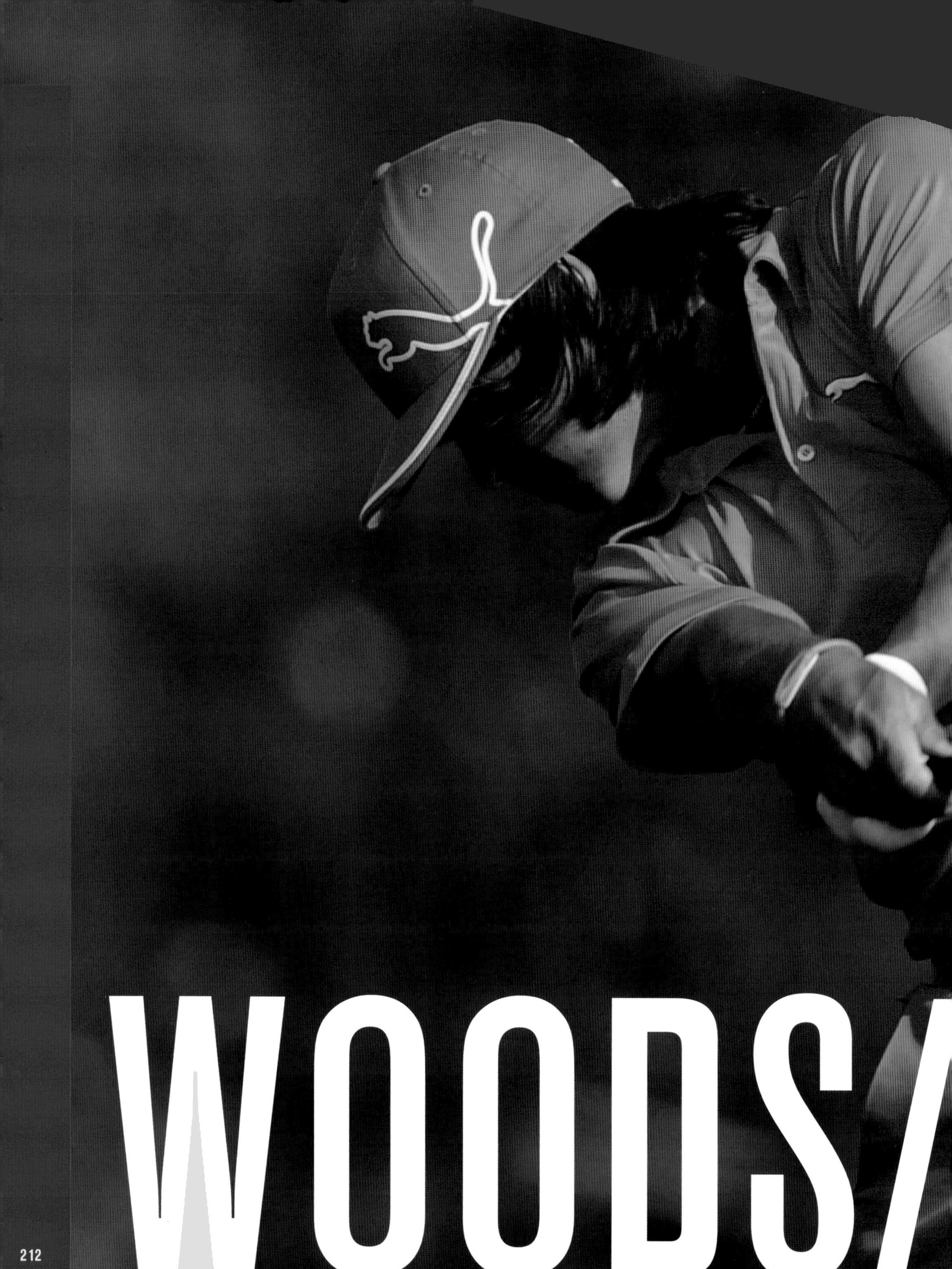

WOODS/

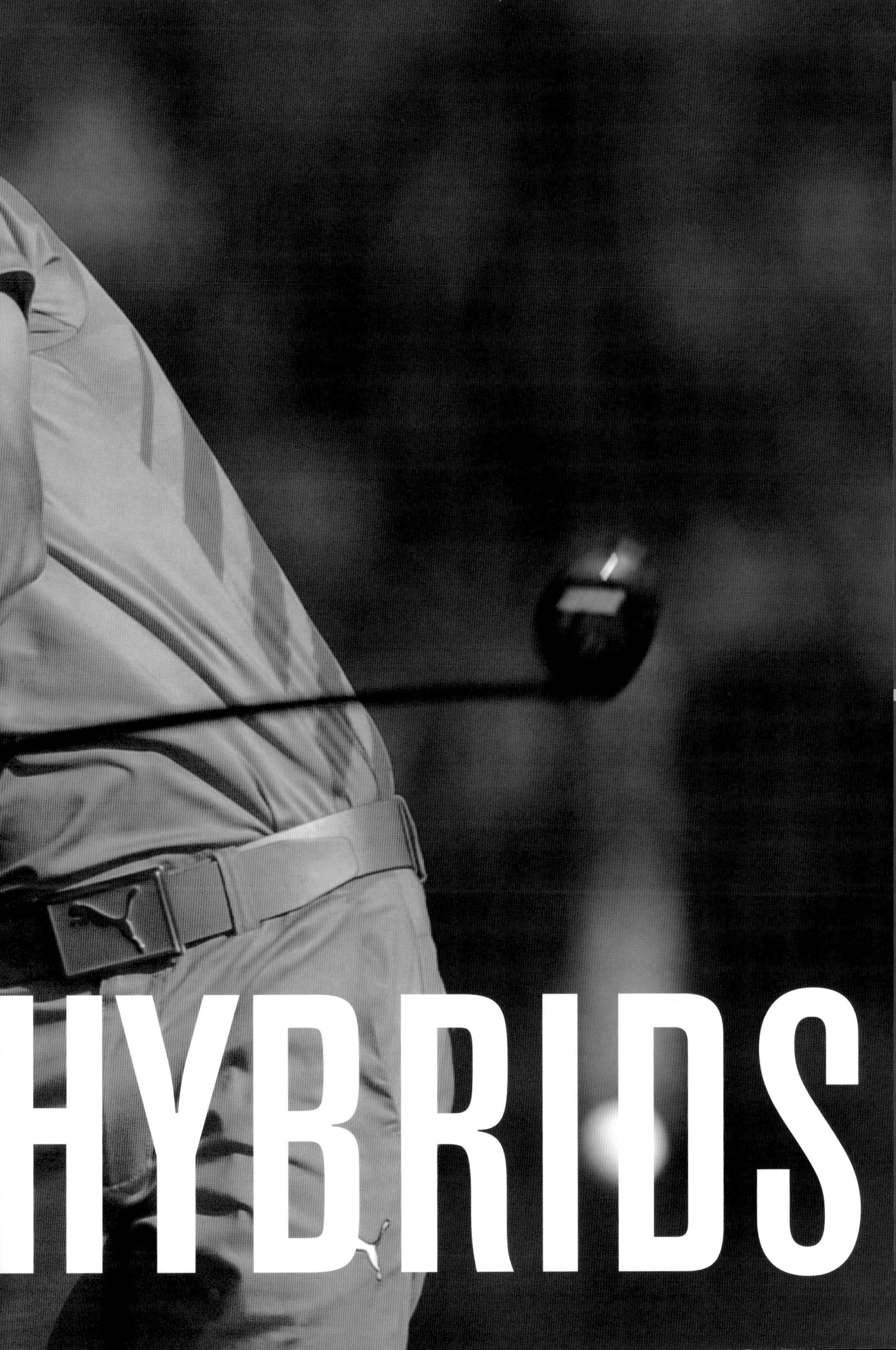

HYBRIDS

PERHAPS THE GREATEST DEVELOPMENT in golf equipment since the modern golf ball was invented is the widespread emergence of hybrid clubs. They are called hybrids because they have some characteristics of irons and some characteristics of fairway woods and are incredibly forgiving when compared to the clubs they were designed to replace—namely the 2-, 3-, and 4-irons.

Hybrids also have helped improve the design of fairway woods in order to keep them relevant and in demand for amateur players. Like modern drivers, fairway woods have gotten bigger and lighter, and some even have adjustable heads to allow players who slice or hook to straighten out their shots.

Now the standard set of clubs might contain a couple of fairway woods and a couple of hybrids, since both are considerably easier to use for higher-handicap golfers. Lower centers of gravity and shallow-face designs help even rank beginners get shots off the turf airborne. And their performance off the tee, in fairway bunkers, even out of thick rough is making long irons obsolete for most.

Both hybrids and fairway woods are effective tools when a golfer needs to hit a high, long-range shot, but the key to mastering either type of club is to make a long, slow, patient swing that allows them to do what they were designed to do. Here is some advice on how to wield a hybrid or fairway wood.

PREVIOUS SPREAD: **Orange crush:** Rickie Fowler rifles a fairway wood shot at the 2010 Memorial Tournament while sporting the colors of his former college—Oklahoma State University.

OPPOSITE: Tiger Woods swing sequence

200 **Maximum yardage at which amateurs have a reasonable chance to hit the green, thanks in large part to hybrids and more forgiving fairway woods.**

- Hybrids and fairway woods can be used for more than 10 different shots, including chipping, fairway bunker play, punch shots, conservative tee shots, etc.
- The average greens-in-regulation percentage on the PGA Tour from 200 yards or longer is 44 percent. The best is 58 percent.
- For average swing speeds (95 mph), a ball hit with a 3-wood carries only 14 percent less (15 yards) than it does with a driver while fairway accuracy improves by 25 percent.

BASICS

STAND TALL AND RELAXED, BUT ATHLETIC

by Jack Nicklaus

Here's the best way for me to explain my thoughts on posture: Stand up as you normally stand; now relax your legs. Bend slightly from the waist. Don't bend or straighten your upper body, just relax. Now hold the club and drop your shoulders. Where your arms fall, that's where the club goes.

I want my back relatively straight, my rear end out a bit, my arms relaxed and hanging down. I also want my chin up so my left shoulder is not restricted as it turns completely under a steady head. Nothing fancy.

Practice Tips

BASICS

TEE HEIGHT IS IMPORTANT WITH HYBRIDS AND WOODS

by Hank Haney

There's a reason they let you tee up the ball only 18 times a round: It's easier to hit a shot that way. When you do get the chance to put the ball on a tee, take advantage of it, and always on par 3s.

When you tee up a ball for an iron or hybrid shot, you're keeping grass from getting between the clubface and the ball, which gives you more control over distance and direction. Whenever anything gets between the club and the ball at impact—like blades of grass or even early morning dew—the ball comes off with less backspin, so it doesn't behave as predictably.

As a general rule, tee up an iron shot so the ball is just above ground level. It should look like the ball is sitting on the top of the short blades of grass on the tee. For a hybrid club, tee the ball slightly higher, about half an inch above ground level. Hybrids have more weight built into the sole, and you want that weight to get under the ball so you're taking advantage of the technology. When you get to a fairway wood, set the tee so a quarter of the ball is above the face.

Be sure to make adjustments to these guidelines based on your swing tendencies. Put a piece of impact tape on your clubface and hit some shots from a tee. If you hit the ball a bit high or low on the face, adjust your tee height to help you hit it flush.

EQUIPMENT

Choosing the right fairway wood

by E. Michael Johnson

Over the last decade professional golf has become a power game, with an equipment focus on golf balls that fly like Flubber and drivers the size of saucepans. Less noticed, however, has been the role of the fairway wood. Quietly, the fairway wood has gone from a club used to reach the green on par 5s and long par 4s to, in many instances, a second driver. As such, lofts on 3-woods have dropped faster than a politician's approval rating. The majority of players who carry a 3-wood are now using less than 15 degrees—although for years that figure was the standard loft.

Although today's lower-spinning golf ball would seem to make a lower loft less desirable, the fact is lower-lofted fairway woods better match the modern tour pros' swing, which produces a high ball speed with enough spin to keep the ball in the air. The standard 15-degree fairway wood can give off too much spin and the ball can shoot up higher than the player wants. In short, the trajectory with these clubs is more important than ever because they're being used off the tee now nearly as often—and, at times, more so—than from the turf.

Low-lofted fairway woods, however, are not for all golfers. In fact, this likely is one area where you should not be playing what the pros play. A study conducted by Golf Digest using the TrackMan radar tracking device revealed that those swinging at 85 mph boosted the height of their trajectory by three yards and added an additional five yards of carry when using a 17-degree 4-wood versus a 13-degree 3-wood. The reason: The shorter shaft on the 4-wood makes it easier to hit the ball solidly while the added loft creates much-needed additional spin at that speed to keep the ball in the air. And low loft or not, a club that works is always in style.

BASICS

SWEEP YOUR FAIRWAY WOODS OFF THE DECK
by Lorena Ochoa

I always went for par 5s in two because I knew I could hit crisp fairway woods. The secret is simple: Keep the clubhead low to the ground in the takeaway and after impact. This ensures a full release where the clubface strikes the ball below its equator, launching it high in the air.

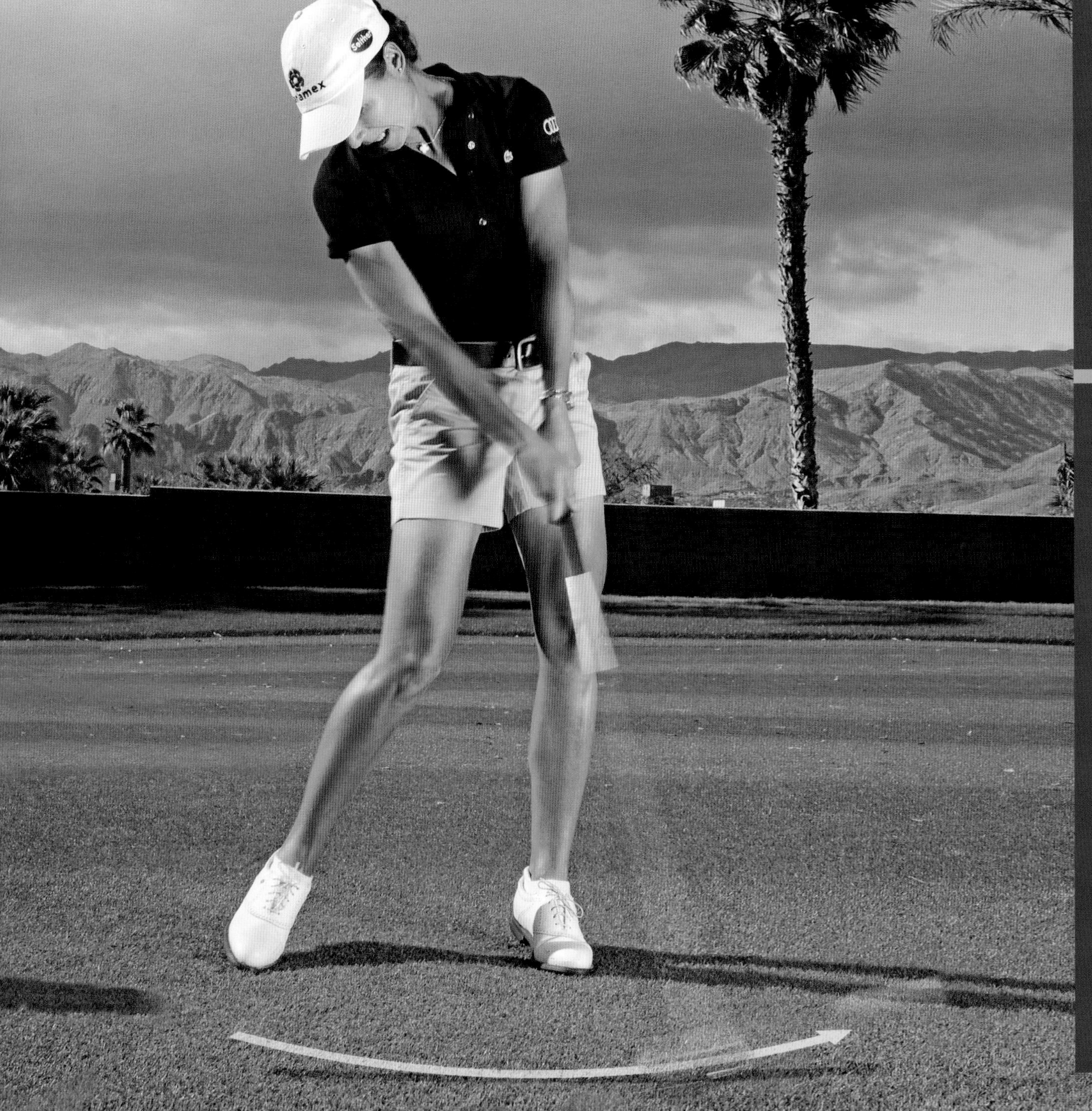

BASICS

STOP TOPPING YOUR 3-WOOD
by Butch Harmon

Hitting a 3-wood off a tight fairway lie brings out the worst in a lot of golfers. Because the club doesn't have much loft, they think they have to help the ball into the air. This mind-set causes them to hang back on their right side and swing up on the ball, even flipping their hands to help it up. The problem is, these moves actually have the opposite effect: The club makes contact on the upswing, and they top the shot.

To make solid contact with a fairway wood, hit with a descending blow, scraping the grass or even taking a small divot. For that to happen, you have to shift your weight to your front side and swing through the ball, letting your arms fully extend. A good cue is to think about swinging to a full finish and not about hitting the ball. Once you start striking it pure, you'll realize the club has plenty of loft to send the ball in the air. So get off that right side and swing through it.

Titleist

BASICS

HOW TO HIT A HYBRID
by Hank Haney

Hybrids replace long irons in your bag, so the tendency is to do the same things with them that you did with your 3- or 4-iron—forgetting why you replaced those clubs in the first place. The main rule of hitting a hybrid is to swing with the same sequencing and mechanics as you do with your 7-iron.

The common urge is to move your arms and hands faster to generate more speed and try to lift the ball in the air. That's not necessary.

Instead, make a full shoulder turn, and swing through to a full finish, so your hips and shoulders are facing the target. Make sure you finish all the way up on your back toe (right), which is a sign you've made it completely through the ball. Trust the loft of the club to get the ball in the air. When you stop turning your shoulders through, the bottom of your swing moves too far behind the ball. That results in hitting shots fat or thin.

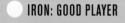

EQUIPMENT

When should you replace irons for hybrids?
by E. Michael Johnson

Using TrackMan ball-flight analysis, we tested middle-handicappers hitting long irons and corresponding hybrids. On average, the players we tested hit the 4-iron and the 4-hybrid about the same distance (180 yards), and the 3-iron just four yards farther (184 yards). But the 3-hybrid went 192 yards, making it an ideal replacement for the 3-iron.

See the chart for more data from our testing.

IRON: GOOD PLAYER
IRON: AVERAGE PLAYER
HYBRID: GOOD PLAYER
HYBRID: AVERAGE PLAYER

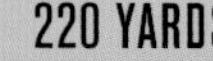

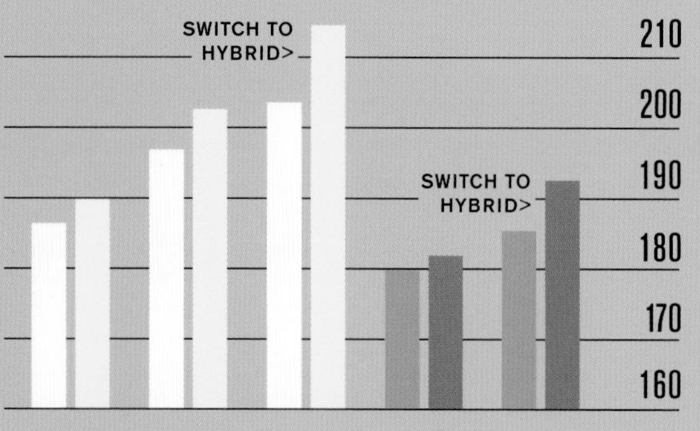

4I / 4H 3I / 3H 2I / 2H 4I / 4H 3I / 3H

BASICS

STABILIZE LOWER BODY TO HIT HYBRIDS

by Jim Flick

Bob Toski and Jack Nicklaus have played a significant role in my approach to teaching and playing the game. Though they have very different body types and golf swings, they both have told me a wide stance is better than a narrow one. I find this especially true with longer clubs and when hitting hybrids from the rough.

A stance just wider than your shoulders gives you a stable platform over which you can turn your upper body. It encourages your hips to stay level throughout the swing; the left hip is likely to drop when your stance is too narrow, causing mis-hit shots. It lowers your center of gravity so playing in the wind is easier—you are less likely to get blown off balance.

Pre-set your right knee slightly inward at address, and keep it there to the top of the swing. You'll find that promotes greater stability, a correct angle of attack, and consistently solid contact.

SWING THOUGHT

When I shot 26 on the front nine of the first round at the 2006 U.S. Bank Championship, I set the tour's nine-hole scoring record. Two of my eight birdies came on long, difficult par 4s. I hit my 23-degree hybrid into both holes at various times during the week, and I'm not sure I would've played them so well without it. It really is a miracle club that I can hit anywhere from 180 to 210 yards, but I did have to acquire a knack for hitting it. You have to hit down on the ball slightly, as though you were hitting a 7-wood. By pinching it off the turf, you hit better shots, get a surer ball flight, and have more variation with trajectory.

COREY PAVIN

ADVANCED

HYBRIDS OR WOODS: LEARN TO HIT DOWN INSTEAD OF LIFTING

by Randy Smith

The best way to be convinced that your clubs have enough loft to get the ball airborne without any lifting action is to prove it to yourself. On the range, place a ball in the middle of a shallow divot and practice hitting fairway-wood or hybrid shots out of it. You might hit a few grounders or thin shots to start, especially when you try to lift the ball by flipping your hands.

But you'll quickly realize that you have to swing the clubhead down to get the ball to go up. That feeling of hitting down on the ball is the one you want for all of your fairway-wood and hybrid shots. Groove it and you'll notice your ball flight improve immediately.

SWING THOUGHT

Amateurs often are afraid to turn their body when swinging down into the ball with a fairway wood. They typically make an arm swing, which lacks power and accuracy. Instead, let your right side release as you swing down and through. This body turn will release energy from the right side into the clubhead and produce the power and consistency you need with longer clubs. JOHNNY MILLER

ADVANCED

FOR BETTER HYBRID HITS, THINK "IRON SHOT"

by David Leadbetter

Hybrid clubs are described as being somewhere between a fairway wood and an iron, but for the purpose of swinging these clubs correctly, think of them as long irons. Play the ball in the middle of your stance, and pinch it off the turf at impact. Don't stand up and try to lift the ball into the air, as many amateurs do. Instead, keep your spine angle constant, and feel as if you stay centered over the ball on the downswing, hitting down on it slightly. The hybrid's wide sole will even allow you to hit a little behind the ball and still produce an acceptable shot.

ADVANCED

THINK "BACK TO THE TARGET" TO AVOID RUSHING

by Tom Watson

Most golfers are shy about turning their shoulders far enough, especially on tight holes where they are scared of not keeping the ball in play with a longer club like a fairway wood or hybrid. But if you're going to hit a fairway wood in play, think of turning your back to the target before starting down.

You have to plant yourself firmly on your right side, keep your right knee flexed, and pivot around it. It's OK to shift your center of gravity a little to your right—just don't let it drift left, toward the target. Swinging with the right side feeling soft promotes a full turn. I want my shoulders behind the ball at the top of the swing, not over it. I try to swing my left shoulder around to where my right shoulder started. I let my right hip turn with my shoulders.

Make a full turn away from the ball, and complete your swing, even on tight holes—especially on tight holes.

SWING TIP

Anytime I find myself struggling during a round, especially with my woods off the tee, I visualize one key image to get back on track: Return the club to its address position at impact.

Why does this help me? It keeps my lower body quiet, my chest facing the ball at impact, and it keeps my spine angle stable so I make consistently solid contact. Another key is keeping my right heel down at impact, which is the same position it was in at address.

SAM SNEAD

Play

ng Strategy

BASICS

HOW TO HIT A 3-WOOD OFF THE TEE

by Annika Sorenstam

Too often, golfers will take a 3-wood off the tee for control, but then try to hit it as far as they hit the driver. When you swing that hard, you give up the 3-wood's control advantage. Yes, it's great to hit the ball straight and long, but keeping it in the fairway is the reason you're hitting with a 3-wood.

When you tee up your 3-wood, follow the same rule used for the driver: Half of the ball should be above the clubhead's crown. Golfers who don't pay attention to tee height struggle to hit 3-woods. Also, play the ball an inch farther back in your stance than you do for the driver.

I'll often hit a fairway wood (I carry a strong 4-wood instead of a 3) when sand or water narrows the driver zone. I'd rather hit a longer club for my second shot than flirt with danger off the tee. It's one shot at a time. Once I pick a driving club, I don't try to stretch it. I stay in balance by swinging every club at one speed: six out of 10 on the effort scale.

DIMENSION
DATA

PLAYING STRATEGY

You can splash the ball out of high grass with a wood by making a more descending swing into the grass two to four inches behind the ball. The bigger wood/metal clubhead with its more tapered hosel glides through and depresses the grass, whereas an iron tends to become tangled in the grass. Another benefit is that the longer shaft of a fairway wood allows you to build clubhead speed with less effort. Too often we try to force an iron out of the rough and wind up dissipating our power and clubhead speed too early. DAVIS LOVE JR.

BASICS

HOW TO HIT A HYBRID OFF THE TEE

by Nick Price

Ideally, you want the clubface covering most of the ball. Maybe a quarter of the ball can be above the face, but that's it. The way the hybrid is weighted, it's easy to get the ball airborne when you tee it low. The only other tip for a hybrid tee shot is to swing as if you're hitting a fairway wood: You want a sweeping approach into the ball.

BASICS

SWING AT 80 PERCENT TO SCORE WITH A FAIRWAY WOOD

by Ernie Els

Even though hybrids are more popular than ever (and easy to hit), you still have to be able to handle your fairway woods to have a complete long game. If you can hit your 3- and 5-woods with confidence from the fairway, par 5s become birdie opportunities and 420-yard par 4s are a lot less scary.

When you're hitting a fairway wood, you've got a lot of real estate to cover to get to your target. Your first instinct is probably to give it a little more power, because you're worried about coming up short. But if you try to hit it hard, you'll tend to speed up your transition at the top and get out of sync. Lunging at the ball from the top leads to a lot of pulls and slices. You'll get better results—and often more distance—if you swing at 80 percent effort.

I almost never hit a shot all out, and I make a conscious effort to swing my long clubs just as I do my wedges. Keep this in mind when hitting your fairway woods.

BASICS

DOGLEG HOLES ARE PERFECT FOR FAIRWAY WOODS

by Laird Small

The water and woods are full of golf balls from players who tried to be heroes on doglegs. Your goal should be to put the ball in play off the tee and have a decent second shot—that's it. Here on Pebble's par-5 18th, aiming left of the trees in the fairway is a risky play, even though it might give you a chance to reach the green in two. Hit the ball in the water, and you're probably going to have to re-tee. Instead, take a club that will put your ball in play right of the trees. You can use a 3-wood, 5-wood, hybrid, whatever you feel comfortable with. If you miss the shot to the right, there's room to recover. And if you pull it, you'll likely still be dry.

ADVANCED

IN THE ROUGH? WHEN TO USE A WOOD INSTEAD OF A HYBRID

by Don Hurter

To get the best result from the rough, you need to understand how woods and hybrids are different. From short rough, the flat bottom on the 3-wood skids easily through the grass—even easier than a middle iron. But in thicker rough, you need the heavier clubhead mass and smaller, more compact head of the hybrid, which helps keep the clubhead stable as it plows through the deeper grass. Most hybrids also have more loft than fairway woods. This helps get the ball up and away from the deeper grass. A higher-lofted wood, like a 7-wood, can be effective out of medium rough, but if it's a borderline call, sacrifice the distance and use the hybrid to extricate the ball from trouble.

ADVANCED

USE YOUR HYBRID TO ESCAPE THE ROUGH

by Lorena Ochoa

A hybrid is such an easy club to play with, so make the most of it–even in tough situations. I try to take advantage of my length, so I hit driver off the tee whenever possible. That's why the hybrid is one of my favorite clubs. It's so easy to hit from bad lies, I can gamble with my tee shots and still salvage a good approach from the rough. The hybrid has a wide, rounded sole and extra weight that makes it easy to slide under the ball without getting caught in the long grass.

You don't have to be strong to hit a crisp hybrid shot from the rough–the club is designed to work for players of all levels. The key is to set up correctly and make a steep swing. I start with a slightly open clubface (right) to add some loft to the club. I vary the distance I hit the ball by changing how much I choke down on the club. (The more I grip down, the shorter I'll hit it.) I put more weight on my left side and play the ball opposite my left heel. Because the face is open, I usually play a fade on these shots, so I aim left of the target and swing in that direction.

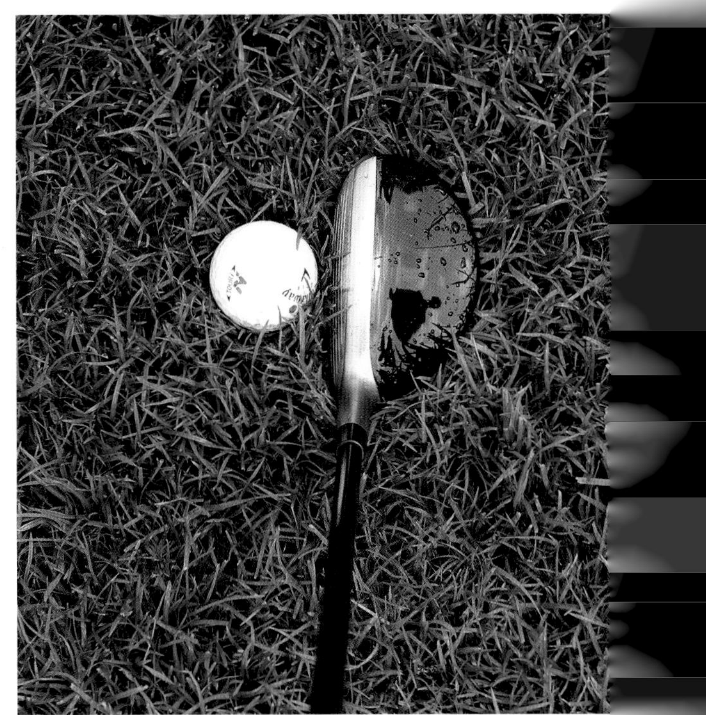

PLAYING STRATEGY

"During the first round of the 1961 L.A. Open at Rancho Park, I made a rather famous 12 on the par-5 18th hole. I hit four consecutive 3-woods out-of-bounds, starting with my second shot. There was O.B. both to the left and right of the green, which made the shot risky–but only mildly risky. It didn't constitute a gamble because my lie was good, I was playing well, and I knew in my heart I could pull the shot off. Only a gust of wind ruined a pretty good shot. And the next one. On the third try, I overcorrected and hooked it O.B. Then I did the same thing again! But to this day, I don't see that strategy as a gamble.

ARNOLD PALMER

ADVANCED

HOW TO FLUSH A FAIRWAY WOOD OFF THE DECK

by Kevin Na

First, pick a small target. When I'm trying to hit a green from fairway-wood distance, I don't think about hitting it just anywhere on the green. I pick a specific landing area. Then, I picture a line from that target to a spot a couple of feet in front of the ball. At address, all I think about is flying the ball over that spot. Also at address, I'll raise my left shoulder a little to help get the ball up. Since this is more of a control shot than a power shot, I also grip down on the club a little.

Make sure you play the ball forward in your stance; I position it just inside my left heel. This allows me to make a fairly level strike with a shallow swing. If the ball is in the rough, I play it back a few inches to make sure I hit the ball before my club twists in the high grass.

Finally, I slow everything down and focus on solid contact. If you hit it solid, you'll get the distance you need without swinging extra hard.

MENTAL TIP

There's a goal that I speak of often. It's called a "process goal." Success comes from patiently and persistently doing the right things over and over. Process goals are the to-do lists of players striving for excellence. The process is what gives you a chance to find out how good you can be. When an amateur tees off with a hybrid or fairway wood, they sometimes fail to commit to the shot the way they would with a driver because they think using the shorter club will make the tee shot easier, almost automatic. You still have to commit to the process no matter what club you are using. And remember to erase doubt. Say this to yourself before you stand over the ball: *I will trust myself and my swing on every shot. I don't have absolute control of where the ball goes. I do have absolute control of whether I trust myself.*

DR. BOB ROTELLA

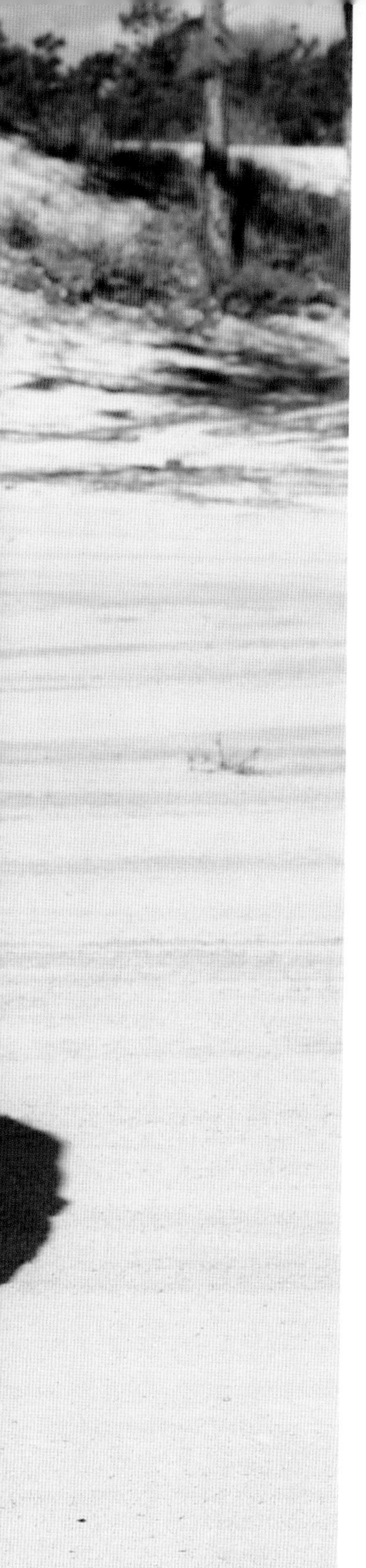

ADVANCED

USE YOUR HYBRID TO ESCAPE A FAIRWAY BUNKER

by Nick Price

From a fairway bunker, the most important thing is angle of attack. Play the ball slightly back of center in your stance, and then swing the club on a shallower path into the ball than you would with an iron. Coming down more from inside the target line will help.

SWING TIP

I used this shot a lot at the Masters, especially when I needed to shoot for the flag from quite a distance. You have to hit it high and land it soft, like a parachute. Here's how:

Stand quite close to the ball at address. This will put your swing on an upright plane so that you can take advantage of the club's full loft at impact. Also, keep your weight back on your heels. This will help you when you turn back to get your body behind the ball, and keep it there. As you take the club back, your hands should move to a high position above your shoulders at the top. This high-hand position is important because it will help you swing down on a steeper angle and hit the ball higher. As you swing down, feel like it's coming sharply into the ball instead of trying to scoop or sweep the ball into flight.

BYRON NELSON

ADVANCED

HYBRIDS ARE AN EASY CHOICE FROM FAIRWAY BUNKERS

by Butch Harmon

If you haven't found enough reasons to trade in your long irons for hybrids, here's one more: They're great out of fairway bunkers. The rounded sole cuts through the sand easier than an iron and they look easier to hit. One warning: Make sure the bunker lip is low enough that you can easily clear it with a hybrid shot.

To play this shot, grip down an inch and twist your feet into the sand about the same amount. This sets your feet lower than the ball so you have to grip down to compensate. Play the ball back in your stance an inch more than you usually do to make sure you catch it cleanly. Next, just before you start to take the club back, lift your chin. With a straighter spine, you'll find it easier to turn. Most players get so tense in the sand, they lock on the ball and their chin drops. Tall posture at address and all the way through encourages a sweeping swing. Finally, don't try to muscle the ball. Swing easy and stay stable with your body.

ADVANCED

HOW TO USE A HYBRID AROUND THE GREENS

by Todd Hamilton

When I won the 2004 British Open at Royal Troon, I got a lot of attention for chipping with a hybrid. I must have tried that shot a dozen times, including in the playoff against Ernie Els, where I knocked it up to tap-in distance to win. The hybrid is a great option when you don't have to get the ball airborne around the greens. You can use it from extreme distances, too, up to 20 yards off the greens and it's still a good play. It hops off the face initially, but then it gets running like a hot putt and is much easier for amateurs to execute than a standard, high-flying chip. Even if you don't hit it quite right, it still has a chance of trundling onto the green.

I recommend playing it much like you would a putt, though you can experiment to find the right grip and stroke. But the key is to make a smooth, back-and-through stroke keeping the clubhead level to the ground throughout. Don't try to hit down on it. The club's loft will get it to hop and then roll.

FITNESS TIP

The drop-step lunge will help sequence your swing

by Mark Verstegen

Hitting good fairway woods and hybrids is largely a result of timing a powerful downswing. Most golfers rush to finish their backswing and this leads to a poor sequencing. To help control your body sequencing better, try the drop-step lunge. It activates and lengthens the hip muscles and strengthens the glutes and also helps generate more swing speed with the correct body rotation.

From a standing position with your hands together in front of your chest, step backward and across with your right foot so it's about three feet behind and one foot outside of your left. Then, sit back and down into a squat position. Stand up, reverse leg positions, and repeat.

DRIVER

at&t
AT&T PEBBLE BEACH
NATIONAL PRO-AM

UNLESS YOU'RE REGULARLY playing 230-yard par 3s or trying to reach 550-yard par 5s in two, the most you'll likely swing your driver is 14 times a round. If you're a 90-shooter, that means drives account for only 16 percent of your total score. Compare that with putting, which takes up roughly 40 percent of your game; or iron play, which accounts for as much as 30 percent. That's why we've saved this chapter for the back of the book.

We're all seduced by the sound and look of a booming drive, but in the grand scheme of learning how to play golf, it should be the dessert and not the main course. Tour pros have a real advantage to hitting their tee shots as far as they can. Why? They have the short games and wedge play to get the ball close to the hole when they are inside of 150 yards. You don't. That's why it's best for you to put a premium on keeping your tee shots in the fairway, no matter how short your drives might be. We'll give you some tips on hitting it farther, but it's always best to remember that control trumps power in amateur golf. Here's what the best of the best have to say about driving.

PREVIOUS SPREAD: **Bomb's away:** Hunter Mahan tees off on the 18th hole in the final round of the 2011 AT&T Pebble Beach National Pro-Am.

OPPOSITE: Rory McIlroy swing sequence

14 **The maximum number of times a golfer will likely use a driver during any given round. Yet it's the club most often used in practice.**

- Amateurs average about 190–200 yards off the tee. For tour pros, it's 250–270 yards.
- A 1 mph increase in swing speed results in an increase of 2.5 yards of distance the ball travels.
- With a lie in heavy rough 150 yards from the green, a 10-handicapper will lose an average of .4 shots to par. Comparatively, a lie in light rough from that distance will cost that player .15 shots to par.

Practice Tips

BASICS

PLACE YOUR HANDS ON THE CLUB NATURALLY

by Jack Nicklaus

Stand with your arms relaxed, and see how they hang at your sides. Now, place your hands on the club without any manipulation. That will be a neutral grip with as few outside forces on the club as possible. The grip in the left hand is diagonally across the palm. In the right, it's in the fingers.

I interlock because it helps unify my hands. Pressure points for me are the last two fingers and the heel pad of the left hand and in the thumb and index finger of the right. It's very important when swinging a driver to keep a lighter, but constant grip pressure to ensure that you release the club, as well as control it.

BASICS

RULE NO. 1: POSITION THE BALL

by Butch Harmon

With the driver, most golfers play the ball too far forward and stand too far away from it. This might feel powerful, but it sets some bad things in motion. The forward ball position shifts the shoulders open to the target, which leads to an out-to-in swing and usually a slice. Standing too far from the ball pulls the upper body downward, leading to a compensating stand-up move through impact, another common cause of the slice.

Here's how to make sure your ball position is correct. Tee it up in line with the logo on your shirt, or just inside your left heel. (For shorter clubs, the ball should stay in line with the logo, but the stance should be narrower, making the ball more centered relative to the body.) As for distance from the ball, the butt of the grip at address should be about six inches from your body. Check this by setting up and then taking your right hand off the grip, moving it about a foot to your right. You shouldn't feel like you have to reach to put it back on the club.

Playing the ball in the correct place takes no athletic ability; it's just remembering to monitor it. Get it right, and your driving will improve immediately.

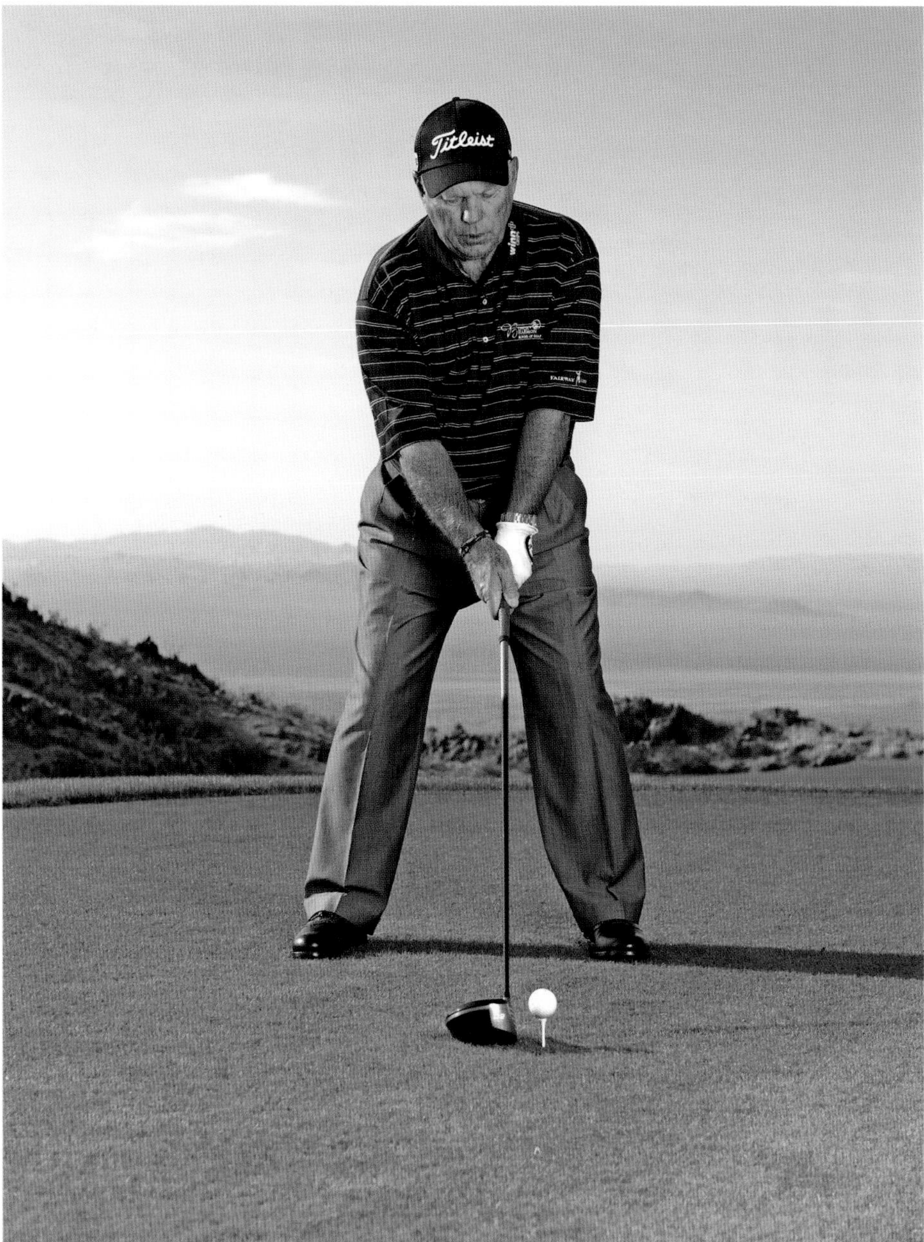

BASICS

FOR POWER, SET UP WELL BEHIND THE BALL

by Dave Phillips

Many amateurs swing into impact on a steep angle and actually hit down on their drives, which is why they pop the ball up. If you want to sweep the ball off the tee like the big hitters do, tee it up in line with the outside of your front foot, and set the clubhead eight or 10 inches behind it. The forward ball position will shallow your path on the downswing, and setting up so far behind the ball will help you visualize the clubhead ascending as it reaches impact.

BASICS

BACKSWING: MAX OUT YOUR SHOULDER TURN

by Stewart Cink

Most amateurs would benefit from increasing flexibility and getting the upper body behind the ball at the top. This leads to better timing–and longer tee shots. So many amateurs I play with struggle with timing, mainly making a poor transition: They start the downswing before finishing the backswing. I realize you can't improve your flexibility during a round, but I'd bet you can make a bigger turn and start down better. Here's my tip: Think about turning your left shoulder over your right foot as you swing to the top.

BASICS

HOW TO SWING THE CLUB TO THE TOP

by Rickie Fowler

I like to draw the club back slow, but not so slow that there's any tension in my forearms. At the top, I want most of my weight shifted to my right side, maybe 70 or 80 percent. With the big shoulder turn I've made, my head has moved significantly behind the ball. From here, I feel I can just step on the gas. It's go time! How far back I move my head is a matter of timing that varies day to day. If I'm feeling super on, I shift back real far.

SWING THOUGHT

Golfers who have developed good hands through years of practice err toward too little use of the body. Less trained players try to make up for their lack of hand speed with excessive body action. As you swing, picture yourself coiling and uncoiling so no part of your torso moves beyond the confines of your feet. In other words, only your hands and arms move beyond the outer edge of your right foot on the backswing and the same goes on the downswing in relation to your left foot.

JACK NICKLAUS

BASICS

LET YOUR LAT START THE DOWNSWING

by Rick Smith

There's some debate about how to generate power as you start down. Many golfers think it comes from driving the legs, but it can be difficult to make consistent contact if your legs get too active. Your legs should play a supporting role, but the real key to starting down correctly is to engage the left side of your torso (for right-handed golfers), particularly your latissimus dorsi, or "lat" muscle.

Big hitters have strong lats, which run from the shoulder blades to the hips. At the top of the backswing, your lead lat muscle should be fully stretched and ready to create that extra burst of clubhead speed needed for a big drive. To tap into this power source, feel that lead lat coiling as you make a full backswing. Then, start your downswing by letting it release and pull your upper body toward the target.

SWING THOUGHTS

How to overcome first-tee jitters

by Eddie Merrins

First-tee jitters are a real problem for people. Always have been, always will be. The best way to calm yourself a little—I say a little, because a little nervousness can work to your advantage—is to toss your golf ball a few inches in the air and catch it while you wait. Do it over and over. It's an amazing little trick, a form of hypnosis, really. Hypnosis is nothing but deep relaxation, and tossing the ball has a hypnotic, calming effect. Just the fact that you're able to catch the ball will give you enough subliminal confidence to get the ball down the fairway when it's your turn to play.

BASICS

LET IT ALL GO TOGETHER
by Ryan Moore

Your golf swing should be a dynamic motion, not a bunch of positions pieced together. It doesn't have to look pretty, but it should be fluid. Make sure you hold nothing back when you swing through the ball. Be athletic and aggressive. Your lower body should be turning hard toward the target, and your hands and arms should feel as if they're being pulled through the ball. Don't resist or try to steer the club. Let it all go.

DRILL

Stand in your normal address position holding something fairly heavy, such as a shag bag full of balls, and try throwing it with some authority toward a target about 15 feet away. How do you naturally perform this action? With your weight equally distributed on the insides of your feet and legs, you would coil your entire upper body–hands, arms, shoulders, and torso together–against the "brace," or set, of your right leg. Your head moves marginally to the right, simply following the spine. As the bag reaches a point just above your waist going back, your weight moves onto the inside of your right foot and right leg. From here, you reverse the thrust of your legs from the ground up. In throwing the shag bag, you have used natural rhythm and coordination in a totally connected tossing action. It is precisely the action in the swing of every great striker of the golf ball.

JIMMY BALLARD

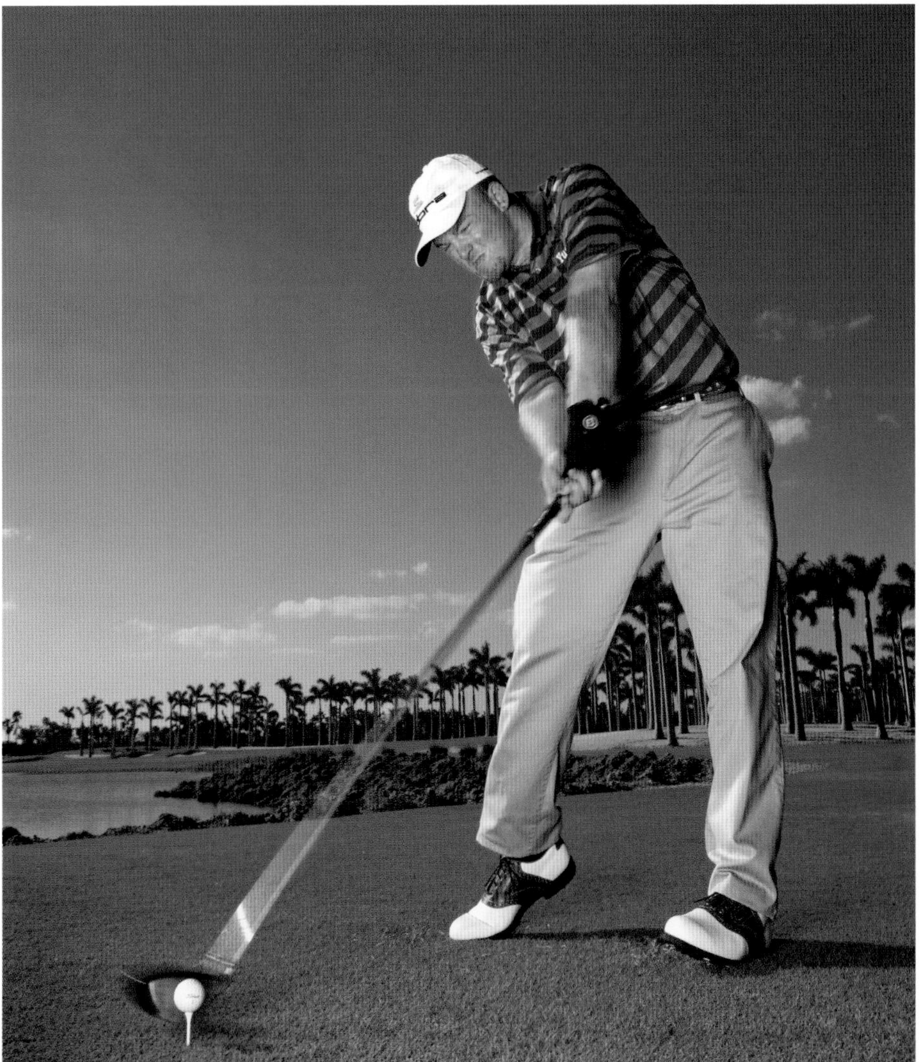

BASICS

SWING IN BALANCE

by J.B. Holmes

Power in the golf swing is balance. If you're off balance, you're not going to get much out of your swing. I start with a wide stance, which gives me a solid foundation. I also stand a bit open–that helps me turn my hips through the ball on the downswing. If I'm open, I can go ahead and swing at it and not worry about hooking.

But average players should work on balance and weight shift. To use all your power, you have to move your weight along with your arms. You have to swing everything in sync. Shift behind the ball as you swing back, and then shift forward coming down, keeping your head behind the ball. Anyone who hits it long has his head behind the ball at impact.

BASICS

SWING A BROOM FOR MORE POWER

by Randy Smith

If I handed you a broom and asked you to sweep a pile of sawdust, would you stick your right elbow out and cast the broom head at the pile? You wouldn't.

Try swinging a broom like a golf club. You'll instinctively support the broom's weight at the top, let it lag on the downswing, and balance it in the finish. But get a club and ball involved, and suddenly there's the urge to lift the ball in the air, and that's where a lot of players lose the power we're all trying to find.

ADVANCED

STOP AT THE TOP
by Sean Foley

Two players I work with—Justin Rose and Tiger Woods—sometimes make what I call a "violent transition" from backswing to downswing, rather than let the change of direction happen smoothly. Their goal is to have the speed of the downswing increase gradually, with the fastest part happening at the bottom. When the transition gets violent, it's hard to square the face at impact.

Many average golfers also suffer from a poor transition. That's mostly because they take the club back too quickly, and then fail to complete the backswing before starting the downswing. If you have this problem, a simple time-tested drill I use with Justin and Tiger will help. Next time you're practicing, when you reach the top of your swing, pause for a second before swinging down.

The reason I suggest doing it on the range is because, if you're quick at the top, this drill will feel very strange and might take a while to get used to. But if you do pause, you can then swing down as hard as you want, and the ball will really jump off the clubface.

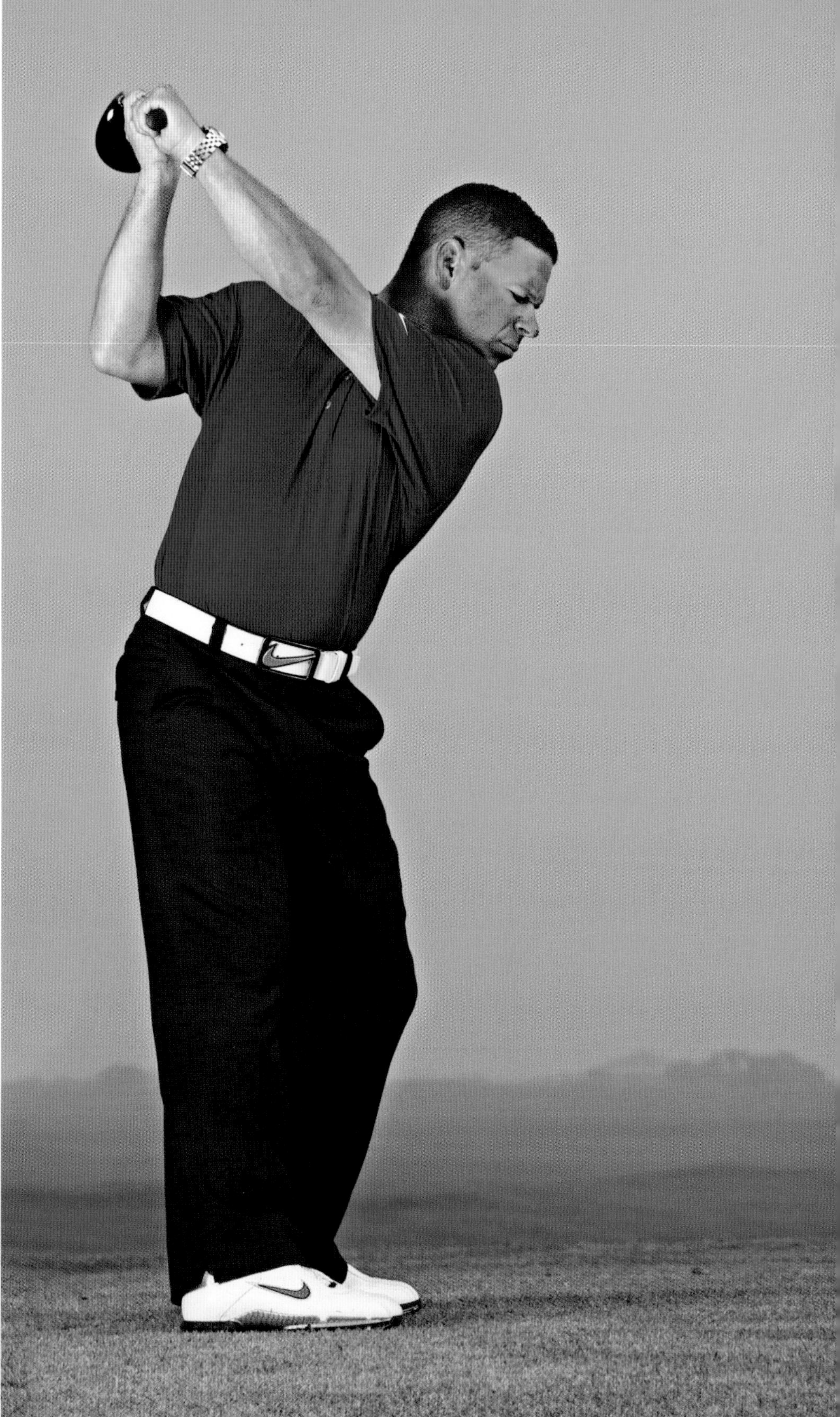

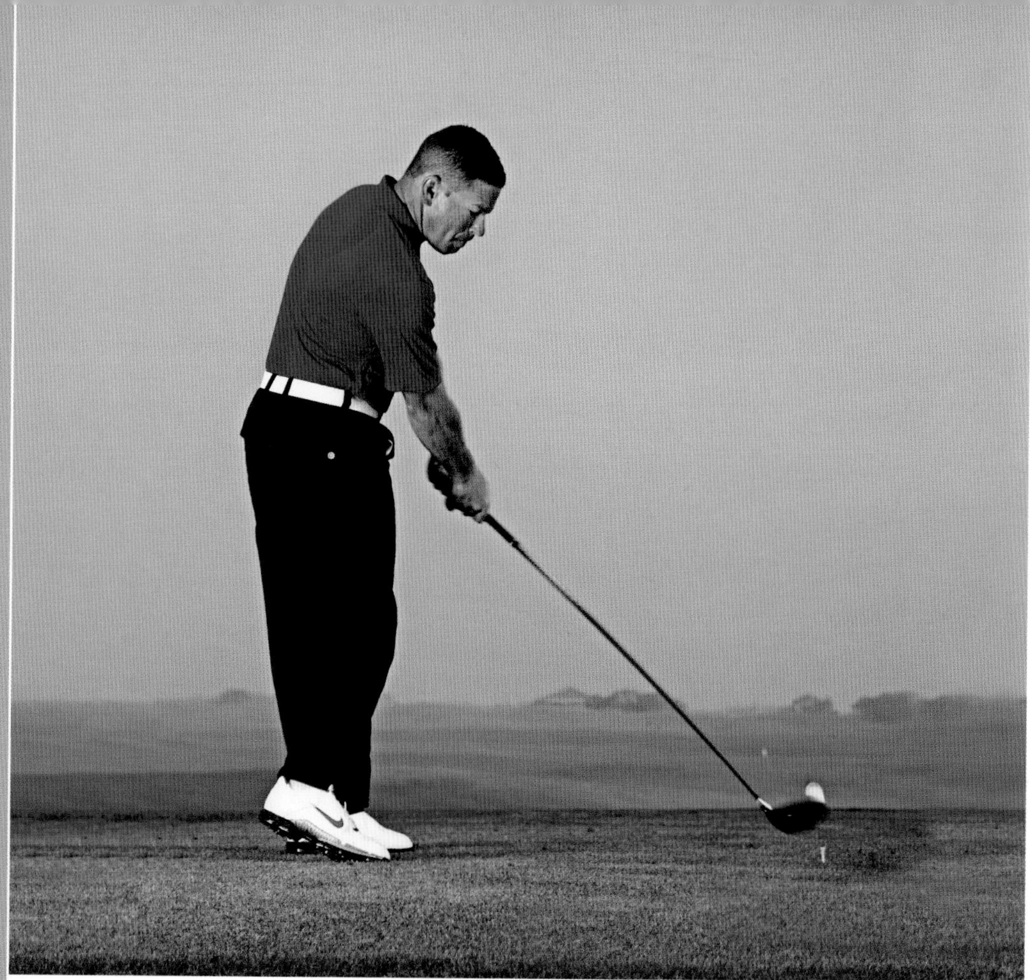

SWING THOUGHT

The shoulder turn occurs on a tilted plane, so the left shoulder should move down as well as around on the backswing. If you've properly tilted and turned your shoulders going back, your left shoulder should point toward the ball at the top of the swing. This backswing turn will put you in the right position to strike the ball squarely and forcefully. Many average golfers, especially those who have played baseball, turn their shoulders on too much of a level plane. Rotation like this makes the swing too flat and limits your chances of hitting the ball with a square clubface.

ARNOLD PALMER

ADVANCED

GET WIDE FOR BIGGER DRIVES

by David Leadbetter

Creating and maintaining good width in your swing will help you hit longer and straighter tee shots. Simply put, a wider swing arc covers more distance than a narrow one and allows you to maximize clubhead speed.

To increase the width in your swing, try this isometric exercise. While standing in your address position, grab a towel at two spots about a foot apart (as shown), keeping a little slack in it. Then, stretch the towel as tightly as you can and maintain that stretch as you simulate your backswing and downswing. Notice how your left and right sides keep their distance from each other as they pull in opposing directions. This is the same feeling of width you want to re-create when you swing.

On the range, alternate between practicing the towel exercise and hitting shots until you get the feel of a wider swing arc. During rounds, you can reinforce this feeling using your golf towel while you wait between shots. Once you learn to maximize the width in your swing, you'll start to produce more clubhead speed at impact and rip those tee shots.

Callaway
GOLF
SAP
Callaway
GOLF
SAP

ADVANCED

USE A HEADCOVER TO IMPROVE YOUR TEMPO
by Martin Laird

When I start to hit the ball poorly with my driver, it's usually because I'm getting quick in the takeaway. I snatch the clubhead back and pull it to the inside, then I have to re-route the club to save the swing coming down.

By adding some weight to the clubhead for some practice swings—either by leaving the headcover on, as I am here, or by wrapping a towel around the head—you force yourself to be more deliberate at the start of the swing. It promotes more of a one-piece takeaway, with your arms and shoulders moving together, and less hand action.

Practice swinging 15 or 20 times—slowly—with the headcover on. When you take it off, the driver will move back in good sequence and on a better path. Plus, the club will feel much lighter and faster on the downswing, which is more than a small side benefit. I hit my longest drives when I feel loose, relaxed, and unwinding smoothly through impact versus trying to rip the clubhead through with a lot of effort.

ADVANCED

IMPACT: HOW TO HIT IT FLUSH

by Stuart Appleby

If you really want to smash the ball, you have to hit it with all your weight behind the strike—this is the key to being sneaky long. To help ensure that your weight stays behind the ball until impact, tee the ball directly under your shoulder joint (see where I'm pointing?) and not under your chin. Then, make a downswing where the club bottoms out under the shoulder joint. Think of that spot on the ground as 6 o'clock and your left arm as the big hand on the clock. When you swing down, your body has to stay back to make the big hand of the clock bottom out at 6.

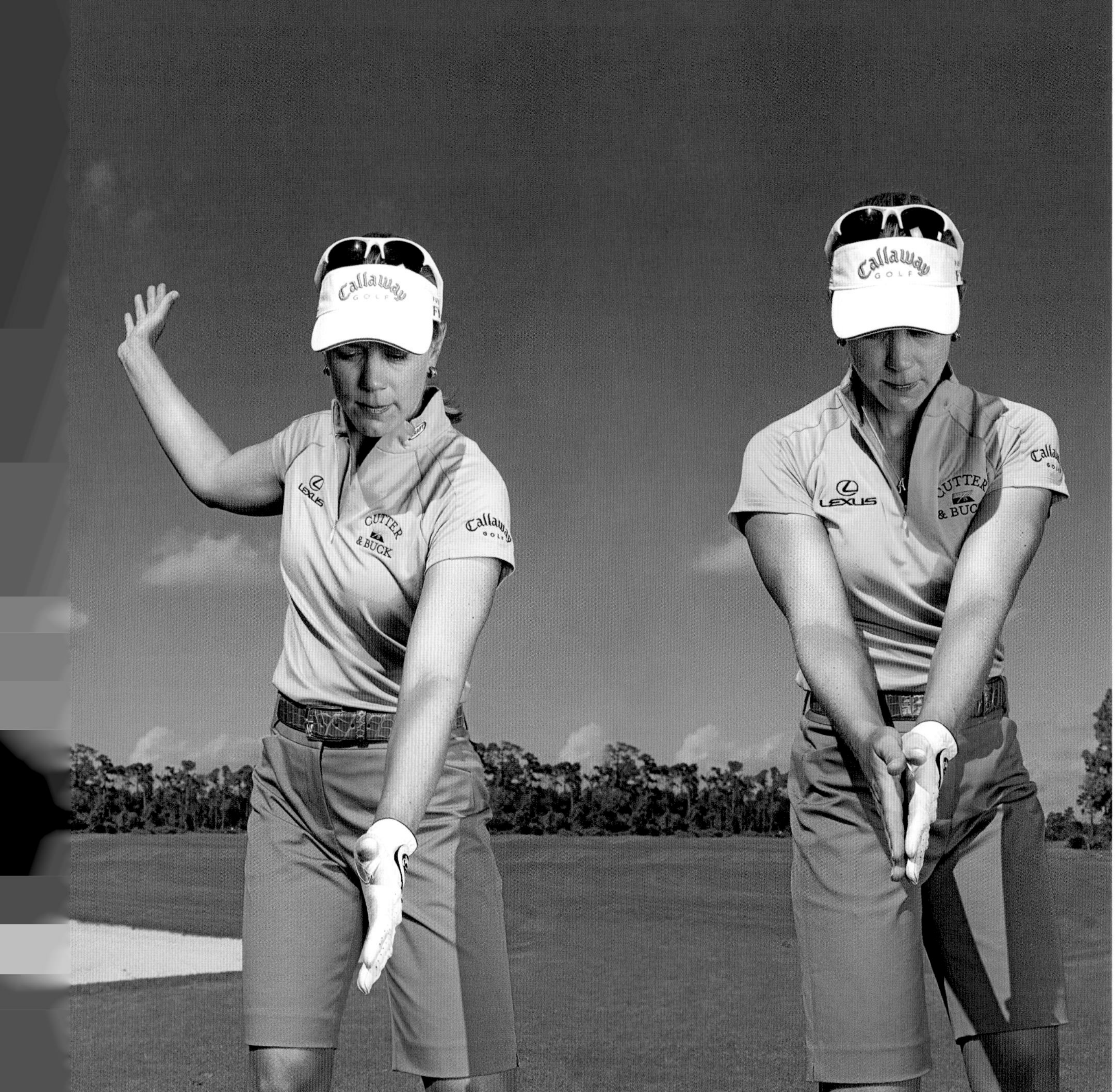

ADVANCED

HOW TO HIT IT STRAIGHTER

by Annika Sorenstam

Most golfers lose the ball to the right because they leave the clubface open at impact. I was having the same problem last summer, so I strengthened my grip, rotating my left hand clockwise on the handle. The key feel for me was the thumb pad on my left hand covering the top of the grip.

Another change I've made on tee shots is a wider stance. This gives me a more stable base and discourages side-to-side movement of the hips. If your hips slide back as you swing to the top, your upper body will tip toward the target. Then, as you swing down, your body will reverse direction, causing an out-to-in path and a slice. Try a wider stance.

I use the drill above to get a feel for square impact. Hold out your left hand, swing your right hand back, then slap your left. Your hands should meet directly in front of you. If your shoulders are open—a slice position—your hands will meet too far forward. Strive for the feeling of square shoulders at impact.

STATISTICS

The real measure of driving accuracy

by Peter Sanders

Which is better, a drive that finishes a few feet off the fairway but is sitting up in the first cut, or a drive that ends up in a tangled knot of thick grass between the roots of a low-hanging oak tree? The answer is obvious, yet the two drives would be recorded as equal under the statistic widely used on the professional tours, "Driving Accuracy Percentage," which simply divides the number of fairways hit by the number of attempts. Because this archaic method has never been updated in the big leagues, it's how most amateur golfers evaluate their own driving. I've created a better system.

If you really want to assess how you're driving the ball, forget about fairways hit. The number you need to know is how many shots your errant drives cost you. Think of this number as a gauge of how much you spray the ball: the lower, the better.

I've done the statistical heavy lifting. Figuring out the cost of your bad drives boils down to a formula I've created where you assign each drive a rating of 0–4, according to how it affects your next shot. Once you've tracked a few rounds, compare your shots lost to your handicap group (see chart below). A good driving round is one that beats the average of your handicap. Here's how it works using the example of Joe, an average golfer.

Joe, an 18-handicapper, went out the other day and shot 90. On his scorecard (below), he gave each drive, except on par 3s, a score of 0–4 points. Joe was careful to score according to how each drive affected his opportunity to hit the next shot (other golfers who handle tough lies better or worse than Joe might have rated the same drives differently). Joe hit three drives in the fairway, four in the light rough, and two in the heavy rough.

In addition, he twice had to chip out sideways, twice had to take a drop from a water hazard, and on one hole drove it out-of-bounds. After the round, we had Joe add up all his points and divide by two. (Using our points system and dividing by two means you don't have to deal with decimals.) Here's how Joe collected the data, made the calculations, and determined how many strokes his driving cost him that day:

1. Assign a point value

Using the scale described, Joe assesses each drive based on the shot it left him, except par 3s.

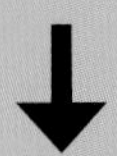

2. Total the points

Joe adds the points for all his drives (16).

3. Divide by 2

Joe divides 16 by 2 and gets the value 8. This is how many strokes Joe's errant tee shots cost him.

4. Compare on the chart

Joe uses the table at right to find out how many shots the average 18-handicapper loses per round (7). Because Joe lost 8, his driving was below average.

HOLE	1	2	3	4	5	6	7	8	9	OUT
PAR	5	4	3	4	4	5	4	3	4	36
YARDS	503	365	160	328	374	603	359	164	381	3237
JOE'S SCORE	6	5	3	6	5	7	4	4	6	46
JOE'S DRIVES (PTS)	1	FW	–	3	0	4	1	–	2	11

HOLE	10	11	12	13	14	15	16	17	18	IN
PAR	4	3	4	5	4	3	5	4	4	36
YARDS	337	176	399	534	364	140	519	347	398	3214
JOE'S SCORE	6	4	4	6	4	4	7	4	5	44
JOE'S DRIVES (PTS)	FW	–	0	2	0	–	3	FW	0	5

YOUR HANDICAP	AVERAGE STROKES LOST TO BAD DRIVES	YOUR HANDICAP	AVERAGE STROKES LOST TO BAD DRIVES
+3	2	15	6.2
0	2.5	18	7
3	3.1	21	7.7
6	3.9	24	8.4
9	4.8	27	9
12	5.6	30	9.6

ADVANCED

HINGE EARLIER FOR MORE ACCURACY

by Ian Poulter

Every now and then I have a tendency to let my drives leak to the right of my target. It's a problem that comes in part from being a fraction laid off at the top of my swing. Being laid off means my clubshaft is pointing well to the left of my target when I finish my backswing, instead of parallel with the target line. My club has actually been laid off all my life, and I believe this hurts my accuracy. I'm working to get the clubshaft on line at the top.

One way I help myself get into a better position is to hinge my wrists early in the backswing. I do it as soon as I take the club back, rather than waiting until I'm nearly at the top of the swing like many golfers do. The early hinge gives me a nice feeling that the clubshaft is pointing where it should at the top. It's one less thing to worry about when I have to put it in the fairway.

BASICS

PLAY TO YOUR STRENGTHS

by Tom Watson

If you hit in the bunkers at Muirfield in Scotland, it's effectively a one-stroke penalty. Those bunkers are so steep, you have to avoid them as best you can, and that was my game plan going into the 1980 British Open.

My strength at the time was my putting—I was making everything. So the strategy of playing away from trouble and to my strength worked, and I won my third Open by four strokes over Lee Trevino.

It was as much a mental process as a physical one, starting on the tee, where I aimed my drives at safe areas, as I'm doing here in this photo. The large bunker on the right is farther than it appears, and because I can't carry it easily I want to play my tee shot well left of it. Next time you play, remember to carefully consider your options this way for every drive and every approach shot. Playing clear of trouble is the key to avoiding big numbers.

That was certainly my approach at Muirfield. It was probably the best putting week I ever had in competition. I played more conservatively off the tee and into the green than I might have if my putting hadn't been so good.

RULES

Rules for the teeing ground

by Ron Kaspriske

Here are five rules to remember before you tee your ball up.

1. You can tee a ball anywhere between the markers—but not in front of them even by the slightest margin. You can also tee a ball up to two club-lengths behind the markers. Picture a rectangular zone.

2. If the ball falls off the tee before you hit it, there's no penalty. Re-tee and play on.

3. You can use anything to tee up a ball, or even leave the ball on the ground. The only requirement is that if you do use a tee, it can't be any higher than four inches and it can't influence the movement of the ball.

4. If you tee off out of order in stroke play, there's no penalty. In match play, your opponent can make you replay the shot.

5. You can stand outside the teeing area as long as your ball is inside it.

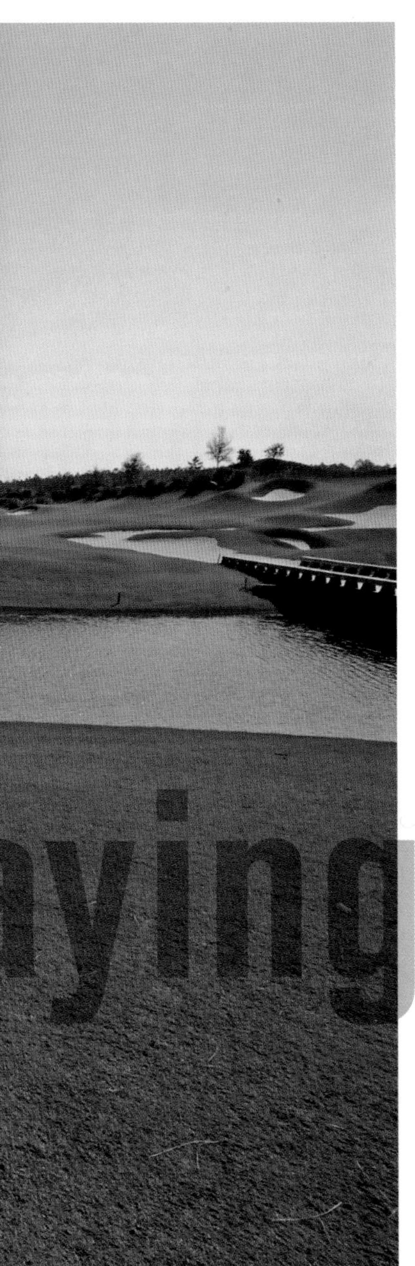

ying Strategy

TaylorMade

BASICS

HOW TO FIND THE TIGHTEST FAIRWAYS

by Fred Funk

On difficult tee shots to tight fairways, make sure you pick a specific target in the distance, like a tree or a bunker, and visualize the shot you want to hit: the trajectory, the curve, etc. Your body will react instinctively to visual cues. You also should maintain your natural rhythm, whether it's slow or fast. Also, feel like you're taking the club back a little longer, slower than normal. You want enough time to square the face. Don't rush it. Finally, it's important to stay in your posture. You might get the urge to stand up too soon and look to see where the ball is going. Keep your address posture through impact and you'll have a much better chance of hitting the ball in the center of the clubface.

SWING THOUGHT

This will help you understand–and feel–the down in downswing. It counteracts the slicer's tendency to start the downswing with a shoulder twist to the left of the target that throws the arms and club outside the line of play. You want your first move from the top of the backswing to be with your arms, wrists, and hands swinging the club straight down. A good way to ingrain that feeling is by imagining you're going to drive a stake into the ground from the top of the backswing. Keeping that stake in mind should give you a feeling for "downward." It also will encourage the proper blending of your arms, wrists, and hands to bring the clubface back to its original aim.

DAVIS LOVE JR.

BASICS

STAY LOOSE ON TIGHT HOLES

by Ernie Els

I'm sure you have a hole at your course where you love to hit the tee shot. You can't wait to get up there and bomb away, because the fairway is wide or the hole always plays downwind. But don't get overexcited on that tee shot–or any other one with your driver–because you can kill your swing with too much tension in your hands and arms. I find that grip pressure and tension hurt my swing more than any other technical problem.

If you squeeze the grip too tightly, you engage all the muscles up and down your forearms and into your shoulders. Tight muscles move slower than loose ones–even if you feel very strong and aggressive when you're holding the club that way. Make a conscious effort to loosen your hands and let your arms feel soft when you're at address. Take the club back a bit shorter, and feel as if you're cracking a whip on the way down–not tensing up to smash something hard.

In this case, less is definitely more. Your longest drives will come when you feel you're swinging at 75 percent.

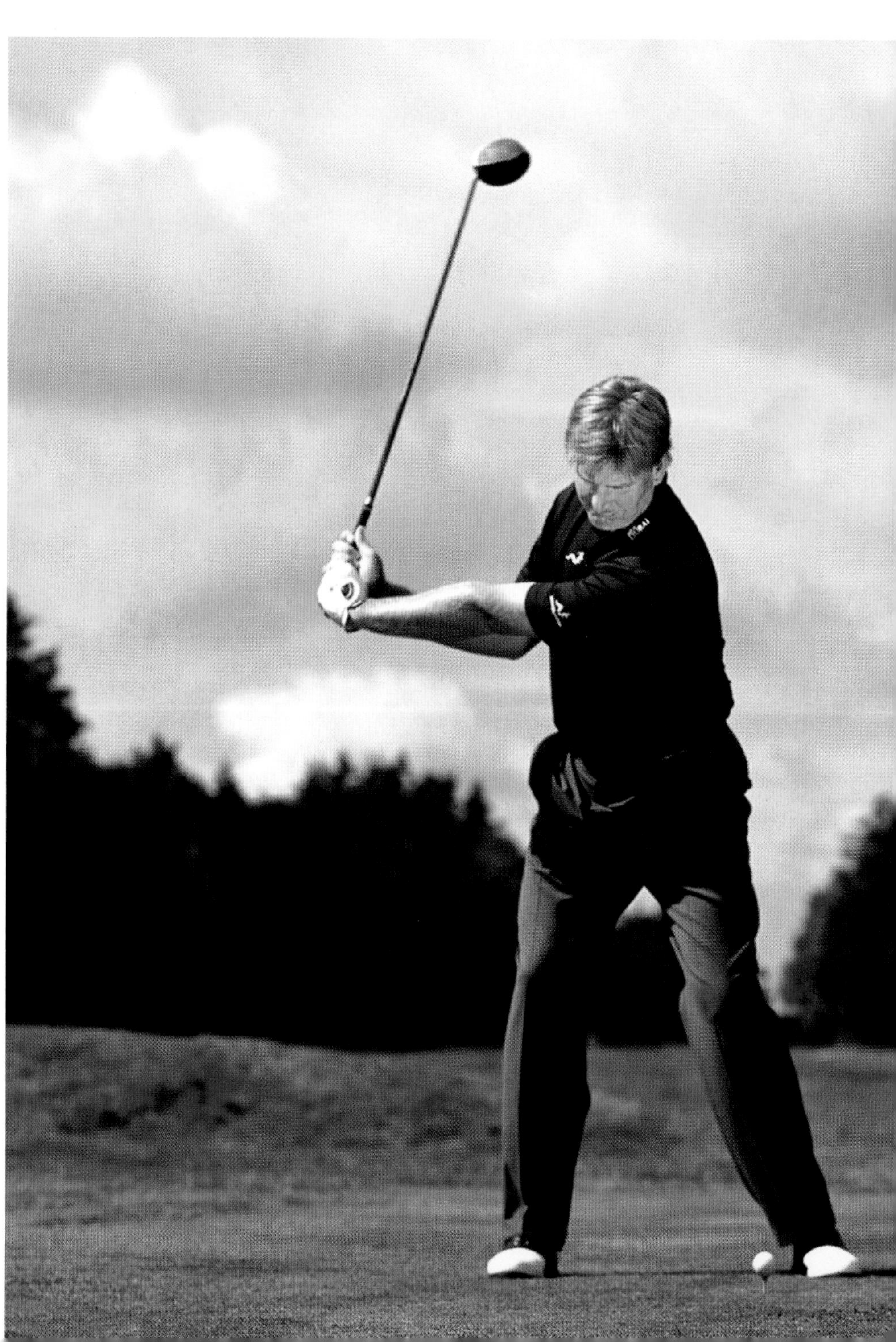

EQUIPMENT

Tee height can help accuracy

by David Leadbetter

If you're hitting crooked drives, an adjustment to tee height can straighten your shots.

Slicers swing down too steeply at the ball, creating too much backspin and sidespin. And if their slices are ballooning, they instinctively tee the ball lower, thinking it will stop the pop-up. This only causes them to swing steeper to get down to the ball.

If you fight a slice, you have to shallow out your swing path. You need to feel as if you're hitting up on the ball, and teeing it higher will promote that. At address, at least half the ball should be above the top of the clubhead. This encourages you to swing more from the inside and to stay back and sweep the ball off the tee.

Hookers, on the other hand, tend to swing too far from the inside and get the club trapped behind them. From there, they have to use their hands to release the club, which, if overdone, produces a hook. Teeing it lower will keep the club more in front of your body on the downswing, helping you swing to the ball on a straighter path.

ADVANCED

WHEN YOU NEED TO DRAW IT, TEE IT HIGH

by Jim McLean

To promote a draw, take a slightly closed stance and tee the ball a little higher. Gripping a touch lighter will help you release the club, which closes the face. Be deliberate at the top of the swing to give the club time to drop to the inside. Your swing shape should be in-to-out through impact. The through-swing is like hitting a big forehand in tennis, with a full rotation of the hands.

ADVANCED

WHEN YOU NEED TO FADE IT, TEE IT LOW
by Jim McLean

To set up a fade, take a slightly open stance and a firmer grip—to hold off the release through impact and keep the face open. I waggle the club along my stance line to pre-set an out-to-in swing; teeing the ball a little lower also helps. Make your normal swing, keeping the clubhead low through impact and your left wrist firm.

ADVANCED

HOW TO TACKLE A DOGLEG LEFT

by Hunter Mahan

When you've got to hit a draw and shape a tee shot around the corner of a dogleg left, the easiest way is by changing your swing path. I'm working to take the club back more inside the target line and turn my back to the target more. This creates a lot of room for my driver to swing down on an in-to-out path through impact. For me, it really feels as if I'm swinging out more to the right of my target. It's an exaggerated move, and the club is actually not going outside the target line through the shot, but that's what it feels like.

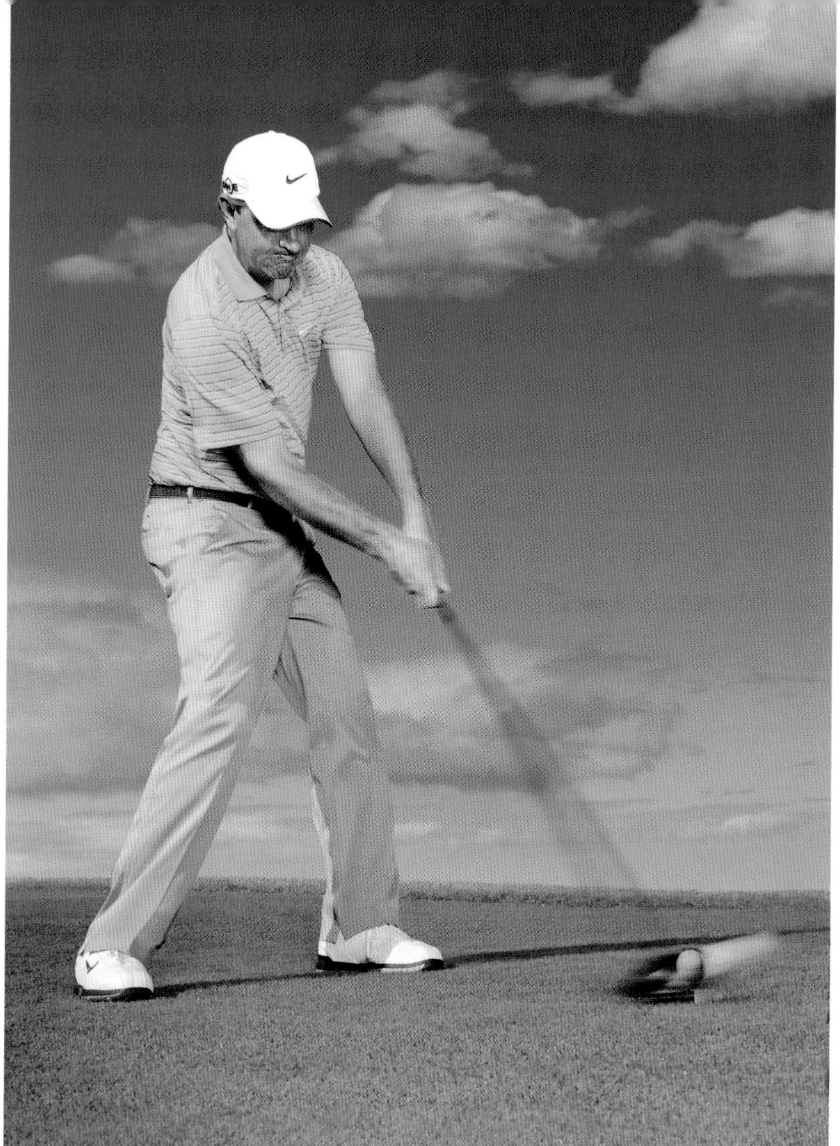

ADVANCED

HOW TO PLAY A DOGLEG RIGHT

by Lucas Glover

I mostly hit draws off the tee because that's my natural ball flight. But when I want to hit a fade, the good news is that I have to make only a couple of swing adjustments to get the job done.

At address, I stand a little closer to the ball. That way, I won't swing at it from inside the target line as much as I normally do. The more your path comes from the inside, the harder it is to curve the shot left to right. I also open my shoulders and hips a bit at address, setting them on the line where I want my ball to start.

Once I'm set up for the fade, I try to make a swing where I feel as if I'm holding the clubface open just a bit through impact. I don't want the toe of the club to turn over the way I would when I'm drawing it. The feeling is, my body's turning toward the target and my hands and club are trailing behind with very little rotation. You can go at it as hard as you want, but you have to complete the swing or you'll risk slicing the ball. So don't stop after impact.

SWING THOUGHT

The shoulder turn occurs on a tilted plane, so the left shoulder should move down as well as around on the backswing. If you've properly tilted and turned your shoulders going back, your left shoulder should point toward the ball at the top of the swing. This backswing turn will put you in the right position to strike the ball squarely and forcefully. Many average golfers, especially those who have played baseball, turn their shoulders on too much of a level plane. Rotation like this makes the swing too flat and limits your chances of hitting the ball with a square clubface.

ARNOLD PALMER

ADVANCED

HOW TO STRAIGHTEN THOSE SHOTS RIGHT OF THE FAIRWAY

by Butch Harmon

Golfers see their tee shots go right and automatically curse the slice. Sometimes those are blocked shots caused by swinging too much from the inside. The slice comes from an out-to-in swing, so trying to fix a slice when you're hitting a block is the worst thing you can do. Here's how to tell the difference: A slice starts left and curves right, and a block flies straight right. Blocks occur when you slide too hard with your lower body on the downswing. The club drops behind you and swings too much from the inside. You have too much lateral motion and not enough turn through the shot.

The best way to promote turn is to take a narrow stance, about a foot wide, and hit drives at 75 percent. With a narrow base, you won't be able to slide much without falling over. You'll make a better turn, and the club will swing straighter down the line, with your arms turning over to square the clubface. You'll beat the block.

ADVANCED

HOW TO CORRECT A HOOK

by Graeme McDowell

Like many good right-handers, I fight hitting it left and have for all of my life. To avoid those hooks, my takeaway thought is to make sure during those first three feet the clubhead works away wide and outside my hands, with a nice bit of loft on the club. When I get it wrong, the club sucks back behind my hands on the takeaway, and from there the club gets stuck behind me. Once the club is stuck on the inside, the only way I can go from there is out and away from me. That's going to put a lot of right-to-left spin on the ball—the dreaded hook.

DRILL

A good way to build strength in your hands and wrists is to take newspaper pages and roll them up into balls with each hand. To use that strength, try for a bigger turn on your backswing. That's what I did in the driving contests or when I wanted a bit more steam off the tee to reach a par-5 green in two.

To increase your turn, make your left hip and left shoulder turn together on your backswing. Do it rather slowly, and keep your hands and arms light. Swinging too fast can tighten them and cut off your flexibility. As you turn away from the ball, let your left knee swing inward to the right so your legs form a K. Then, start your downswing with your right knee swinging to the left to form a backward K in the opposite direction.

SAM SNEAD

ADVANCED

CONTROL THE CLUBFACE WITH THE BACK OF YOUR LEFT HAND

by Steve Stricker

My consistency off the tee really started to improve when I switched to a neutral grip so the back of my left hand is facing the target at address. My main focus now is trying to swing my left hand into that position as the club hits the ball. Since the back of the left hand mirrors the clubface position, you can control the clubface simply by focusing on the position of that hand as contact is made. I feel as if I'm returning my left hand at impact so it faces the target again.

If you prefer a weaker or, more likely, stronger grip, check where the back of your left hand is facing at address and then try to match that position at impact and your accuracy can improve, too.

ADVANCED

COVER THE BALL ON WINDY DAYS

by Jerry Kelly

The wind always seems to be a big factor in the winter. That's when I rely on my wind-cheater off the tee. If you get the ball up into the breeze, it's not going very far. Even worse, it's a lot easier to miss the fairway because a wind into you exaggerates any sidespin on the ball. A gentle fade turns into a mean slice, and a controlled draw becomes a vicious hook. So lowering your ball flight is a must.

One of the first things I do into the wind is grip down on the club a bit. The shorter shaft helps keep the ball down and gives me a better feeling of controlling the swing. Then, I try to keep my body and my hands a little ahead of the ball as the club makes contact. I want to feel as if I'm covering the ball with my body and club.

Actually, it's a lot like playing a shot from a fairway bunker. I feel as if my lower body is fairly still and I'm staying on top of the ball as I swing through impact.

SWING KEY

"To maintain good tempo, you have to be totally relaxed. Also, there's no such thing as too slow a backswing. If the average player would remember those two points, he'd improve his game immediately. If you take the club back slowly, you'll start it down slowly. I even think that if you can learn to pause at the top of the swing, it's a great thing. If you rush it at the top, you never know where your clubface is. JOHNNY MILLER

ADVANCED

HOW TO PICK UP 10 MORE YARDS OFF THE TEE

by Dustin Johnson

I play a power draw when I need some extra distance. The ball seems to fly as far as a fade, but also rolls out more when it hits the ground because it doesn't have as much spin on it.

To hit a power draw, the club has to swing down from inside the target line. I feel as if I'm creating space between my body and the ball for the club to travel. That's the big feel for me. To do that, your lower body must lead the way through. If you have room on the inside, you'll have an easier time turning it over.

But honestly, you can't think about all of that when you're playing. So what I do when I want to draw the ball is visualize the shape and then allow my body to make it happen. One more thought: Try not to swing too much harder than normal, because you will lose your rhythm and timing. It's better to focus on hitting the ball solidly and picture that draw.

FITNESS TIP

Throw a medicine ball for more distance

by Mark Verstegen

To improve your swing speed and hit longer drives, grab a medicine ball and find a solid wall to throw it against. Take the ball with both hands and stand perpendicular to a wall, in your address posture. Bring it down alongside your hip and then thrust your legs up as you toss it into the wall—simulating the down and through-swing you would make with a driver. Once you catch the rebound, drop it down alongside your other hip and repeat the motion to train both sides of the body equally.

Why it works: This activates and strengthens the hips and torso. It also improves your recoil action through impact and allows you to compress the ball by swinging against a firm left side.

THE NEXT ST

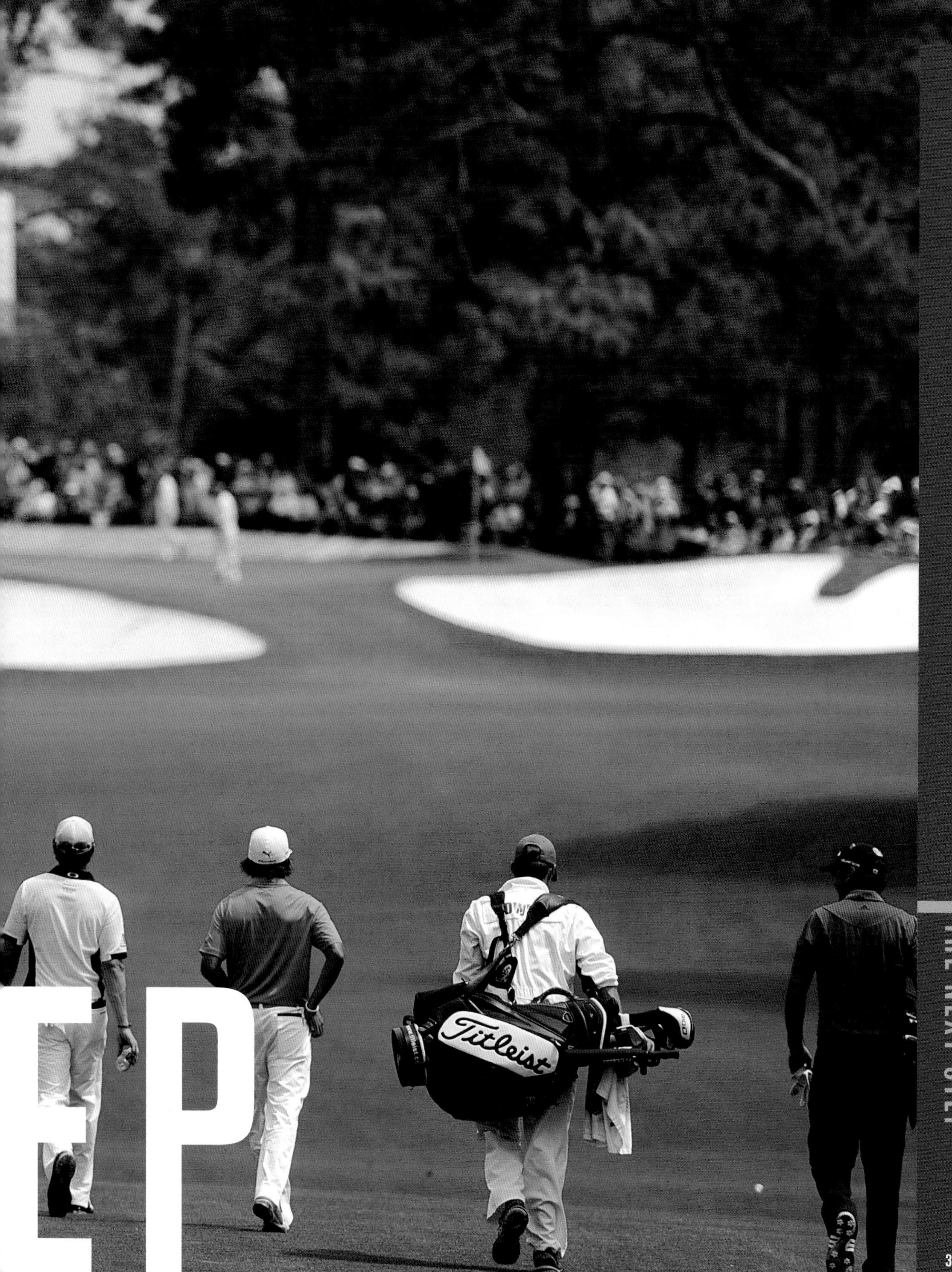

EP

PREVIOUS SPREAD: **Youth movement (from left):** Rory McIlroy, Rickie Fowler, and Jason Day approach the seventh green at Augusta National during the 2011 Masters Tournament.

NOW THAT THE BEST GOLFERS AND TEACHERS have given you the foundation to play this game from green to tee, it's time to take the next step and learn all the golfy bits that make this sport so special. Assuming you're new to golf, you probably feel like a stranger in a strange land when you observe all the nuances and listen to the golfspeak. Don't fret. While the game can seem intimidating and veteran players unwelcoming, there really isn't a great deal you have to know in order to look and feel like you belong. And the rest you can pick up as you go.

To save you some time in the learning process, we've asked the experts to share some of the most important information to get you started. In this chapter, you'll get a better understanding of the game's rules, etiquette, equipment, and attire, as well as advice on demeanor, taking care of the course, and giving back to the game in a broader sense. Think of this as CliffsNotes and your next round as the big test. Wait. Scratch that. That last thing anyone wants is to equate their recreational hobby with their English literature midterm from sophomore year. What we're trying to say is that the following information is your shortcut to what would normally take years to learn. Presumably, you came to the game for enjoyment. Hopefully these tips will help you achieve it.

FINAL THOUGHT

Perseverance is to continue in a state of grace until it is succeeded by a state of glory. SEYMOUR DUNN

MY 10 RULES FOR GOOD ETIQUETTE

by Arnold Palmer

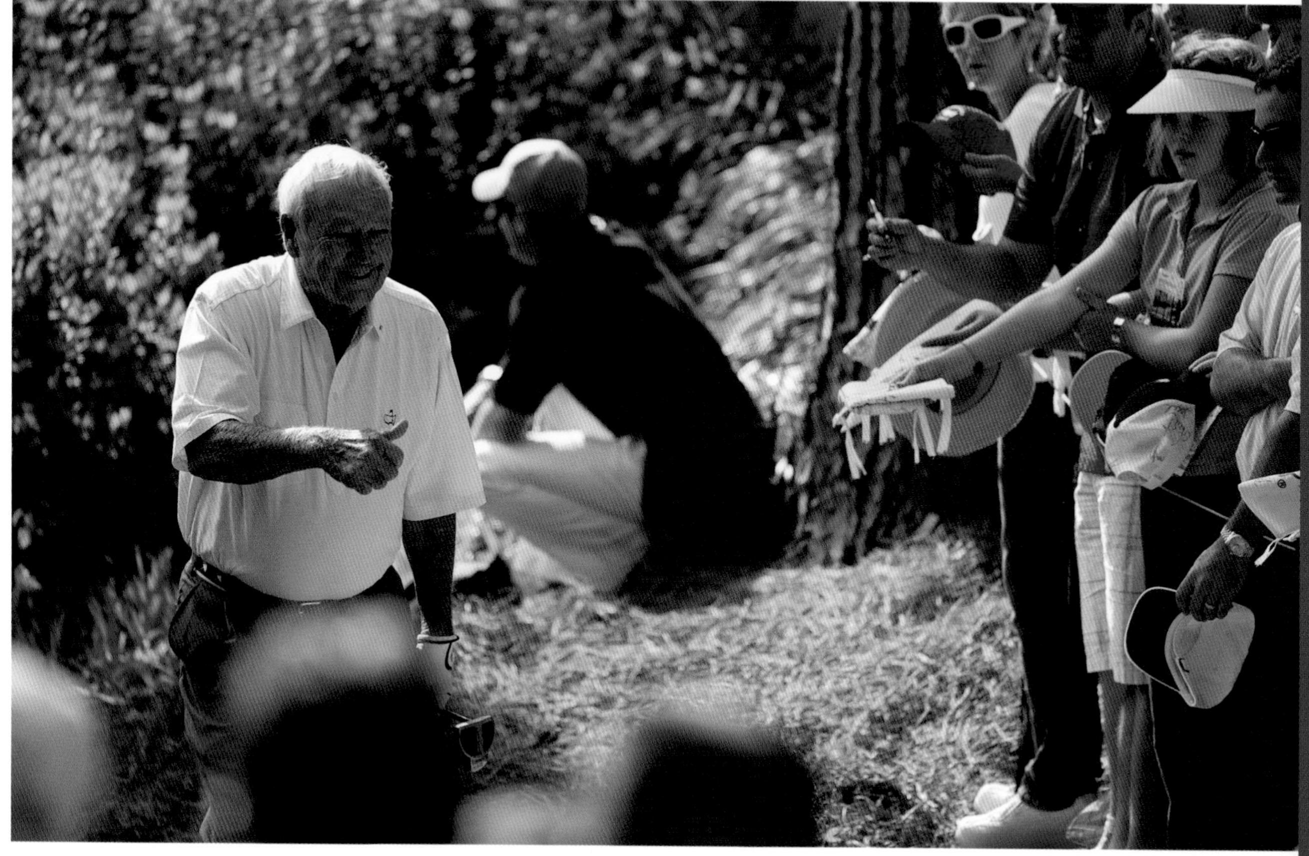

1. DON'T BE THE SLOWEST PLAYER If you're consistently the slowest one in your group, you're a slow player, period. Encourage everyone to move quickly enough so you find yourself right behind the group in front. Remember the old staples of getting around in good time: Play "ready golf" (hit when ready, even if you aren't away) until you reach the green, be prepared to play when it's your turn on the tee and green, and never search for a lost ball for more than five minutes.

2. KEEP YOUR TEMPER UNDER CONTROL: We all have our moments of frustration, but the trick is to vent in an inoffensive way. Don't throw clubs or curse.

3. RESPECT OTHER PEOPLE'S TIME: There are few good reasons for breaking a golf date. Deciding last-minute to clean the garage on Saturday, or getting a call that the auto-repair shop can move up your appointment by a day, just doesn't cut it.

4. REPAIR THE GROUND YOU PLAY ON: I have a penknife that's my pet tool for fixing ball marks, but a tee or one of those two-pronged devices is fine. As for divots, replace them or use the seed mix packed on the side of your cart. Rake bunkers like you mean it.

5. **BE A SILENT PARTNER:** Know where to stand and when to keep quiet. Position yourself directly across or at a diagonal from a player setting up. Never stand on the line of play, either beyond the hole or directly behind the ball. When a player is about to hit a shot, think of the fairway as a cathedral, the green a library.

6. **MAKE YOUR GOLF CART INVISIBLE:** Your goal when driving a cart should be to leave no trace you were there. Because we tend to look where we're going and not where we've been, it's easy to damage the turf and not realize it.

7. **ALWAYS LOOK YOUR BEST:** From Bobby Jones and Walter Hagen to Ben Hogan and Sam Snead to Tiger Woods and Phil Mickelson, the best players have been meticulous about their appearance. Your appearance speaks volumes about you as a person. The neatly appointed golfer, like a businessman or someone headed to church, gives the impression he thinks the golf course and the people there are special.

8. **TURN OFF THE CELL PHONE:** I don't know all the gadgets and settings on those phones, but do whatever you have to do to keep it quiet. And if you absolutely have to make a call, move away from the other players.

9. **LEND A HAND WHEN YOU CAN:** It's easy to help out your fellow players, if you just pay attention. One obvious way is looking for lost balls—or better yet, watching errant shots so they don't turn into lost balls. Pick up that extra club left on the fringe or the headcover dropped next to the tee, and return it to its owner.

10. LEARN THE LITTLE THINGS: There are a hundred bits of etiquette I haven't mentioned, like laying the flagstick down carefully, tamping down spike marks when you're walking off a green, letting faster groups play through, and so on. All of these things are learned by observing with a sharp eye and a considerate heart. Just know that golf has a way of returning favors, and every piece of etiquette you practice will be repaid tenfold.

SOMES RULES TO GET YOU STARTED

by Ron Kaspriske, Golf Digest Rules Editor

1. DON'T MOVE YOUR BALL: Unless you're on a putting green, don't move your ball under any circumstance. Play it as it lies unless it's interfered with by an obstruction (man-made object), ground under repair, or casual water. And if you're not sure what any of these things are, it's perfectly acceptable to ask the head pro or an experienced golfer. On the putting green, you have to mark the ball's position before lifting it, usually with a coin or a small ball marker.

2. STICK WITH YOUR OWN BALL: If you see a ball that's not your own, you might think, "Hey, free ball!" What you should do is leave it. Believe it or not, you're not the only golfer on the course who is hitting his ball to unintended locations, so it could be another player's ball from another hole.

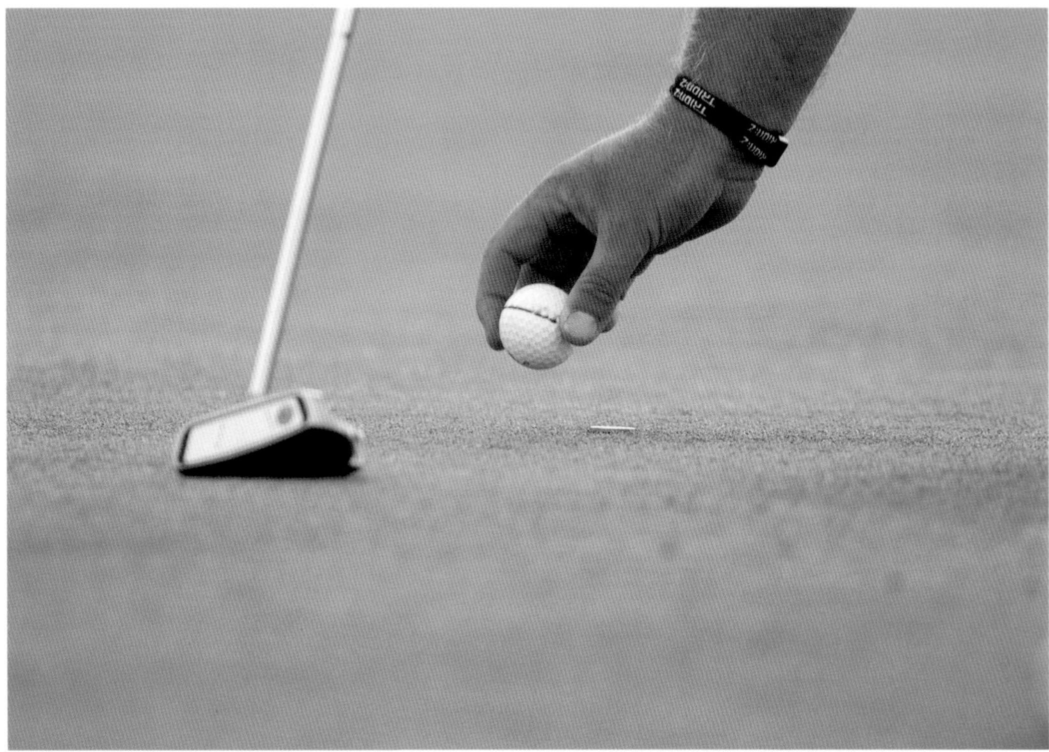

3. IT'S (MOSTLY) OK TO PLAY FROM ANOTHER HOLE: If your shot lands in another fairway, you can play the ball as it lies as long as that fairway is not designated as out-of-bounds (white stakes or lines). If you don't see white stakes or lines, you can play back to the hole you're playing. Just don't interfere with players on that particular hole. Let them play through unless they give you permission to go first. If your ball is outside the out-of-bounds markers, take a one-stroke penalty and play another shot from the spot you just hit from.

4. ONLY TAKE FIVE MINUTES TO LOOK FOR A BALL: If you hit a shot and you can't find the ball after five minutes of searching, take a one-stroke penalty and play another shot from as close as possible to the last spot you played from. This might require you to drop a ball. If so, extend your hand at shoulder height over that area, simply drop it, then play from there.

5. PLAY WITHIN THE GOLF COURSE: If you ever hit a shot out-of-bounds (white stakes or lines), you have to replay a shot from as close as possible to where you just hit and add a stroke penalty to your score. So, for instance, if you teed off and hit a shot out-of-bounds, take a stroke penalty and play your third shot again from the tee. If your ball is in a hazard (marked with white or red stakes or lines) in a bunker, you cannot ground your club until you hit the ball. If you do, it's a one-stroke penalty.

WHAT YOU NEED TO KNOW ABOUT CLUBS

by Mike Stachura, Golf Digest Equipment Editor

1. YOU ONLY NEED A FEW CLUBS: You're allowed to carry as many as 14 clubs in your bag, but you won't need nearly that many when you're first learning. Instead, start with a driver, a putter, and a sand wedge (it's the club that has an S on the sole or a loft of 54 to 56 degrees), and supplement these with a 6-iron, an 8-iron, a pitching wedge, and a fairway wood or hybrid with 18 to 21 degrees of loft. These are the clubs that are the most forgiving and easiest to get airborne. You can find used and new titanium drivers for as little as $75 and putters for much less online, but most larger golf and general sporting goods stores also offer racks of discounted or used clubs.

2. **DON'T GUESS—TRY BEFORE YOU BUY:** If you're an absolute beginner looking to buy clubs, go to a larger golf shop or driving range and ask to try a 6-iron with a regular-flex and a stiff-flex shaft. (Generally, the faster and more aggressive your swing, the more you will prefer a shaft that is labeled S for stiff.) One of the two should feel easier to control. That's the shaft flex you should start with for all your clubs. Once you get serious about the game and are able to make consistent contact, a clubfitting will enable you to get the most out of your equipment.

3. **THE MORE LOFT, THE BETTER:** Unless you're a strong and well-coordinated athlete experienced with stick and ball sports (baseball, softball, hockey, or tennis, for example), opt for woods that have more loft. Why? The extra loft generally means it will be easier to get the ball in the air and also can reduce sidespin so shots fly straighter. Go for drivers with at least 10 degrees of loft and fairway woods that start at 17 degrees, not 15 degrees.

4. **TAKE ADVANTAGE OF CLUBS MADE FOR BEGINNERS:** Some types of clubs are easier to hit than others. For one thing, you're better off with hybrids instead of 3-, 4-, and 5-irons. And irons with wider soles (the bottom part of an iron) will alleviate the tendency for the club to stick in the ground when you hit too far

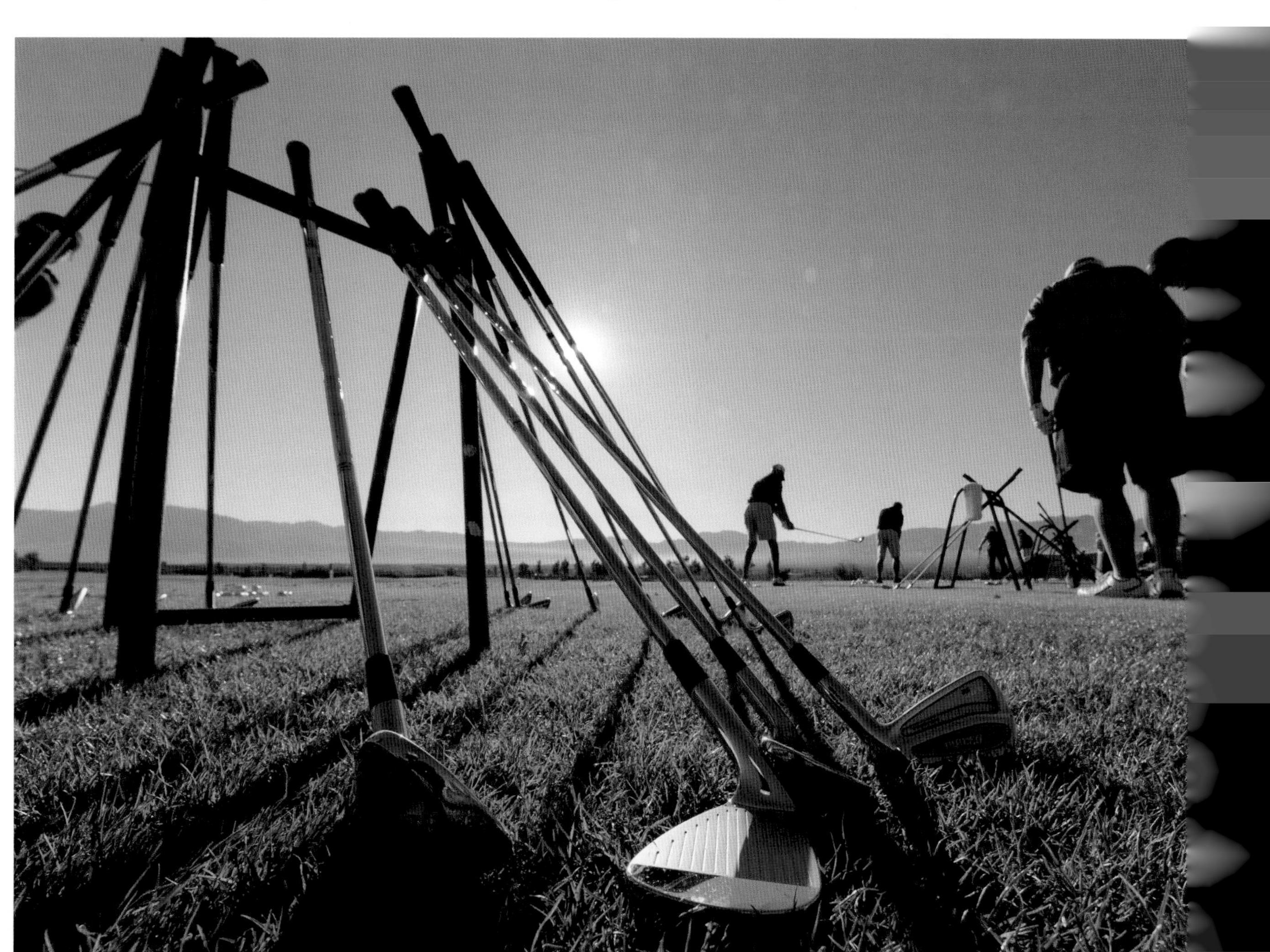

behind the ball. Also, with more weight concentrated in the sole, the iron's center of gravity will be lower and this will help shots launch on a higher trajectory. Generally, a more forgiving iron will feature a sole that measures about the width of two fingers (from front edge to back). If an iron's sole measures less than one finger width, you only should be playing it if you're paid to do so.

5. **CHOOSE THE RIGHT BALL:** Buy balls on a sliding scale based on how many you lose in a round. If you've never played before or lose two sleeves or more a round, buy balls that cost around $20 a dozen (if you can't decide between two brands, try putting a few to see how they feel coming off the putterface). When you cut the number of lost balls back to maybe three to five balls a round, buy balls that cost less than $30 a dozen. Only if you're losing less than a sleeve a round should you consider the $40 a dozen balls.

WHAT TO WEAR

by Marty Hackel, Golf Digest Style Editor

Learning how to play may be the most important part of becoming a golfer, but not to be overlooked is knowing what to wear. Your attire matters for a variety of reasons: because most golf courses enforce some kind of dress code (some stricter than others); because you'll be spending at least four hours outdoors; and because, frankly, who doesn't want to look sharp? With that in mind, we provide five pointers to make sure you're outfitted right for the course.

1. **PICK THE RIGHT COLLARED SHIRT:** Most courses, even public ones, require that men wear a collared polo (women are more often allowed to play without a collared top). There are two main types of collared shirts: those made of cotton, and others made of more technical fabrics. If you feel more comfortable in a traditionally cut polo, stick with cotton. But if it will be hot on the golf course, collared shirts made of technical fabrics, such as those made by Adidas, Nike, and Callaway, will help keep you dry by wicking moisture away from your skin.

2. **STICK TO KHAKIS:** Hands down, these are the most comfortable pants to play in, especially since khaki fabric is more breathable than ever before. You won't find a golf course that doesn't allow you to wear khaki pants. Most courses, save for a few traditional private clubs, now allow shorts as well, although some are iffy on cargo shorts. As for jeans, it's best to leave those at home. Even if a course allows them, they're uncomfortable for golf.

3. **PREPARE YOURSELF FOR THE ELEMENTS:** If all goes well, you won't be spending your entire round punching your ball out from under trees, so shielding yourself from the sun will be important. A basic baseball cap never fails, and when it's time to buy sunglasses for golf, make sure the lens blocks UVA and

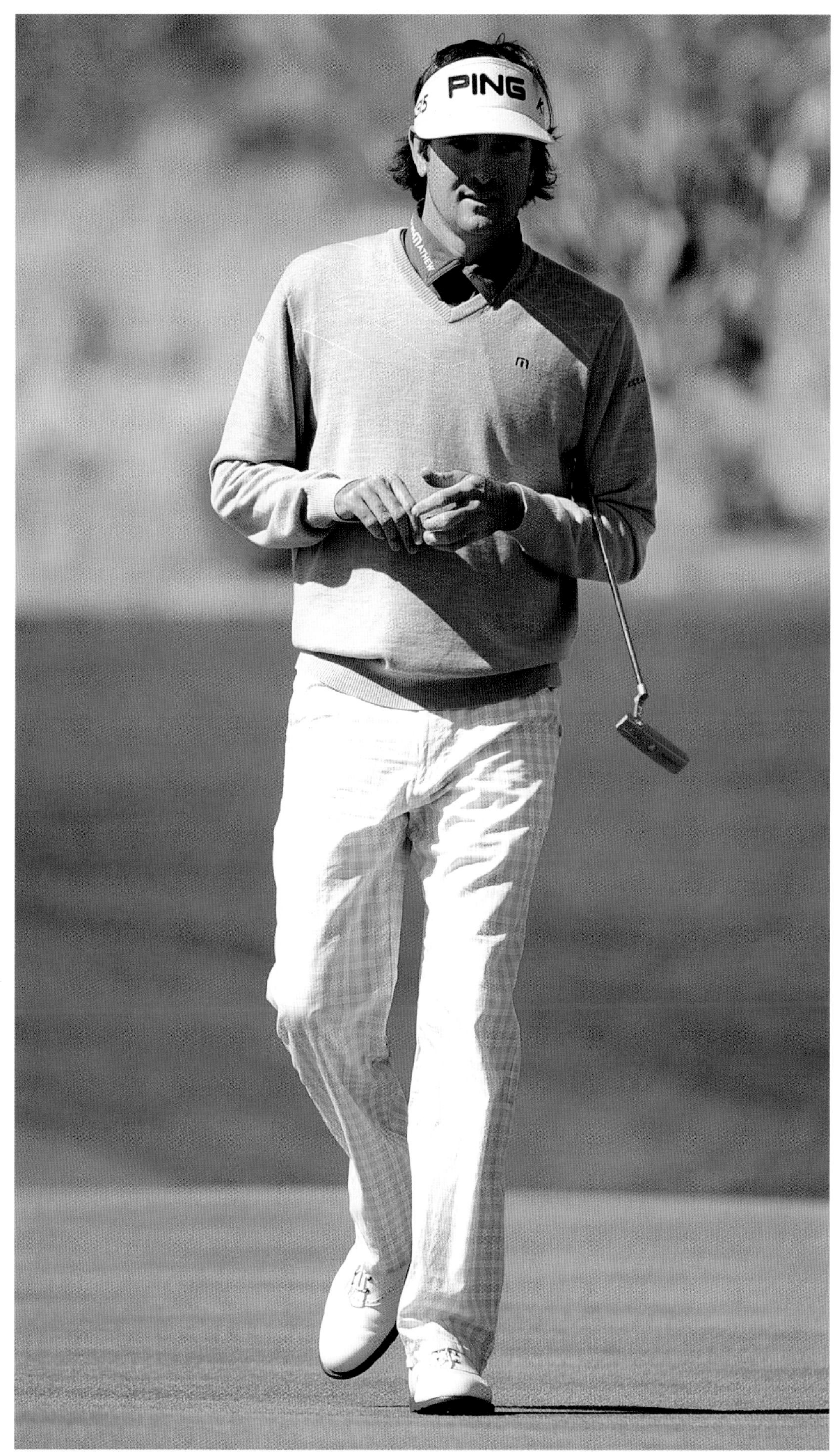
PING

UVB rays, and that they wrap around your eyes to offer complete coverage. Of course, golf is played in all kinds of weather. You'll need a good rain jacket for wet conditions, and you should always carry a dry towel to keep your grips dry.

4. **FOR STARTERS, GO WITH SNEAKERS, NOT GOLF SHOES:** Hold off on purchasing golf shoes until you become really serious about the game. Stick with sneakers, which you'll be able to use on and off the course. Since you'll want to stay as level to the ground as possible, make sure you don't wear running sneakers, which have too much cushion under the heel of your foot.

5. **APPLY SUNBLOCK:** A must-have accessory for all golfers. You'll need to apply sunblock 30 minutes before your round and again at the turn, since the SPF in sunblock wears off after a couple of hours. Look for a sunblock with an SPF of at least 30. Also, try a spray sunblock when you reapply during your round, since you can apply it without making your hands slippery, and don't forget to apply a lip balm with SPF as well.

WHEN YOU'RE READY FOR THE GOLF COURSE

by Pete Finch and Matt Ginella, Golf Digest Senior Editors

So now that you've got some clubs and you've learned the basics of golf rules and etiquette, you're thinking about testing yourself on an actual golf course. Great, but it's not as if you should step right onto the same course the pros play. If you want to make sure your early experiences on the golf course are positive ones, it's best to know your limitations, then build yourself up. Here's what to keep in mind.

1. **START SMALL:** Golf is hard enough without needing eight shots just to get to the green. Start on a par 3 or "executive" course before you try an 18-hole championship course. On a par-3 course, all the holes are par 3s—that is, usually less than 200 yards. Executive courses typically have multiple par-3 holes and their par 4s and 5s are shorter than what you'd find on a championship course. Give yourself some time to get acclimated here before taking on a bigger challenge.

2. **PLAY THREE HOLES:** In a way, golf is its own kind of an endurance sport, and you need to build yourself up to playing 18 holes. Consider starting by playing three holes of a nine-hole course late in the afternoon when the course is less crowded and rates are cheaper. The course might not charge a three-hole rate, so just play until you start getting frustrated, then come back another day.

3. **CHOOSE THE RIGHT COURSE:** Don't start on Bethpage Black, or any course that's going to have you discouraged before you reach the first green. A good beginner course is flat, short, and doesn't have many hazards or

forced carries—that is, waste areas or hazards you have to hit over to get to the fairway. There'll be plenty of time to test yourself on tougher layouts, but for now, give yourself a chance to gather some positive momentum.

4. **MOVE ON UP:** Forget about ego, and feel free to play from the forward set of tees. Playing the course at 5,500 yards or less will save you time, frustration, and golf balls. And you'll be in good company: There's a nationwide push for recreational golfers of all levels to be playing courses from shorter distances.

5. **KEEP UP THE PACE:** Most golf courses ask that you finish 18 holes in 4½ hours, but you can do better than that. One way to maintain a decent pace is to limit yourself to a certain number of strokes per hole. (We suggest a maximum of seven strokes per hole.) As a beginning golfer, there's nothing wrong with picking up your ball if you're holding your playing partners up.

WARM-UP GOAL: HIT IT SOLID

by David Leadbetter

On the practice tee at a British PGA Championship in the late '70s, I asked Gene Littler what he worked on before he went out to play. He told me his only goal was hitting the ball in the center of the clubface. Off-line shots didn't concern him as long as they were solid, because he could always adjust for accuracy. Mis-hitting shots was more worrisome to him. Littler's tempo is legendary, and probably stemmed from his desire to hit the ball flush. Concentrate on solid contact; it'll set up a great day.

PLAY MORE THAN YOU PRACTICE

by Johnny Miller

Shortly after I turned 14, in 1961, I became the first junior member (whose father was not a member) at the Olympic Club in San Francisco. Playing Olympic day in and day out made me the good iron player I turned out to be. You never seem to get a level lie at Olympic. You're required to hit a lot of awkward shots, such as playing a fade with the ball above your feet. You can't work on shots like that on the practice tee, which is why I always played more than I practiced. A lot of things I learned at Olympic defied conventional teaching. For example, from a sidehill lie with the ball below you, the tendency is to pull it dead left—not slice it, as most instructors say—because you straighten your right arm to reach the ball, and you swing over the top. Don't be one of those driving-range superstars: players who can make their irons sing on the practice tee but are only so-so on the course. Get out and play.

EMBRACE YOUR PLAYING STYLE

by Justin Leonard

Not everyone can bomb the ball off the tee, hit the high draw on command, and spin wedges. So play to your game. An example: The 16th at Firestone, where we play a WGC event, is one of the longest par 5s we face, stretching more than 650 yards. It's obviously a lay up for me, and an awkward one at that because the second shot is downhill to an area that is also downhill. In the first round last summer, I laid up to about 100 yards. The second day, I laid up again and noticed my divot from the day before—three feet away. I got it right on those lay ups: They left me a fairly level lie for my third. Although I don't fixate on leaving myself a favorite yardage, laying up to a wedge distance you like is a way you can get an advantage over other players. Learn to pick out landmarks, such as trees, bunkers, and, of course, yardage markers, in your lay-up zone. And if you have a GPS device, use it on lay-up shots.

NEVER SWING WITH MORE THAN 80 PERCENT EFFORT

by Nick Faldo

My first teacher, Ian Connelly, gave me a lesson I've never forgotten. He had me hit six 7-iron shots as hard as I could. He then had me hit six 7-iron shots so easily they flew only 100 yards. He then asked me to increase the distance in 10-yard increments, six swings for each. Before I knew it, I was hitting the 7-iron the original maximum-swing distance, but with hardly any effort. It proved that good rhythm, not sheer power, is what makes the ball go long—and straight.

MY ADVICE ON COMPETING

by Michael Jordan

1. **FOCUS ON THE LITTLE THINGS:** I always told myself to focus on the little things because little things added up to big things. I equate making putts with making free throws, and my biggest mental challenge shooting free throws was in 1986, when I had a 63-point game against Boston in the Garden. I had to make two free throws to send the game into overtime, and all I focused on was the basics—I'm not going to be short. I'm going to extend and reach for the rim. Golf is no different. Don't assume, for example, that any putt is good. Make sure you putt every three-footer with conviction.

2. **BE CONFIDENT IN WHAT YOU CAN DO:** If you have 100 percent confidence that you can pull off a shot, most of the time you will.

3. **DON'T THINK ABOUT THE PRIZE; THINK ABOUT THE WORK:** Prepare, practice, and perfect it. Do the work, and the prizes will come.

4. KEEP IT SIMPLE: There are a lot of correlations between basketball and golf, especially on the mental side. Whenever I played a big game, I tried to stick to things I knew I was capable of doing. I do the same in golf. Keeping it simple works especially well in pressure situations.

5. CONTROL YOUR EMOTIONS UNTIL THE ROUND IS OVER: Celebrating during a round can be a good thing if it inspires you to keep doing great things. But be careful not to overdo it. Sometimes, celebrating too much adds pressure and makes you feel like you›ve got to live up to it the rest of the round. Worse, your celebrating can motivate your opponent.

6. NERVOUSNESS IS NOT A BAD THING: I was nervous a lot of times before games. The key is, does that nervousness go away once the ball is thrown up because of your preparation and your routine? Once the game started, I was back in my routine. Golf can work the same way if you put in the work to prepare. Yeah, you're going to be nervous on the first tee, but all it takes is one good shot, and that nervousness goes away.

HOW TO CHOOSE THE RIGHT TEES

by the Editors of Golf Digest

If you're playing on a course for the first time and you're not sure which tees to play from, do yourself a favor and ignore the yardages on the right side of the scorecard. Columbia University professor Lucius Riccio says check the Slope Rating. Riccio, who has served on the USGA's Handicap Research Team since 1979, says length is not the determining factor—difficulty is. For example, a big-hitting, 20-handicapper would get crushed playing a tee set with a Slope above 135. Follow the chart above to determine your tee box. Note: If you're struggling, or don't know what your handicap is, keeping moving up until the game becomes enjoyable.

HOW TO AVOID CHOKING

by Johnny Miller

Serious choking—extreme stage fright—doesn't necessarily set in on the first tee. Often the player, although nervous, finds a way to get the ball around for the first hole or two. Then, out of nowhere, he hits a horrible shot—skulls a pitch 40 yards over the green, shanks one into the gallery, or muffs a series of chips from the greenside rough. It's like a bomb going off. Deeply embarrassed, he collapses completely and a long series of disasters ensues. The amateur can diffuse the bomb by using smart course management and not trying to play shots he has no business playing. If he can play within himself and find some kind of rhythm, he can prevent his nervous system from detonating.

IGNORE UNSOLICITED SWING ADVICE

by Dr. Bob Rotella

Not too long ago, I was working with this player who was struggling. But a couple of strong finishes had him feeling better. At the next tournament he made, like, eight birdies in the first round. Now he was feeling really good. He stopped by the putting green to hit a few, and a player he knows walked up to him and said: "I don't know what you're doing with your putting, but that's not the way you used to set up." A few minutes later, another player came over: "You don't have your eyes over the ball the way you used to." Now my guy didn't know what to think. He went from making everything he looked at to being a mess the next day.

You'll have lots of well-meaning friends who want to give you advice. Don't accept it. In fact, stop them before they can say a word. Their comments will creep into your mind when you're on the course. If you've worked on your game, commit to the plan and stay confident.

IF YOU'RE SHANKING, GET HELP NOW

by Jim McLean

The shank is the worst of all shots because of the instant and indelible imprint it leaves on your psyche. The fear of doing it again is so great that many golfers can't diagnose the problem. My advice: Don't even try to figure it out on your own; see a teacher right away.

When I was the head pro at Sleepy Hollow Country Club in New York in the early '90s, I had a member who started shanking almost every shot. He'd get a basket of balls, go to the range, shank the whole basket, and go home. I'd never seen a golfer so discouraged. After some badgering, he let me give him lessons. I did six sessions with him, starting around the greens.

There are four ways to shank. His was a nasty over-the-top loop with an open clubface. I told him to keep his elbows attached to his rib cage from start to finish, so his arms couldn't drift from his body far enough for the hosel to reach the ball. He did this on every swing, and it cured his shanks.

HOW TO PREPARE FOR YOUR FIRST TOURNAMENT

by Max Adler, Golf Digest Staff Writer

IF YOUR INDEX IS....	THE CORRECT SLOPE IS....
PLUS	146
0-5	140-145
6-10	135-139
11-15	130-134
16-20	125-129
21-25	120-124
26-30	115-119
31-36	110-114
37+	109 OR LESS

The legendary amateur golfer Bobby Jones once said, "There's golf and then there's tournament golf, and neither one resembles the other." If you're signed up to play in an organized golf event or outing for the first time, don't let those words unnerve you. All Jones meant is that standing over shots that matter is an experience far richer than just hacking around with buddies. It's fun to feel butterflies in your stomach, to feel your hands shake. Even if you shoot a million, here are five points to help you look like you've played tournament golf before.

1. **KNOW THE FORMAT:** Such as with darts and billiards, there are lots of different ways to score golf events. While the goal of getting the ball in the cup in the fewest strokes possible never varies, understanding how your group's round is being tabulated will help you maximize strategy and save time. For events in which the ability levels of participants are widespread, the most common formats are a Scramble and Best Ball. Because team formats are designed to reward aggressive play, you'll often be in a situation where only a one-putt will suffice (so don't leave the putt short), or, after several bad shots, your score on a hole will likely not count, in which case you should pick up. When in doubt, ask your group's scorekeeper how to proceed.

2. **USE THE RIGHT GEAR:** Besides clubs, two essential items for tournament play are a Sharpie and a coin. Use the Sharpie to draw unique dots or lines on your ball. Simply knowing what brand and number you're playing (Titleist 1, Callaway 2, Nike 3, etc.) is not enough to reliably distinguish your ball from the balls of other competitors. Have a ball ready with a slightly different marking in case you need to hit a provisional. You'll use the coin, or a plastic ballmarker, to mark your ball on the greens. A tee will not do. Golfers are finicky when it comes to marking. Know that replacing your ball with anything less than full care signals that you're either a novice or a cheater.

3. **ANNOUNCE WHEN YOU'RE PICKING UP:** If you've topped consecutive shots or pumped two balls out-of-bounds, there's no shame in picking up. In fact, your playing partners will appreciate this effort to maintain pace of play. However, not clearly announcing your intention creates an awkward situation. Your playing partners will be uncertain if they should wait, help you look for your ball, or play on.

4. **MAINTAIN A SENSE OF HUMOR:** This is probably the most critical element of playing in a golf outing. Enjoy the pressure and challenge of hitting golf shots that are counted toward a prize, but remember, these are casual events and no one cares if you play poorly. Since you are not a professional golfer who practices daily, the only expectation others have is that you offer pleasant company. Sulking and cursing are unacceptable, and especially ridiculous if you're a beginning golfer.

5. **NEVER GET A LESSON THE DAY BEFORE AN EVENT:** Winning's fun, and it's natural to want to play your best when it counts. However, resist the temptation to get a lesson or otherwise revamp your swing the day before an event. "I'll arrive to the course early and figure out my swing on the range" are universal famous last words. Golf swings take time to settle, and it's virtually guaranteed you'll play miserably if you have a lot of new thoughts in your head as you try to simultaneously cope with the experience of playing in a tournament. Go with what you know.

PLAY TO WIN, NOT FOR A SCORE

by Hunter Mahan

As a junior golfer in southern California, I had two goals: beat my dad, and break par. But something always happened near the end of rounds that stopped me from doing either. Then, on my 12th birthday, my dad took me to Alta Vista Country Club. I was playing well, and as the round went on, my desire to beat my dad got so intense, I forgot about my score. I did beat him that day, but only when we got inside did I notice I'd shot 71—one under par. If you're struggling to break through a scoring barrier, have a second goal going at the same time.

DON'T GO IT ALONE

by Butch Harmon

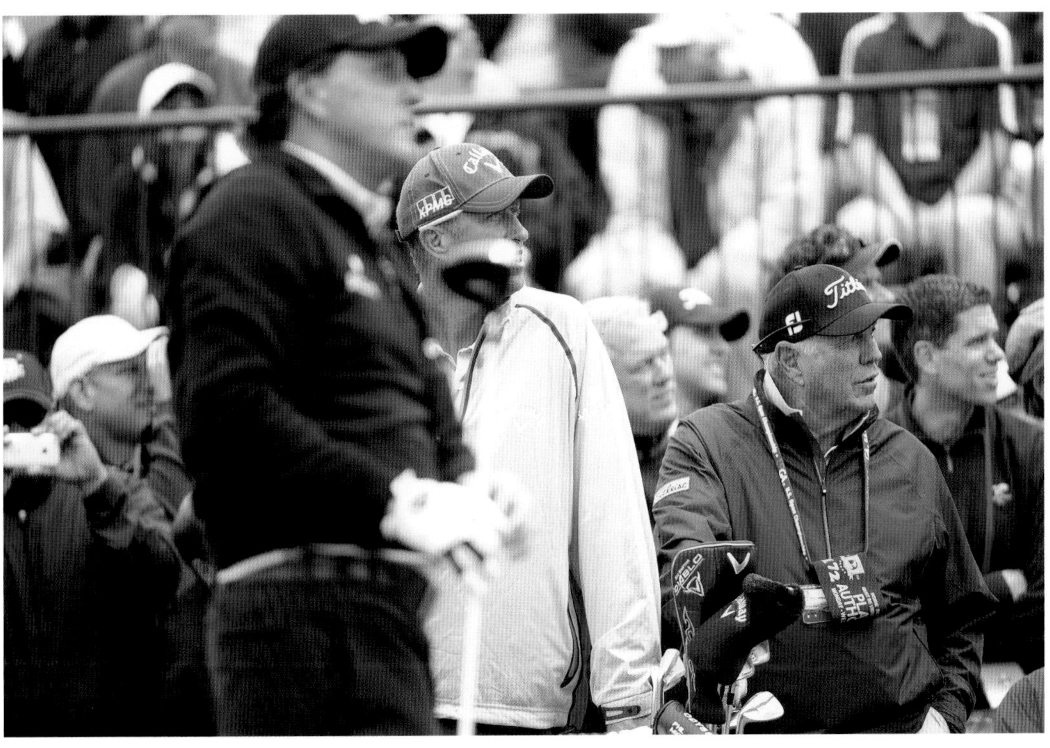

There's a saying among teachers: "Feel and real are never the same thing." In other words, what you think you're doing with your swing and what you're actually doing are a lot different. You've got to see a PGA pro to help you make an accurate diagnosis and identify the right change for you. And don't limit yourself to one or two lessons. You need the pro's eyes to check your positions, because you can't see yourself swinging—and you can't videotape every subtle change. I don't know of a single modern tour player who has made a big swing change by himself, so for the average player to go it alone will probably do more harm than good.

Charl Schwartzel celebrates his victory at the 2011 Masters Tournament.